Beyond the Frame

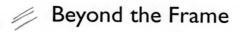

Beyond the Frame

Women of Color and Visual Representation

Edited by

Neferti X. M. Tadiar

and

Angela Y. Davis

palgrave
macmillan

BEYOND THE FRAME
© Neferti X. M. Tadiar and Angela Y. Davis, 2005.

First published in 2005 by
PALGRAVE MACMILLAN™
175 Fifth Avenue, New York, N.Y. 10010 and
Houndmills, Basingstoke, Hampshire, England RG21 6XS
Companies and representatives throughout the world.

PALGRAVE MACMILLAN is the global academic imprint of the Palgrave Macmillan division of St. Martin's Press, LLC and of Palgrave Macmillan Ltd. Macmillan® is a registered trademark in the United States, United Kingdom and other countries. Palgrave is a registered trademark in the European Union and other countries.

ISBN 978-1-4039-6533-2   ISBN 1-4039-6533-1

Library of Congress Cataloging-in-Publication Data

Beyond the frame : women of color and visual representation / edited by Angela Y. Davis and Neferti X.M. Tadiar.
     p. cm.
Papers originally presented at a conference sponsored by the Humanities Research Institute, University of California, Santa Cruz, entitled "Women of Color and Visual Representations" held in spring of 1999.
Includes bibliographical references and index.
ISBN 1-4039-6533-1 (alk. paper)
   1. Minority women—United States—Social conditions—Congresses.
2. Photography of women—United States—Congresses. 3. Marginality, Social—United States—Congresses. I. Davis, Angela Y. II. Tadiar, Neferti Xina M. (Neferti Xina Maca), 1964–

HQ1421.B49 2005
305.48′8′00973—dc22   2005043132

A catalogue record for this book is available from the British Library.

Design by Newgen Imaging Systems (P) Ltd., Chennai, India.

First edition: September 2005

10 9 8 7 6 5 4 3 2 1

Printed in the United States of America.

Transferred to digital printing in 2008.

For Gloria E. Anzaldúa

Contents

List of Figures   ix

About the Contributors and Editors   xi

Introduction   1
Neferti X. M. Tadiar and Angela Y. Davis

Part I   Popular Culture and Advertising

1. *"The East Side Revue, 40 Hits by East Los Angeles Most Popular Groups!"* The Boys in the Band and the Girls Who Were Their Fans   13
   Keta Miranda

2. The Commoditization of Hybridity in the 1990s U.S. Fashion Advertising: Who Is *cK one?*   31
   Laura J. Kuo

3. Albita's Queer Nations and U.S. Salsa Culture   49
   Darshan Elena Campos

4. Beyond Pocahontas   61
   Joanne Barker

5. "Come Up to the Kool Taste": Race and the Semiotics of Smoking   77
   Sarah S. Jain

Part II   Self/Identity, Memory/History

6. Conjuring up Traces of Historical Violence: Grandpa, Who is Not in the Photo   107
   Naono Akiko

7. "The Face Value of Dreams": Gender, Race, Class,
   and the Politics of Cosmetic Surgery   131
   Victoria M. Bañales

8. A Fraction of National Belonging: "Hybrid
   Hawaiians," Blood Quantum, and the Ongoing
   Search for Purity   153
   J. Kēhaulani Kauanui

Part III   Resistance Images

9. Bearing Bandoleras: Transfigurative
   Liberation and the Iconography
   of la Nueva Chicana   171
   Maylei Blackwell

10. Aztec Princess Still at Large   197
    Catrióna Rueda Esquibel

11. Embodied at the Shrine of Cultural Disjuncture   207
    Luz Calvo

12. "¿Soy Punkera, Y Que?": Sexuality, Translocality,
    and Punk in Los Angeles and Beyond   219
    Michelle Habell-Pallán

Index   243

List of Figures

1.1 Front cover of *East Side Revue: 40 Hits by East Los Angeles Most Popular Groups!*   14

2.1 "Jenny, Kate, and Company," prototype for the *cK one: portraits of a generation* advertising campaign, released in September 1994   33

3.1 *Albita: No Se Parce A Nada*   51

3.2 *Albita: Una Mujer Como Yo*   58

4.1 "A New Kind of Warrior," U.S. Secret Service Advertisement   62

5.1 Cover (L) and Inside Cover of *Ebony*, August 1967   82

6.1 Late Spring 1972; from top left (clockwise): Grandma's elder sister, Grandma, Dad, my brother, myself, Mom   109

7.1 Ana Ponce exits a plastic surgeon's office in Lima, Peru after undergoing rhinoplasty   132

8.1 "Chinese-Hawaiian Girl," 1930 photograph included in papers of William A. Lessa, National Anthropological Archives   155

9.1 "La Soldadera," *Chicana Student Movement* newspaper, 1968   172

10.1 "Ixta Ponders Leverage Buyout," Robert Buitrón, 1989   198

11.1 Laura Aguilar's *Three Eagles Flying*   208

12.1 Flyer insert for *Pretty Vacant* (dir. Jim Mendiola, 1996)   220

12.2 Still photo for *Pretty Vacant* (dir. Jim Mendiola, 1996)   222

About the Contributors and Editors

A doctoral student in Literature at the University of California-Santa Cruz, **Vicky Bañales** is finishing her dissertation, entitled "Twentieth Century Latin American and US Latina Women's Literature and the Paradox of Dictatorship and Democracy." Her research interests include: Latin/a American women's dictatorship novels and testimonial narratives, women's social and literary movements in the 1980s, Third World feminisms, and gender and race studies. Vicky has been a member of the Research Cluster for Women of Color in Collaboration and Conflict since 1997, and is affiliated with the UC-Santa Cruz Chicano/Latino Research Center and the Feminist Theories in the Latin/a Americas Research Cluster. She teaches women's studies and literature/writing courses at UC-Santa Cruz, and is a past Ford Dissertation Fellow.

Joanne Barker (Lenape) completed her Ph.D. in the History of Consciousness Department at the University of California, Santa Cruz, in 2000 where she specialized in indigenous jurisprudence, women's/gender studies, and cultural studies. She has published articles in *Wicazo Sa Review: A Native American Studies Journal, Cultural Studies, Inscriptions,* and *This Bridge We Call Home: Radical Visions for Transformation.* She has edited a collection of essays entitled *Sovereignty Matters* that is being published by the University of Nebraska Press for 2005. She is currently working on energy policies and conservation issues in relation to California Indian tribes with the California Energy Commission and California Indian Legal Services. She is Assistant Professor in American Indian Studies at San Francisco State University.

Maylei Blackwell is Assistant Professor in the César E. Chávez Center for Chicana/o Studies at the University of California, Los Angeles. She is an activist-scholar whose research examines how racial and sexual difference shapes the challenges and possibilities of transnational organizing in the Americas. She completed a Ph.D. in the History of Consciousness Department at the University of California in Santa Cruz. Her current research and teaching explore how women of color in the United States and indigenous women in Mexico organize to resist the conditions created by globalization. Her recent publications include "Contested Histories: las Hijas de Cuauhtémoc, Chicana Feminisms and Print Culture in the Chicano Movement, 1968–1973," in *Chicana Feminisms: A Critical Reader* (Duke University Press), a coauthored article entitled, "Encountering Latin American and Caribbean Feminisms," which appeared in *Signs, Journal of Women in Culture and Society* (Winter 2002), and *Time to Rise: US Women of Color—Issues and Strategies*, a report to the UN World Conference Against Racism, available at <www.coloredgirls. org>, which she coedited for the Women of Color Resource Center.

Luz Calvo is Assistant Professor of Ethnic Studies at California State University, East Bay. She earned her Ph.D. in the History of Consciousness at UC Santa Cruz. Her article "Art Comes for the Archbishop: The Semiotics of Contemporary Chicana Feminism" appears in *Meridians: Feminism, Race, Transnationalism* (Autumn 2004). She is working on a manuscript entitled, "Border Fantasies: Race, Sex, and Mexican Bodies."

Darshan Elena Campos is a media arts educator. Activism fuels her scholarship. She programs cultural events and writes as often as possible. Social justice, which means political, social, cultural, and psychic liberation for all oppressed and colonized peoples, is her goal. Her dissertation considers independent women of color filmmaking as a form of cultural criticism and grassroots political organizing. She is a Ph.D. candidate in the Department of History of Consciousness at University of California, Santa Cruz.

Catrióna Rueda Esquibel is Assistant Professor of Ethnic Studies at San Francisco State University. Her work has been published in *SIGNS: Journal of Women in Culture and Society, Chicano/Latino Homoerotic Identities, Tortilleras: Hispanic and Latina Lesbian Expression, Velvet Barrios: Popular Culture and Chicana/Chicano Sexualities*, and in her book, *With Her Machete in Her Hand: Reading Chicana Lesbians* (University of Texas Press, 2006).

Michelle Habell-Pallán is Assistant Professor in the Department of American Ethnic Studies at the University of Washington, Seattle. She is author of *Loca Motion: The Travels of Chicana and Latina Popular Culture* (NYU Press) and coeditor with Mary Romero of *Latino/a Popular Culture* (NYU Press). She is a recipient of research fellowships from the Rockefeller and Mellon Foundations. Her book-in-progress is a comparative study of women of color's participation in the punk and new wave music cultures of the 1970s.

Sarah S. Jain is Assistant Professor in the Department of Social and Cultural Anthropology at Stanford University. Her publications include *Injury*, Princeton University Press, 2005.

J. Kēhaulani Kauanui is Assistant Professor in American Studies and Anthropology at Wesleyan University in Connecticut. In 2000, she earned her Ph.D. in the program of History of Consciousness at the University of California, Santa Cruz. Kauanui has been awarded several fellowships supporting her research and writing, including those by the Woodrow Wilson National Fellowship Foundation, the University of California Pacific Rim Grant, the Smithsonian, the Rockefeller Archives Center Research Grant, the National Science Foundation, and the School of American Research. She is currently completing her first book, *The Politics of Hawaiian Blood and the Question of Sovereignty*. She has numerous publications which appear in the following journals: *American Studies, Political and Legal Anthropology Review, Social Text, Women's Studies International Forum, Amerasia Journal, Pacific Studies*, and *The Contemporary Pacific*. With Dr. Caroline Sinavaiana, she is coediting a forthcoming special issue of *Pacific Studies* called "Women Writing Oceania: Weaving the Sails of the Waka."

Laura J. Kuo is Assistant Professor and Program Director of Theory as Practice in the Department of Fine Arts at Otis College of Art and Design in Los Angeles, California. Her research has been supported by the Whitney Museum of American Art Independent Study Program Fellowship in Critical Studies, the Bolin Predoctoral Fellowship in Women's Studies at Williams College, and the Institute of American Cultures Postdoctoral Fellowship in Asian American Studies at UCLA. Kuo's current research explores the transnational underpinnings of post-9-11 activist art by Arab/Muslim/Iranian/American artists addressing Western imperialism in Central and Southwest Asia and North Africa in their work. Articles, including "Transnationalism,

Interdependency, and Consciousness in the Art of Abdelali Dahrouch: 'Desert Sin, Revisited,' " have been published in *Third Text* and *Estrago*; she has published numerous reviews in art catalogues and magazines, and has articles and reviews forthcoming in the art journal *X-tra* and in *Third Text*. Kuo is currently developing a manuscript entitled, *Contested Visions: Transnational Cartographies of Feminism, Multiculturalism, and Postmodernism in Contemporary Cultural Production*.

Marie (Keta) Miranda is Assistant Professor at the University of Texas, San Antonio in the Mexican American Studies Program in the Bicultural-Bilingual Studies Department in the College of Education. She graduated from the History of Consciousness Department at the University of California at Santa Cruz in 2000. She is the author of a study of girls' culture, entitled *Homegirls in the Public Sphere* (University of Texas Press, 2003).

Naono Akiko is Associate Professor of Graduate School of Social and Cultural Studies at the University of Kyushu, Japan. She received her Ph.D. in Sociology from the University of California, Santa Cruz. She has been a post-doctoral fellow at the Japan Society for the Promotion of Science, a visiting research fellow at the Hiroshima Peace Institute and she established and served as the Project Director of the Nuclear History Institute at American University in Washington, D.C., a project that won the North American Association of Summer Sessions Award for Creative and Innovative Programs. She is the author of *"Genbaku No E" To Deau: Komerareta Omoi Ni Mimiwo Sumashite* [Encountering the drawings of the atomic bomb survivors] (Tokyo: Iwanami shoten: 2004) and *Hiroshima/Amerika: Genbakuten Wo Megutte* [Hiroshima/America: on the atomic bomb exhibit] (Hiroshima: Keisui sha, 1997), which won the 1997 Award of the Peace and Cooperative Journalist Fund of Japan.

About the Editors

Angela Y. Davis is known internationally for her ongoing work to combat all forms of oppression in the United States and abroad. Over the years she has been active as a student, teacher, writer, scholar, and activist/organizer. She is a living witness to the historical struggles of the contemporary era. Professor Davis's long-standing commitment to prisoners' rights dates back to her involvement in the campaign to free the Soledad Brothers, which led to her own arrest and imprisonment.

Today she remains an advocate of prison abolition and has developed a powerful critique of racism in the criminal justice system. She is a member of the Advisory Board of the Prison Activist Resource Center, and currently is working on a comparative study of women's imprisonment in the United States, the Netherlands, and Cuba. She is the author of five books, including *Angela Davis: An Autobiography; Women, Race, and Class; Blues Legacies and Black Feminism: Gertrude "Ma" Rainey, Bessie Smith, and Billie Holiday;* and *The Angela Y. Davis Reader.*

Neferti X. M. Tadiar is Associate Professor of History of Consciousness at the University of California, Santa Cruz. She is the author of *Fantasy-Production: Sexual Economies and Other Philippine Consequences for the New World Order* (Hong Kong University Press, 2004) and *Things Fall Away: Philippine Literature, Historical Experience and Tangential Makings of Globality* (forthcoming from Duke University Press). Her work broadly addresses questions about the role of gender, race, and sexuality in discourses and material practices of nationalism, transnationalism, and globalization, as well as explores the potential of non-Western knowledges for thinking about the politics of minoritarian cultural practices. She was the project director of "Feminisms and Global War," the inaugural project of the Institute for Advanced Feminist Research.

Introduction

Neferti X. M. Tadiar and Angela Y. Davis

A History and Project of Collaboration and Coalition

Beyond the Frame emerges out of the vision and hard work of a group of graduate students actively involved in the Research Cluster for the Study of Women of Color in Conflict and Collaboration based at the University of California, Santa Cruz. As both contributors to this anthology and members of the editorial collective (originally composed of Victoria Bañales, Luz Calvo, Cecilia Cruz, J. Kehaulani Kauanui, and Keta Miranda), these students, many of who are now assistant professors at other universities, are entirely responsible for the conceptualization of this collaborative project, which seeks to interrogate dominant regimes of visual representation from the perspectives of women of color feminist criticism. They also solicited the papers and organized the Humanities Research Institute–sponsored conference, "Women of Color and Visual Representations," held in the Spring of 1999, where the initial papers were read, discussed, and critiqued by invited scholars in a collaborative effort to sharpen the political intervention which they sought to make. Such an intervention was articulated by the contributors themselves as "a critical interruption of the conception of 'women of color' identities as a historical, fixed, or essential" through the interrogation of photographic images. The choice of photographs as a point of departure was predicated on the recognition that processes of identity-formation are mediated by images—and indeed reified in and through photographs. The contributors are also interested in exploring how such identity-images are pressed into service for the dominant realisms of our time. In critically engaging a single photograph, each essay attempts therefore to look at those complex processes of identity-production and subject-formation, which shape both dominant and alternative meanings of the chosen image—to look, in other words, at what moves and takes place "beyond the frame" as a constitutive aspect of what is inside of it.

As a project undertaken by the Research Cluster for the Study of Women of Color, *Beyond the Frame* is the product not of an isolated initiative, but rather of a social and political context and community. The University of California at Santa Cruz has been the site of significant work by women of color feminist critics, most notably Gloria Anzaldúa and Chela Sandoval, but also a great many more scholars, activists, and students involved in the connected struggles against racist, sexist, and homophobic forms of domination. Since its founding in 1991, the Cluster has attempted to introduce visual images into debates around the meaning of the category "women of color." Thus this project is linked to such efforts as the annual Women of Color Film and Video Festival, founded by a former Cluster member, Margaret R. Daniel, which has been screening films and videos by, about, and for women of color for more than a decade. The work of such artists as Lourdes Portillo, Trinh T. Minh-ha, Pratibha Parmar, Renee Tajima-Peña, Sylvia Morales, and Julie Dash, has helped to constitute a community of images that have shaped new social and political identities, as well as critiques of identity-based politics. Engagement with this work has encouraged scholarly and popular reflection on what it means to self-consciously inhabit image environments.

The Cluster has also sponsored a multiyear curriculum development project, which has resulted in the offering of three undergraduate courses on women of color: the first focused on genders and sexualities, the second on visual representation, and the third on violence. What this present project has in common with these other activities, besides a "common context of struggle," is a commitment to a politicized and politicizing education that is interdisciplinary and antiracist. Indeed, one of the aims of this present anthology is to provide a broad audience with accessible critical tools necessary for the transformative understanding of the images that fundamentally shape the media-dominated society in which we live.

This anthology thus reflects historical and contemporary conversations about scholarly, artistic, and organizing strategies associated with women of color feminism. The methodological insistence on multiple, concurrent, interlinked modes of analysis emerged precisely in order to develop otherwise unavailable understandings of "women of color." At the same time, as the contributors to this anthology recognize, the object "women of color" was itself constituted through these crosscutting, intersectional analytical and organizing strategies. In other words, even as we tend to employ the term "women of color" to refer to women or groups of women who are located by dominant racisms at the margins of the social order, this anthology rejects such easy, positivistic assumptions. Indeed, what is most important about this term is its theoretical and practical imperative to bring together such categories as gender, race, class, sexuality, and nation, asking how they always work in mutually constitutive relations.

In so far as the designation "women of color" is a political category emerging out of U.S.-based struggles, it cannot be expected to travel easily beyond these national boundaries. Nevertheless, within this context it has enabled a political coalition of diverse, particular histories of struggle—Native American, Chicana/o, African American, Hawaiian, Asian American, as well as immigrant Third World women struggles. These alliances have not been without their share of contradictions and tensions. Indeed, the essays in this volume continue the practice within the research cluster itself of exploring the productive force of those contradictions and tensions, which emanate from the diverse, particular histories out of which the political formation of women of color emerges. It bears repeating that the category of women of color does not pertain to a collection of racialized women. The essays challenge this very notion by analyzing the ways in which women of color are fixed as unchanging, intrinsic, and exchangeable identities within dominant cultural representations. One of the ways that they accomplish this is through placing emphasis on the different histories that comprise, challenge, and escape any unifying narrative of liberal, multiculturalist democracy. The essays also foreground the processes of production of racial, gender, and sexual difference, and the ways that these historical differences have been deployed both by state and civil apparatuses to secure various cultural logics of domination and by marginalized social groups struggling against those cultural logics to bring about social transformation.

With the exception of Akiko Naono's essay, which is most explicitly situated outside of, though certainly in relation with, the U.S. context, most of these essays are located in U.S.-based struggles. Nevertheless, because of their critical positions in relation to U.S. hegemony, as a consequence of long and continuing histories of marginalization and colonization, all of these essays necessarily interrogate the naturalized unity and borders of the U.S. nation, not to mention the figural practices of an insidious U.S. nationalism. For example, Kehaulani Kauanui and Joanne Barker highlight the histories of colonization of Hawaiian and Native American peoples within the United States; Luz Calvo and Catrióna Esquibel write on and about the borders of hegemonic U.S. national fantasies; and Maylei Blackwell, Michelle Habell-Pallán, and Darshan Campos underscore the constitutive role of transnational movements across the Americas and Africa in the production of counterimages and alternative socialities. In effect, the essays attempt to find new places from which to interpret the images before them, places that are necessarily "beyond the frame" of the dominant U.S. nation.

Women of Color and Visual Images

All of these essays present critical interdisciplinary readings of photographic images inasmuch as gender, racial, and sexual structures of oppression and domination are deeply shaped not only by such images but also more generally by orders of visual representation. In doing so they also reflect on the complex processes of visuality, or of seeing and being seen, and their relation to social power. While a couple of contributors are located in visual studies, most are writing out of different disciplines. The goal of this project in fostering such crossing of disciplinary borders is the understanding and viewing of visual representations not as a matter of scholarly expertise, but rather as a manner of creating and exercising historical agency. This means developing a kind of fluency that includes but is not limited to what might canonically be understood to be theories of the visual. Indeed, one of the goals of the book is to encourage a new kind of popular fluency in reading images, a fluency that intersects with but is not fully contained within the disciplines of visual studies, such as art history and film theory. The contributors draw their methodological tools for reading images from the broader, multidisciplinary critical interpretative practices of antiracist, feminist writing. Their analyses do not only issue out of an awareness of the conventions of normative interpretation—dominant, gendered, racialized, and sexualized ways of seeing and reading images. In order to further enabling practices of understanding our visual environments, these analyses also greatly depend on alternative interpretative categories provided by communities in struggle. For example, in the context of reading the image of an American Indian Warrior Woman used in a U.S. Secret Service advertisement, Joanne Barker, takes "sovereignty and cultural autonomy as the primary frames of reference for a hermeneutics of Indian women's representations." Barker develops an investigative path that diverges from the familiar one of "getting to the facts" and from the familiar, putative history presented by the figure of Pocahontas. Informed and inspired by the political interpretative strategies of other Indian women, her investigative path leads, instead, to a deconstruction of the facts and a story of how history might be otherwise. By drawing on interpretative categories used by communities in struggle, these essays thus contribute important sources of hermeneutical tools for reading images.

Very importantly then, the development of visual literacy also means rethinking the category of "visual theory" through "women of color." In this regard, "women of color" stands less as a racialized, gendered identity and more as a set of critical reading strategies or a problematic implying particular modes of theoretical and political analysis for addressing racializing, sexualizing, and gendering forms of oppression. These critical reading strategies, which are forged through the inflection of "visual theory" by "women of color," thus fundamentally relate to other important paradigms associated with scholarly work on, about, and by women of color such as "differential consciousness" (Chela Sandoval) "intersectionality" (Kimberlé Crenshaw) and "border consciousness" (Gloria Anzaldúa), even as they address intersecting social and political concerns of postcolonial, Third World, and transnational feminisms, queer studies, and cultural studies. Such scholarly work associated with women of color feminism has attempted to acknowledge the very histories of struggle that have enabled these theoretical concepts, histories that are unfortunately often disappeared by narrow academic citational practices. By not confining their contexts of theoretical reference to particular academic disciplines and fields and drawing on analytical tools they acknowledge as the product of communities of struggle, the essays in this book show themselves to be interdisciplinary in a broader sense. It is this enlargement of citational practices by women of color feminism that we need to encourage among emerging scholars.

The strategies for confronting and interrogating images used by the book's contributors include the placing of seemingly static or frozen products of visual culture back into the dynamics of history. One strategy is to foreground the erasures and rewriting of "other" histories that dominant representational practices, as embodied by the photographs, accomplish. Laura Kuo writes about the work of "hiding" relations of exploitation and histories of struggle that are carried out by images of hybridity and multiculturalism in Calvin Klein advertisements. She demonstrates, moreover, the psychic and social ambivalence and difference that the postmodern liberalism of the ads depend on and co-opt but that also harbor possibilities for subversive appropriation. In this way, Kuo points to a wider history of social contestation in which the photograph takes part. In her essay on a photograph accompanying a news article on cosmetic surgery in Peru, Vicky Bañales also writes about the "hidden" power relations underpinning both the actual phenomenon of Third World cosmetic surgery and the ideological narratives about Third World women, which are offered and naturalized by the photograph and the news article's representation of Third World cosmetic surgery. Like Kuo, Bañales brings in the global context of international economic relations to understand the politics of representation at work in what appears to be a simple photographic illustration of a "news" feature.

Indeed, many of the essays use the photographs as a point of departure or an illustration for a much broader discussion of the social, historical, economic, and cultural conditions that produce such representations, thereby emphasizing the embeddedness of the photograph in a thicker, more complex, and more contradictory world than the photograph and its embodied ways of seeing leads us to see. In her essay exploring the issues of economic racism and racialized injury raised by a lawsuit filed in behalf of Black smokers against the tobacco companies, Sarah Jain places a cigarette ad in *Ebony* magazine in the messy context of the emergence of an African American middle class, intensifying Civil Rights struggles, the growth of tobacco corporations and the rise of U.S. consumerism in the post–World War II period, in order to suggest the complexity of actors and institutions accountable for the production of "race" and racialized injury. Beyond mere contextualization, the strategy of restoring the photographs to a dynamic history foregrounds struggle, conflict, and contradiction as the conditions of the photographs' production and reception and, very importantly, of their meanings and functions within social worlds structured by racism, sexism, homophobia, and capitalist exploitation. As Darshan Campos's essay on the images on the CD album cover of the Cuban American singer Albita reveals, photographs of popular culture often play at least two tracks, two trajectories of political meaning and desire, at once—one of transgression of normative discourses of gender, race, and sexuality and another of capitalization on such transgressions and the gendered state racisms that support it. Two tracks symbolize not so much a Manichean world of absolute divisions and antagonisms as the conditions of contradiction and ambivalence—indeed, the very conditions of the borderland—that characterize the positions of the subjects interpellated by these photographs. Similarly, Keta Miranda's essay on the album cover of a collection of early 1960s East

Los Angeles bands, highlights the processes of cultural negotiation of identities, meanings, and desires engaged in by Chicano/a youth during a period when the War on Poverty, the war in Vietnam and the Civil Rights struggles raged, serving to heighten the paradoxical experience and social contradictions of the American Dream for emerging Chicano/a subjects. Focusing in particular on the album cover's photographic depiction of the bands' screaming girl fans, Miranda attends to the dynamic process of articulating an emergent identity for Chicano/a youth prior to the Chicano Power movement, the growth of possibilities of middle-class citizenship for Mexican Americans in Los Angeles and "the non-productive and uncontrollable expression of desires beyond meeting and satisfying needs" that are part of the politics of the subcultural moment depicted in the photograph.

Another strategy employed by the essays, which works against the objectifying tendency of photographic images, is the subjectification of images. This means looking at the meanings images bear for alternative social subjects or, put another way, viewing images as signifying practices that help to constitute not only dominant but also alternative forms of subjectification. The "I" voice evident in all of the essays here is not a matter of private, individual reflection but rather a matter of social subjectivity, which implies an interested and affective view, as against the self-evidence and empirical realism that photographs have long been associated with. J. Kehaulanui Kaunui's essay opens with a "scientific" photograph that was part of a Rockefeller-funded ethnological research project on race-mixing in Hawaii. Kaunui's discussion dwells on the historical and social conditions of the photograph in order to unveil the racist project of "remaking" of Hawaiians that the study in question was an important part of and, further, to show how the issue of the blood quantum requirement for Hawaiians continues to shape Hawaiian dispossession in the present moment. Moreover, she searches the photograph for its evocative meanings for today's Hawaiian sovereignty struggles, for clues to what eludes the dominant modes of identification shaped by this dominant racist history, for alternate ways of understanding what constitutes Hawaiian-ness and its invoked terms of belonging. In contrast to Kaunui's essay but very much in keeping with this subjectifying strategy, Naono Akiko's essay opens up with a private family photograph, which records a personal loss, the death of her grandfather from radiation sickness. As Naono writes of this loss, however, the haunting absence marked by the photograph becomes an opening into a different understanding of a too-well understood public event, the bombing of Hiroshima. Caught between two imperialist governments and their nationalist state violence, between the roles of "victim" and "victimizer" demarcated by prevailing political narratives, and trapped in the deathly embrace of either innocence or guilt, Naono's figure of absence troubles the familiar political landscape in which present-day Japanese have learned to navigate and, in doing so, makes space for other, yet unforeseen, possibilities for political action and political subjectivity to emerge.

Plying the terrain between personal and public fantasies, Luz Calvo approaches a photograph by Chicana artist Laura Aguilar with a similar affective movement toward open-endedness, in lieu of analytical closure and political conclusions. Calvo unravels the signifying strands of the fantasy staged by Aguilar's photograph not from a disinterested perspective but rather from a subjective position bound up in the very same psychic, social constraints that shape and are represented in the photograph. In this way, Calvo stages the very ambivalent social and psychic dynamics that images provoke in the subjects they interpellate. Reading images subjectively means engaging questions of who the photographs are for—what kind of subjects they presume and produce, how "we," as viewers, are enticed to see the world, and how the way we see the world and each other might matter. Photographs stir the imagination, and beyond any "objective" restoration of the conditions of their production, the histories out of which they emerge and are embedded in, they work by evoking memories, speculation, dreams, and desires on the part of viewers. These subjective aspects of images perform the affective and ideological work necessary to maintain as well transform the worlds of social injustice that we live in. In these essays, besides history, the viewer is also what lies beyond the frame but nevertheless compels our attention. The authors foreground their own subjectivity as a practice of women of color criticism, a practice of situating hegemonic histories and objectified reality in alternate, unrecognized social contexts through subjective means. Speaking as political and personal subjects at the intersections of racial, gendered, and sexual oppression and freedom, they foreground their subjectivity as a critical enactment of difference, making the photographs a presentation of difference and possibility—a "may-be"—rather than a representation of sameness and reality—an "is."

These strategies of reading photographs are about looking and looking again in ways that enable the telling of different stories, the reviving of histories that are either actively lost or obliterated, and the making of new histories and new futures. The reconfiguration of dominant ways of looking thus means the creation of new lenses that mobilize images and make possible impeded fantasies and desires,

lenses that can also bring into focus alternative images which threaten
to disappear from history even as they offer alternate possibilities of
experience, life, and political action, some lost, some yet to be gained.
All these authors hold out for such possibilities, even if only the possibility of seeing the social injustice and historical wounds that are obliterated from hegemonic sight but that continue to haunt the dominant
visual representations of our real and imagined worlds. Photographs
become a spur to refigure prevailing notions of who or what one is as
a people, a community, a woman of color. As the contributors envisioned for this project, photographs become a tool for interrupting the
conception of women of color identities as "ahistorical, fixed or essential." They become tools in a continuing struggle.

Most of the essays in this book demonstrate this simple but crucial
premise: images are sites as well as instruments of social struggle. In
the last section, in particular, the authors focus on the importance of
images for creating communities of struggle and shaping the terms of
political participation, solidarity, and liberation. Maylei Blackwell
writes, for example, on the way the figure of la Soldadera was used by
Chicana activists to refigure women's political agency within the
Chicano movement. Blackwell argues that the visual tropes and icons
deployed in struggle "are not just 'representations' of what already
exists within Chicano culture but rather, political and cultural practices which play a constitutive role in the domain of culture." Chicana
feminist iconography reworked the dominant gendered tropes of
Chicano nationalism as Chicanas negotiated their own political subjectivities and historical agencies and opened up new social spaces and
oppositional publics. Catrióna Rueda Esquibel builds her discussion
of struggle around the legendary figure of the Aztec princess
Ixtacihuátl depicted in a photograph by artist Robert Buitrón. Like
Calvo, Esquibel unpacks the social fantasies that the photograph
ambivalently plays upon. She inquires into the pleasures obtained
from the prevalent images of the Aztec princess circulating in popular
Mexican and Chicano/a cultural environments and demonstrates the
provocative pleasures and challenging counter-fantasies that Buitrón's
image offers in their stead. In this way, Esquibel highlights the importance of counter-images of Native women for spurring the alternative
imaginations that accompany social struggle.

Michelle Habell-Pallán also takes a female icon of struggle—the protagonist figure of Jim Mendiola's 1996 independent short film, *Pretty
Vacant*—as the point of departure for a discussion of Chicana feminist
cultural production. Like the image of female fans in Miranda's essay,

the image opens up a discursive space for Habell-Pallán's analysis of the politics of Chicana punk music in East Los Angeles and Hollywood during the 1970s and 1980s. For Habell-Pallán, the press photo from the film encapsulates and stages the transnational political sensibilities that shaped Chicana feminist struggles during this period. As she writes, "The photo functions as a visual allegory for the way Chicana feminists and artists—as women of color—at the turn of the century, have turned a critical eye on the public sphere, and in doing so, have envisioned new subjects and subjectivities, as well as mapped out affiliations with racialized-as-non-white women within and across national borders." Focusing on an image of a woman of color, now placed at the center of the frame, Habell-Pallán's essay might itself serve as an allegory for this book as a whole insofar as the contributors all seek to place what is conventionally beyond the frame—histories, subjectivities, struggles—at the center of our attention, pleasure, and concern as a way to envision our worlds differently.

As editorial participants in this project, we hope *Beyond the Frame* contributes to new ways of image-making as well as new ways of looking. The essays here show that readers of images can also reframe and refocus dominant images, through critical analysis, historical research, counternarratives, countermemories, imagination, and fantasy, and thereby participate in the photographic process beyond the reproduced photographic image itself. Viewers are enjoined to be active interpreters and alternative producers of their meaning-making visual environments. In this way, we hope this project contributes to what we might call visual modes of resistance, whereby counter-images are deployed in the furthering of transformative social movements. And we hope it contributes to new strategies of resistance reading or reading practices that create, support, and expand the social struggles within which, ultimately, this endeavor is most meaningfully located.

Note

We acknowledge Kianga Ford as well as the editorial collective for their important work in organizing the conference. Other participants whose essays did not make it into this volume but whose work and involvement in the project were absolutely crucial to the project's realization include: Annie Laurie Anderson, Kale Fajardo, Noelani Goodyear-Kapoua, Jarita Holbrook, and Deborah Vargas. We also thank Gina Dent, Jennifer Gonzales, Avery Gordon, Saidiya Hartman, and Deborah Wright for their helpful and generous advice and mentorship during the conference.

Part I

Popular Culture and Advertising

"The East Side Revue, 40 Hits by East Los Angeles Most Popular Groups!" The Boys in the Band and the Girls Who Were Their Fans

Keta Miranda

The early 1960s East Los Angeles music scene—garage bands, rock and roll shows, car club sponsored dances, cruising down Whittier Blvd., Mod style and original dance steps—was a synergetic public space of cultural hybridity.[1] An artifact of the period between 1963 and 1968 is the recording and album cover of the *"East Side Revue: 40 Hits by East Los Angeles Most Popular Groups!"* The two record set album's first release was in 1966 and reissued in 1969 to commemorate LA's East Side Sound—in clear wax for audiophiles. In each release the album cover remained constant [see figure 1.1].[2] There are twenty photos of the garage bands that participated in the recording effort; the photographs are publicity shots produced in photography studios. In the majority of twenty, the band members are professionally positioned for the group shot. The studio photos of the band members align along the edges of the album cover create a frame, encasing the album title and the larger, center picture.[3] In this center photo there are women standing, dancing, arms waving in the air, with their mouths wide open—screaming. These girl fans evoke the "mania" of the early 1960s—the uncontrollable idolization of stars and fandom gone rampant. In most accounts of rock and roll, fandom (mania) is isolated from the musicology and from the musician's personal-career history. Fandom, separated from the musical form and the histories of the performers, stands outside as an incongruous phenomenon. Yet, here in this photo montage

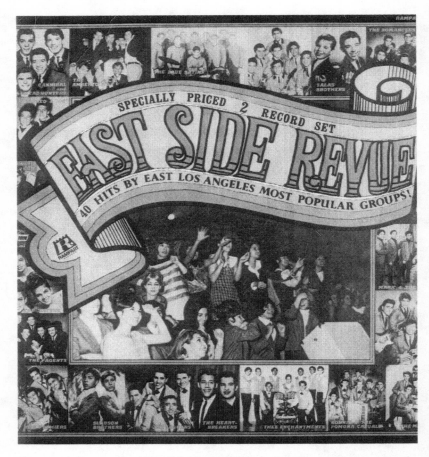

Figure 1.1   Front cover of *East Side Revue: 40 Hits by East Los Angeles Most Popular Groups!* (specially priced 2 record set). Released through Rampart Records Label, 1969. Used by permission, Hector Gonzalez.

of band members and fans of a local and regional music that made up the East Side Sound, a different understanding of fandom in relationship to the distinctive Chicano musical style can be decoded. In this essay, I make a particular kind of turn, a movement that centers the fans of the East Side Sound, specifically the teenage girls who were the fans of the boys in the bands. Focusing on the fans will mark a decided shift from the usual paradigms about rock and roll history and analysis of local, regional musical style.

In the exceptional works of Stephen Loza, *Barrio Rhythm* (1993), and David Reyes and Tom Waldman, *Land of 1000 Dances* (1998), the authors' primary projects are to situate Chicano music in relation to mainstream rock and roll as a dominant American musical style. Each of the social history treatises examines the influence of Chicano artists and music upon the mainstream (and vice versa). Additionally, Loza, Reyes, and Waldman critique the recording industries inability to market the music of Mexican American artists. While such a market critique may bring about an interpretation in which Chicano music is relegated as a subordinated culture attempting to cross over, the authors instead register a different paradigm to understand Chicano music. Through interviews with Chicano musicians and producers, the music that constituted the East Side Sound reflects their attempt not only to seek inclusion to the mainstream, but also to transform the dominant. Thus, the authors recognize culture as a site of counter-hegemonic practice. Moreover, the authors suggest a workable understanding of the Chicano musical style as a hybrid form. The hybridity is of particular importance to defining the distinctive character or style that produces the Chicano sound of the East Los Angeles rock and roll bands during this period. However, the photo of the girls on the album cover offers a different approach to reconstruct the history and interpretation of the local, regional music of the East Side Sound.

Providing a methodology to interpretation of history, Emma Pérez's *The Decolonial Imaginary: Writing Chicanas into History* (1999) calls for researchers to examine the interstitial space, or the third space, which is a location for articulating new identities.[4] In her critique of the processes and methodologies that ignore these areas, Perez conceives of these spaces as emergent points of historical transition. In this sense, this arena for historical recovery is silent because it has been silenced becoming an unarticulated space. Utilizing her proposition, I contend that the centrality of the girls in the photo and their voices, which are heard in various hit recordings by the bands, are fundamentally constitutive of the sound and scene of the early 1960s Mexican American youth culture. While the Scream and the bodies in movement can be read as nonproductive and uncontrollable expression of desire, this essay examines the Scream and the bodies in movement in order to reconsider—the spaces of cultural production—where meaning is made.

An album cover is part of product packaging, thus it works as advertisement. The cover of an album solicits, beckoning the consumer to "buy me." This album cover juxtaposes the bands and their fans in a complex interrelation in the production of the East Side Sound. While an image could produce multiple meanings, the conjunction of image and text produce and "fix" the meaning.[5] The caption, "most popular bands," privileges as the preferred meaning the bands over and above the visual representation of the girls. The alignment of the professionally produced studio photos of the bands works as a frame for the album, encircling the girl fans and fixing popularity to the heteronormative boy–girl relationship. The caption and the visual representation of the East Side scene connect to an already existing sign system—the star system. The text signifies the metalanguage of the 1960s captured through the song, "So you want to be a rock and roll star." Using the structure of the meta system of mainstream rock and roll (and the general star-system produced by the media), this local Mexican American musical scene signifies a claim to fame and stardom.[6] The caption and photo of the girls connect rock and roll music-making with popularity and for the boys: inevitable popularity with girls.

The album cover as advertisement works to set itself apart from all other recordings; inducing the consumer to register the difference and therefore to buy it. The cover as advertisement enunciates two conceptions for two different consumers: boys and girls. One way of examining the consumptive practice would be to read the juxtaposition between the bands and girl fans as masculine or dominant meta system stardom. The frame of studio photos is a signifier of fame, fun, participating in making the scene. Making the scene is to live outside the mundane everyday life of teens. Making music is productive and not just hanging around like the majority of youth. Through the involvement of arranging songs, understanding a sound and composing a performance for an audience, making music places a value on self-expression therefore is a means to defining an individual identity for the performer.[7] The added attraction is getting girls. Since the preferred meaning of the album cover constructs the girls as consumers, they are restricted to consuming the commodity.

Notwithstanding the dominant meaning of the album cover, that is to set it off from all other albums, the frame of the bands, additionally, sets boundaries and distinctions between the fans and the bands. The frame encloses the girls as an act of containment, controlling these unruly, vocal, dancing girls. Does the containment also signify competition as to what makes up the East Side Sound? Does the enclosure reveal a conflicting history about the production of the East Side Sound?

A second way of studying the album cover as advertisement is to examine a different kind of desire that is produced by the location of the girls at the center of the album. What meta system is generated to have the girls buy the product? The photos of the bands are small. One cannot sit and dote on one's favorite band or favorite band member. Through the juxtaposition, the work of the girls and their social relation to the production of "the most popular bands" is revealed. The center photo changes the relationship for the young women: We are central to this. Our attendance, our presence makes this scene happen. Fandom is acknowledged. Generally, musical historiography recognizes fans through their buying power, or as idolization from afar or as irrelevant to the creation of the artists. In this instance, the juxtaposition centers the girls who make the bands popular. As decoders of the advertisement, the centrality of their fandom is a reassertion of the self as producer. The hidden social relation of production—the general unacknowledged fan—is revealed in the montage of photos and caption.

However, there is another production process that remains hidden or overlooked in the descriptive histories of what created the East Side Sound. The work of the fans establishes not only the scene but also the musical style. This hypothesis adds another element to the cultural economy of fandom. While the fans are essential to the East Side Mod scene through their bodies, their voices—the noise and the screams—are constitutive of the East Side Sound. Their screams, their voices make the music categorized as the East Side Sound. Primary evidence of my contention is provided by an interview with Eddy Davis who produced some of the best recordings among the Mexican American musicians during the 1960s. In an interview conducted by Lee Joseph in October of 1992 with the assistance of Carmen Hillebrew for the liner notes for the CD compilation, *The East Side Sound*, Eddy Davis describes his role in producing the recordings and consequently the development of the Chicano Sound. Describing how he became familiar with local Chicano rock bands, Davis inadvertently discusses the participation of the girl fans in the recording of "Farmer John." A hit for the Premiers, this 1964 song rose to number nineteen on the Billboard chart, one of the highest showings by a Chicano band of that time. Working with Billy Cardenas, the manager of several East Side predominantly Mexican American bands, Davis describes his relation to the Premiers:

> Anyway, I broke down one night and let The Romancers on the show and I was impressed with the feeling they had in their music. That was my first experience with a Mexican-American group playing Motown

and R&B. So then we tried another Mexican-American band of Billy's, the Premiers. In a casual conversation I happened to mention to Billy about the song, "Farmer John" by Don and Dewey. Two weeks later Billy calls me to tell me he wants me to hear something. I went over and he had the Premiers play "Farmer John." I told him that I wanted to record it and we did.

Recounting the production problems, as well as the problem with the band, Davis goes on:

> The Premiers were the greatest groove band in the world. All their music they played with a groove, but they couldn't sing for shit! The vocal on the record was so bad, I just didn't know what to do. When I recorded my Rainbow album I used Wally Heider, who's now a famous technician. At that time he had just got his first remote 8-track and he did my first album "live" from the Rainbow Gardens in Pomona. I was interested in live sounds, trying to develop that, so I suggested that we record "Farmer John" live. We got a crowd and we took them over to the studio and we just overdubbed the music with a party going on. That's how that happened . . .
>
> ". . . It's a very groovy single and we made it live. All those voices screaming, *nobody had ever done that*. They were a girls' car club called the Chevelles that used to follow the Premiers. They were cholitas. They would scream and holler for the Premiers." [My emphasis]

Through this haphazard refinement of the product, through this winding tale Davis mentions one of the principle characteristics of the East Side Sound—the inclusion of the audience, *girls!*, in the recording. Davis further explains his use of the claim "Recorded live" was a way to publicize the dance clubs he was promoting. It also made the band's music available to the consumer. In Davis's scheme the youth attendance at the clubs and the possibility of participating in a recording "caused excitement. It seemed to work . . . They were coming just like that."

Through this ingenuous production, the hidden social relations between stars and fans reveal not only the consumptive practices, but also the fans who created the rock and roll phenomena of Chicano bands and the East Side Sound during the 1960s. The relocation of fans in the cultural production of the East Side music differentiates the product from all other garage band recordings. While the music history of these proto-punk rockers feature the artists and their music, the sound of the 1960s for Mexican American youth in Los Angeles embodies the girl fans through the noise that they make: the screams.

Rock music is indebted to its roots from African American traditions of gospel and blues. In the liner notes for the CD compilation, *The Grandson of Frat Rock, Volume 3*, Richard Henderson notes that Ray Charles's 1959 musical arrangement of "What'd I say" formulated a staple of pop music:

> Little remains to be said about Ray Charles, as he has become the revered institution he always deserved to be. However, "What'd I Say," a Jerry Wexler production dating from July 1959, contains some neat innovation that helped secure its success, and that have long been regarded as part of the furniture in the pop market place. I'm speaking of the infectious call and response vocals exchanged between Ray and his backup singers, The Raeletts, which were common to inner-city gospel churches, but were very new to the AM radio of the day. (Liner notes, 1991, Rhino Records)

Additionally, at the very end of the recording, the voices of the studio band and Raeletts emerge as Charles finishes the song abruptly. The voices of protest are for Charles to continue as well as expressions of a great session. The affection of the audience, in this instance the singers and the musicians in this call and response relationship, produce a "live" quality. The singer in this relationship "belongs" to the audience who wish Charles not to stop, but to keep going.

The call and response that produces a performer "belonging" to the audience occurs in Davis's "recorded live" from the Rainbow Room, accentuating the relation between fans and bands in the Premier's 1964 national hit. The utilization of the audience influenced a later national hit by Cannibal and the Headhunters, "Land of 1000 Dances" in 1965. Like the Premiers's cover recording, the song was first recorded by Rythm and Blues artist, Chris Kenner (I Like It Like That). The song became a staple in the repertoire by the East Los Angeles singing group. Most interviews contend that Garcia (the Cannibal and lead singer of the Headhunters) brought in the unforgettable, and contagious "Na, Na, Na, Na, Na, Na" refrain because he forgot the words to the music. Nonetheless, what is rarely celebrated, is the "live" audience that participates in the recording. Reyes and Waldman corroborate the following:

> Everybody, it seems, has a story to tell about the recording of "Land of 1000 Dances." The most accurate accounts are probably those of Frankie Garcia, Billy Cardenas, and Eddie Davis . . . As with many songs produced by Davis and Cardenas, this one was recorded under

simulated live conditions. The team would typically import both friends and strangers into the studio to whoop, holler, and shout encouragement, providing the background noise that takes place at a concert. The idea was to recreate the excitement of an East LA show without any attendant risks of taping an actual performance, such as an audience that is too boisterous to allow for the musicians to be properly heard. (Reyes and Waldman, 71)

Unlike the Premiers recording on a three track tape, the audience background is muffled until the moments in which the call and response of the singer and audience, "Na, Na, Na . . ." commences one quarter through the set. The two songs went national, thus the location of the fans, particularly the girl fans who make the most raucous noise is located in the production. Thus, Davis's idea of "live" is one of the most singular qualities of the East Side Sound that the rest of America heard.[8] Examining "the East Side Sound" through the voices of the girl fans provides a way to examine the Mod scene among Mexican American youth during that decade.

While the album cover as advertisement reveals a set of production relations, the photo montage also offers an entry to examine the social context of the musical phenomenon. It is to consider the wider meaning of the album cover as emergent points of historical transition. In this instance, the text of the album cover must relate to the broader sociopolitical relationships in which both fans and bands are embedded. Thus, the body language of the girls and their scream becomes a key site for examining the articulation of identity in the 1960s.

What is of particular interest to me is that the screaming, in chaotic fandom, is not for the Beatles—a band that was successfully marketed by the record companies. Nor are these young women screaming for Elvis who is not only successfully marketed but given the aspect of "star-dom" transcends the local community to acquire national fame. Instead, these girls are screaming for the boy who lives down the street. A boy whom the girls go to school with. A boy who is their best friend's brother or cousin. This local fame presents some interesting ideas to consider. Fame in its U.S. sense is attached to fortune and glamor. Fame is a representative of the North American Horatio Alger's success story: every poor boy has the opportunity to fame and fortune. What does local fame then signify?

Screaming out the band member's name—Willie! Ray! Eddie!—registers a close identity with the performer. The performer is a "star" who is not nationally marketed and therefore far from them, but rather for a Chicano youth who is close by. Local fame expresses the shared status between the local star and the local fan. During the period between 1963 and 1968, when the first wave of East Los Angeles Rock and Roll revues occurred, the dominant social paradigm of social injustice was framed in terms of Black and White. The racial and social issues framed between these two terms then devalues the experience of the Mexican American youth and empties occurrences in which identity—racial, ethnic, or national—is articulated. (Thus, even though the state attempts to prescribe identity and race, it can fail at the local level.)

Since the young men are local (immediate), community (Mexican American) boys, the screaming (body) registers the space, an interstice, within the state-regulated discourse about ethnicity and race, constraining the ways that individuals and groups can articulate identity. At the time, census forms did not include the term "Mexican American" as a way to claim ethnic-national identity. Thus, many Chicanos marked the box—Caucasian. Yet, their everyday lives were anything but the experience of White-ness. Dominant discourse framed racial/ethnic identity through social problems of poverty, racism, employment, and education, bringing forth a mixed and complicated relation to national identity.[9] Screaming not for Elvis but for a young man who could be their neighbor, configures the paradoxical experience about the myth of the American Dream. The scream can then be understood as articulated identity during a period when there is a War on Poverty, a war in Vietnam, and warring sides in the burgeoning Civil Rights movements and the emergent youth and student movements.

The body of the fans becomes a preeminent (consummate?) concern. The screaming bodies articulate the oneness of their local experience with the growing population of Mexican Americans in Los Angeles. The body in this sense speaks when subjective emotion is proscribed, when dominant discourse has structured other terms for naming identity. The screaming bodies, hundreds of Mexican American girls gathered in the auditoriums of high schools and union halls, converge into a singleness of uproarious clamor. Hundreds of bodies become the social body.

The screaming bodies are juxtaposed to the fluency of style that the youth participated in. Most of the boys in the bands wore the dress of the British Mods and the fans appropriated the style. This reworked Chicana/o aesthetic style may not be so unusual in most of our minds, since the early 1960s media was saturated with the Mandarin-collared suit coats, tight fitting trousers and the longer hair for boys, as well as the Mary Quant makeup of thick black eyeliner, straightened hair, long straightened bangs, of precision-asymmetrical haircuts, and the Twiggy style for girls. Such mediated style was taken up by the majority of youth. The image was everywhere.

One can argue that the Mod style is disguised orientalism. Orientalism, as described by Edward Said (1978: 12), is a "will or intention to understand, in some cases to control, manipulate, and even incorporate, what is a manifestly different (or alternative and novel) world." In this instance it is not the stereotypical "mysterious Orient" of danger, darkness, and fear, but the Orient of demeanor, gentility, and precision that is appropriated. The style conflicts with the raucous mood of rock and roll. (Could this be an instance of packaging rock and roll to control the stormy mood and turbulent bodies of youth?) Yet, the style cannot contain the music or the bodies or maintain the boundaries of nation-states. The Mod scene arrives along a convoluted course from England, from its eastern colonies back to a failing imperialist Britain to the United States. Similarly, the music was Rhythm and Blues, moving across the Atlantic and returning to the United States. with a particularly Mod influence on the sound.[10] The musical travel—the course of the sound from African American Rhythm and Blues to Britain back to the United States—registers the distinction of between-ness, of fissure, within the American social paradigm of Black/White relations.

The Mod style as it operated for Chicano youth in Los Angeles offers a possible interpretation of oppositional politics where youth grasp the style to signify opposition to the state project of patriotism and Americanism. The state's discourse of integration and economic mobility requires assimilation—loss and erasure of culture and history. The style and music were important markers of identity for the Chicano youth of Los Angeles in the early 1960s. The American sound of Surfer music was replaced by the British beat. It offered an oppositional style to a grouping that was outside of the surfers' socioeconomic background.[11]

Notably, the style and music taken up by Chicano youth in Los Angeles, the Mod scene, seem to register a rejection of Americanism as typified by Hollywood produced surfer. However, it is not a rejection of the surf sound (like that of Dick Dale and the Deltones et al.). The rejection was more about the kind of music produced by the taming of the Beach Boys and definitely the surfer sound of the "beach" movies featuring Frankie Avalon and Annette Funicello. These portrayals of youthful frolicking produced the suburban sound subduing youth sexuality and adventure.[12] The bands and youth who took up the Mod dress would lead one to conclude that it was an oppositional style, that is, oppositional to the dominant White middle class, U.S. culture.

The Mod style as it operated for Chicano youth in Los Angeles offers a more complex approach than orientalism. While one possible interpretation can be seen as oppositional politics—to oppose the state projects of patriotism and Americanism, a hegemonic national identity—there is another form of "assimilation" occurring. The Mod style is at the same time a desire, a wish to enter the middle class. The period between 1963 and 1968 was one in which economic mobility reached greater numbers and in particular through economic programs and affirmative action, produces economic mobility that performs a *class assimilation* that is different from the function of ethnic/racial/nationalist assimilation.

Thus, to look at the girl-fans, to investigate their expressions and modes of behavior, their style, introduces a different path of class mobility. It marks the psychological preparation for middle-class citizenship for Mexican Americans in Los Angeles. The music scene is the interstitial space in which Mexican American youth were reconstructing their racial-ethnic and class identities in the period just prior to the Chicano Power movement. The cultural politics of that moment, depicted in the moving, dancing bodies and the scream, is generally excluded as a nonpolitical digression. This neglected and excluded history, particularly the practices of the girls, offers a way to examine the political, economic, and racial factors at play at the moment of producing a rising middle class.

Hence, I note one other form of antithesis at work during the early 1960s. The Mod style was also a rejection of the *cholo* image and the *cholo* style. *Cholo* was the term used to identify what we now call gangbangers. The *cholo* image—Pendelton shirt and bell-bottomed khakis or bell-bottomed jeans—dominated the youth style in the late 1950s and early 1960s in Los Angeles among Mexican American youth. The move by youth to take up the Mod style, marks a particular turning point for identity as a minority in the United States. The postwar economy that hit the United States finally came to the barrio of Los Angeles in the mid-1960s. But it was a postwar boon that was bolstered by state intervention with programs like the War on Poverty. It was a moment when economic mobility was a real possibility for a community that had been relegated to the margins of subsistence for generations. It was a moment in which a new social class outlook and sensibility could be formed given the possibility of mobility.

Turning away from the *cholo* style, the patois, the language, and English-Spanish code switching suggests the trend toward assimilation by the Mexican American youth. However, I believe that it was not necessarily an assimilative intention. Grasping the British Mod subcultural style was a device for marking difference arising from its resistance meanings in Britain.[13] Therefore, it maintains some of its nonconformist character among the Chicano youth in the United States. Not Black and not White, not *cholo* and not surfer, the Mod style presented a hybrid cultural form for Angeleno youth who eclectically brought together musical forms and cultural style to register difference in a period where ethnic/racial and social identity are constrained. It was a transitional moment. It marked not only opposition to the dominant culture but also registered difference from the former class identity to an emerging class identity.

This liminal identity, not a *cholo*, is why I focus on the young women who carved out a social space for their social expectations. One of the features of the Mod sound was its celebration of self. In this manner the critics of music register the hedonism of youth subcultural style. Yet, I think that for the period between 1963 and 1968, there is another reasoning emerging, particularly for the girls. The sound of the 1950s could be generally characterized by the notions of unrequited love, of personal investment to tragic love, and of the completed self in love relations. While the Mod/Mersey Beat and Soul/R and B music did repeat and reproduce these notions, there were at the same time the notions of freedom and even chaos and uncontrollability. These sounds and words offered enjoyment and pleasure at a point when a consumer culture extensively diffuses throughout society. The scene, in combination with the postwar economy, offered new consumptive practices formerly unavailable to a large section of the Mexican American community. And, at the same time, the celebration of self, male or female, boy or girl, offered distinct new concepts of self for the young women. One's identity did not have to be locked/contained in the dynamic of the love duo.

Choosing a different style indicates the politics of representation. As Donald Lowe has noted, the peak stage of the perceptual revolution happens simultaneously with the postwar growth of capitalism with the expanding and accelerating rate of capitalist production and consumption in the boom economy.[14] Representation becomes the site of struggle to express interests, of meeting and satisfying social needs—beyond material needs and wants. The Mod style, while it may be marked as extraneous need, signifies social aspiration. Additionally, the consumptive practice is placed upon the body, over the body. It is important to register the differences between body practices and style as representation. Style as a representational practice differs from body practices. The bodies of the Mexican American youth are racialized in social practices of exclusion and discrimination in higher rates of unemployment, lower educational attainment, segregated residence and high rates of police brutality. Clothing the body enters the realm of symbolization, like the written sign. Representation symbolizes in order to depict or portray a reconstructed identity.

"Not a *cholo*," marks the socialization process in which the young women as fully conscious agents of change demand that their boyfriends and girlfriends change their fashion style and socially refigure themselves in a society that is able to incorporate a large grouping into its middle class.[15] The shift in style registers the fact that a sizable number of Mexican Americans were becoming economically mobile. The socialization process of getting ready for the social mobility needed a psychological factor, to incorporate the middle-class concepts of propriety and behavior (the bourgeois-ification of the lower income working class to a middle-class mind-set).

I am aware that this formulation about the role of young women as agents of socialization—the woman behind the man—is problematic. The social roles for women in this early 1960s period were expanding, particularly as more women entered the employment field outside the home. Work outside the home was still conceptualized as work supplemental to the male head of household income, or "pin-money." This notion of work therefore constructs an identity of complementarity for young Chicanas. In fact, this way of thinking was considered progressive at the time. With social roles defined as, and limited to, work in the home, the drive toward middle-class norms can be viewed as an important role that young Mexican American women helped to accomplish. While it seems as if there is a lack of agency, or returning to a subordinate role, the opposite may be considered. The role of wife and future mother under a new set of economic (social production) relations prepared the way for the social mobility that was now possible for a large number of Mexican Americans. In this way, the young women participate in the psychological and ideological shifts.

During the early 1960s, Klein categorized Chicano youth as either *cholos* or squares.[16] While the typology is problematic, that is, there is a greater variety of youth between the categories, nonetheless, one can utilize Klein's categories to investigate the subcultural notions that did operate in such dichotomies. The Mod style was a space to act out hipness. Mod style was an exaggeration of neatness; the dress was conventional yet exaggerated to undermine conventions. As Dick Hebdige (1979) has noted about the Mod style, "it undermined the meaning of conservative dress through a style that pushed neatness to the point of absurdity." Predominantly a working-class youth culture in postwar England, many Mods had jobs "which made fairly stringent demands on their appearance, dress and 'general demeanor' " enabling them "to negotiate smoothly between school, work and leisure." The style disrupted the orderly conventions of clothing, underneath was a " 'secret identity' constructed here beyond the limited experiential scope of the bosses and teachers, [it] was an emotional affinity with black people." The affinity to the "Black Man" was a form of subversion for the Mods: to bend the rules to suit his own purposes, elaborate different codes, and use language skills to conceal as well as invert the "straight" worlds values, norms, and conventions (52–54).

Attention to the latest dance, the latest song, the latest fad marks the social ability to become consumers of superfluous commodities. At the same time, by consuming certain cultural goods, they in turn resisted certain cultural and ethnic stereotypes. These are practices located in the social relations of consumption. Attention to the latest craze, the subcultural style allows for a greater number of youth to become not only consumers of marketable commodities but also makers of purposeful choices.[17] Thus, resistant practices may be understood as blocks and obstacles to racial or ethnic assimilation, not necessarily oppositional to economic assimilation.

Situated in this Mod scene are music, style, and dance. Dance in particular is an aspect of culture that is usually considered nonproductive and therefore generally not critically studied in social science research. Dance is usually researched as either high art or folk art. Focusing on dance yet again offers an examination of emergence. The body becomes a critical element to understand the structures of feeling operating in the barrios of Los Angeles. Again, dance and the body are the other forms of communicating the incommunicable. For me, the dance also symbolizes the ability to articulate one's identity in a society that racializes bodies.

In *The Body in Late Capitalism*, Donald Lowe argues that nonexchangist social and cultural values are destabilized under the capitalist endeavor to constantly create new markets for consumption. While including the role of mass media that creates new desires for consumption, he argues that these elements transformed the past established patterns of meeting and satisfying human needs. Marking the 1950s as the point of no return, he argues that the consumption of lifestyle radically refigures individual subjects and how they respond to state capitalism. In many ways, I do agree with his overall hypothesis. However, the study of the music scene in Los Angeles among Mexican American youth would delineate the areas of subjects as citizens (i.e., rights), subjects as agents of choice (consumers), and change (rights and social agency), and bodies (i.e., subject to structures, economic, state, and to ideological) that are acted upon by the material conditions of living and the state. A study of the subcultural style of the East L.A. Mod scene accounts for the challenge to racist and stereotypical representations because of the wide-range of signifiers that are not only marketed but can also be stolen from the vast array of images and messages. The musical scene includes the bodies of youth in dance or the screaming body offering a different range of signification, somewhere outside of base, exchange value and consumption. The Scream and the dance of this period could be seen as if it is the nonproductive and uncontrollable expression of desires beyond meeting and satisfying needs. However, the Scream and dance can also be considered the interstitial space where meaning can be interpreted.

Notes

1. This essay sketches out a future research project about the East Los Angeles Mod scene. In a book project tentatively titled, *The Boys in the Band and the Girls who were their Fans*, I will examine the subcultural style in order to locate a site of transitional identity politics during the years between 1963 and 1968. The shift from the bands to the fans focuses on the agency of the women who carved out space for a social identity. By focusing on the social milieu, investigating the lives of the youth in their own lived contexts, examining a wide range of consumptive practices, I hope to characterize the youth subculture and determine the historical location of racial/ethnic, class, gender, and sexual identity. By shifting emphasis to the fans, to the local community, to the relations between the fans and the band, I examine consumptive practices during postwar capitalist development. What's more, the local context becomes the salient feature to situate identity, race, class, gender, and sexual identity, in the context of state institutional projects of assimilation, the inclusionist policies that attempt to erase difference in the name of liberalist national identity. Thus, I attempt to look at those spaces where culture is negotiated, where identity is created when there is pressure to erase the local and particular locations of identity production.

2. The album cover has been reproduced in the 1999 four volume CD collection, *The East Side Sound* (Rampart; distributed by American Pie as LP 3303; 1966 (1969)). All of the covers for this collection reconstitute the format of the earlier record albums, however differences are the center photo of fans who are boys and girls or as in volume four the producers of the rock and roll shows are centered. The third volume CD cover is the picture of the girls, however photos formatted along the album cover are different band members as well as the labels of the local recording companies that distributed the records of the local bands that constituted the East Side Sound.

3. The one photo of The Sisters, a local singing group who sang for various bands, is pictured just under the banner that announces the album. The Sisters have been interviewed by Stephen Loza, *Barrio Rhythm: Mexican American Music in Los Angeles* (Chicago: University of Illinois Press, 1993), and by David Reyes and Tom Waldman, *Land of 1000 Dances: Chicano Rock 'n' Roll from Southern California* (Albuquerque: University of New Mexico Press, 1998).

4. See Emma Pérez, *The Decolonial Imaginary: Writing Chicanas into History* (Bloomington: Indiana University Press, 1999).

5. See Roland Barthes, "Rhetoric of the Image" in *Image, Music, Text* (essays selected and translated by Stephen Heath NY: Hill and Wang, 1988 (1994)).

6. The star system is a highly manufactured relation between the consumer and artist produced by the media. The system depends on the presentation of images from commercial pop culture. Fantasy in this relation places the fan in a subordinate role, in awe of the male performer. See Angela McRobbie, "Girls and Subcultures" in *Feminism and Youth Culture: From Jackie to Just Seventeen* (Boston, MA: Unwin Hyman, 1989).

7. See Simon Frith, "The Cultural Study of Popular Music" in *Cultural Studies*, edited by Grossberg, Lawrence, Cary Nelson, and Paula Treicher, 1992 (New York: Routledge, 1992: 174) who summarizes the ethnographies of British rock artists by Sarah Cohen, "Society and Culture in the Making of Rock Music in Liverpool" (Unpublished Ph.D. Thesis. Oxford University, 1987), and Ruth Finnegan, *Hidden Musicians* (Cambridge University Press, 1989).

8. While live albums are now part of the mainstay of top rock bands, the history of live recordings begin in 1963 with James Brown's *Live at the Apollo, Vol. 1* [King K826] followed by the Animal's 1965, *On Tour*. Live albums do not take up the repertoire until 1970, when technological innovations allow the recording of live performances—the interaction between audience and performer.

9. See Thomas Holt, *The Problem of Race in the Twenty-First Century* (Cambridge, MA: Harvard University Press, 2000), on race making at the everyday level of peoples lives that links national and local.

10. See Paul Gilroy, *The Black Atlantic: Modernity and Double Consciousness* (Cambridge, MA: Harvard University Press, 1993), who discusses the hybridity of music and the ineffaceable essential meaning of Black music.

11. Surf music particularly the sound was rehabilitated for the Beach movies, arises from the concern of White middle-class parents who did not want their children patronizing Black musicians. The Beach movies and subsequent musical genre were intended to keep their children away from Black soul

music—the transgressive energy of funk. It was a cultural intervention in the lives of White youth by their parents (i.e., the establishment to tame the flaunting bodies of delinquent "animalism"). See Susan Douglas, *Where the Girls Are: Growing Up Female with the Mass Media* (New York: Times Books; Random House, 1994 (1995)).

12. Note also the "whitening" of Italian American youth that erases ethnicity in Southern California. As a cultural space of homogenization, Hollywood de-ethnicizes the East Coast Italian American experience of ethnic and urban identity. Therefore, Mexican American style signals resistance to assimilation to dominant culture not to class mobility.

13. Dick Hebdige explains style as a signifier rather than distinct cultural expressions. Since style takes place in a complex relation to social existence of its followers, the objective of style is to be out of step with mainstream dominant culture in *Subculture: The Meaning of Style* (New York: Routledge, 1970).

14. Donald Lowe, *The Body in Late Capitalism* (Durham, NC: Duke University Press, 1995: 12), discusses the perceptual revolution that began in 1905–1915 and fully developed in the second half of this century. New epistemes emerged where representations of identity and difference were ordered in spatial terms.

15. The point here is that capitalism is in its productive capacity, its drive for markets and profit brings about a larger base of people into social production. However, the term "society" may be questionable because it connotes civil society and forms of law and justice. "Society" then may not be the term to use. Society is attempting to resolve issues of civil liberties and human rights—through the struggles of the Civil Rights organizations—at a time in which capitalist growth is changing society in a postwar economy.

16. Malcolm W. Klein presents the subcategories found among Mexican American youth in *Street Gangs and Street Workers* (Englewood Cliffs, NJ: Prentice-Hall, 1971).

17. I engage an idea by Nancy Chen, *Breathing Spaces: Qigong, Psychiatry, and Healing in China* (New York: Columbia University Press, 2003), who notes that the rituals of the state, the statist body or body politic, acts upon and transforms the body. Her example provides an examination of the Chinese state that intervenes in the production and development of commodities enabling consumption. As a result, there is the growth and expansion of student demonstrations and movements for democracy. Individual bodies or the social body flows into the social economy. Thus, state policies and projects transforming consumptive practices can enact much different responses to the intents of the state.

2

The Commoditization of Hybridity in the 1990s U.S. Fashion Advertising: Who Is cK one?[1]

Laura J. Kuo

> *. . . an important caveat follows for postcolonial practices, namely the risk that hybridity might be re-colonised by the apparatus of power as either compensation for our losses, or as the velvet glove of enjoyment that goes hand in hand with the iron fist of exclusion.*
>
> —*Kobena Mercer*

How does a concept like hybridity travel within different economies—between the academy, activist arenas, and the media, for example—and what forms does it take on within these smart mutations? Is the adoption of a complex concept like hybridity by the media the simple appropriation of culture by capital? The usages, travels, and permutations of hybridity are more complex and elaborate than a blanket confiscation of its political value. After all, capital *is* culture (among other things) and hybridity *is* another sign within postmodern commodity systems. By engaging the structure of these systems we can begin to identify the ways in which hybridity operates within—and in the service of—the dominant logic of postmodern capitalist neoliberalism, and its massive contradictions. In this essay I investigate hybridity as a site of possible transgressions of fixed identities, and as a potentially productive space that has been recolonized by market multiculturalism—a space that views everyone as mixed and thus elides structural differences and persistent hierarchies of race, class, gender, and sexuality.

Specifically within the context of advertising, hybridity becomes, at one level, a strategy that stabilizes discursive power relations within transnational capital. For example, there are complex relations between multinational corporations in the United States and U.S./Third World and gendered immigrant labor practices on the one hand, and the co-optation of political coalitional work on the other. At another level, images of hybridity in advertising generate value in a global world where these commodities circulate. Certainly, a racialized economic hegemony is stabilized through appropriations of racial diversity discourses within market multiculturalism. Yet it is too easy to declare that global capital exploits the labor of women of color in the Third World and in the United States, that advertising hides this exploitative relationship, and that the images therefore should be criticized and dismissed. Instead, I am interested in the way in which this practice of "hiding" constitutes a necessary vector of postmodern difference that enables the dominant logic of late capitalism, which in turn depends upon exploitation, appropriation, and difference. Advertising hybridity becomes complicitous with the act of hiding, yet at the same time images of hybridity open up new communities of possibilities for people who take up the ads within their specifics of home and place, looking toward new forms of identifications and affective communities *within* capitalism's cultural logic.

The observations in this essay are based on the principal photograph of the *cK one* advertising campaign, which has been displayed prolifically on billboards and in magazines. This photo (see figure 2.1), which served as the prototype on which other early *cK one* ads were based, is called "Jenny, Kate & Company" in the Calvin Klein Cosmetics press packet. Using this ad as a sort of case study, I investigate how images of hybridity and multiculturalism in advertising serve to conflate race, class, gender, sexuality, ethnicity, nation, and culture within a totalizing logic of neoliberalism.[2] I call the discursive practice of homogenizing race, class, nation, gender, sexuality, ethnicity, and culture—and the elision of the specificities of their individual locations and their intersections—*commoditized hybridity*. Commoditized hybridity is a manifestation of a particular practice of the relentless marketing of race. It is informed by processes of consumption of race within postmodern capitalism. Commoditized hybridity also can be represented under the guise of "multiculturalism."[3]

The staging of hybridity in fashion culture is inextricably bound up with the heterogeneity and plurality that are features of identity and culture—both past and present—in the United States. My specific

Figure 2.1 "Jenny, Kate, and Company," prototype for the *cK one: portraits of a generation* advertising campaign, released in September 1994.

interest concerning the performance of commoditized hybridity in popular culture foregrounds the treatment of U.S./Third World racialized, gendered, and cultural hybridity in the staging of hybridized racial relations, a phenomenon that is well-illustrated in the photographs that comprise early *cK one* advertisements.

Calvin Klein fragrances are distributed throughout the world via a network of affiliated and nonaffiliated distributors. When *cK one* was released in September 1994, CK fragrances—*Obsession, Obsession for men, Eternity, Eternity for men, Escape, Escape for men, cK one, and cK be*—dominated the domestic and international marketplace with 1994 world sales in the range of $500 million.[4] The *cK one* line of perfumes/colognes entered the market following *Obsession '85, Eternity '88* and *Escape '91*.[5] The photographic images promoting *cK one*, entitled "portraits of a generation," were widespread, appearing on billboards and television coast to coast and inhabiting the pages of magazines and newspapers nationally and internationally.[6] A series of black and white *cK one* photo of the same nature appeared steadily until late 1998, each image presenting a different arrangement of men and women lined up side by side, spanning two and sometimes three or four full magazine pages.[7]

Although my analysis here focuses on *cK one*, there was a prolifer-ation in the early to mid-1990s of similar marketing campaigns, which reached their zenith in 1995–1996 with hybridized imagery permeating the pages of fashion magazines and playing a cardinal role in contem-porary mainstream fashion culture itself. The shifting roles race occupies as both resource and foil in the United States are illuminated when these cultural texts are situated within larger sociohistorical and political contexts in late-twentieth-century America. Issues of diaspora and citizenship, and belonging and displacement, that are evoked through images like those found in Calvin Klein advertisements are utterly familiar; yet they are also strangely unsettling—why hybridity, why now?[8]

Does the image of multicultural difference as represented in the ad campaign's prototype (and its offshoots) valorize a particular state of cultural hybridity? Or does this instance of racially hybrid fashion photography merely masquerade as a homage to race, or as magna-nimity to racial difference? Despite the complexity and allure of its exhibition, is this image merely the utilization of race as code to turn a dollar? Does this image represent anything more than the panning, homogenizing, and flattening of racial vicissitudes—and hybridized relations, experiences, and identities—in contemporary U.S. culture? Do Calvin Klein's "Jenny, Kate & Company" ads subvert the binary racial formations that deny notions of hybridity being mapped by contemporary activists and cultural theorists? In staging the array of bodies that constitute the nation of hybrids, does Calvin Klein create an ideological space of hybridity? Is *cK one* a concession to the force of hybridity in culture? Is this progress? Or is this advertisement an example of what Kobena Mercer warns us against, specifically, a recolonization of hybridity? In this case, are the answers to these questions mutually exclusive, or can Calvin Klein intend all of these readings at once—that is, simultaneous progress and recolonization?

I am interested in possible interpretations and receptions of this photograph, and more importantly the ad campaign it represents, in relation to the construction of hybridity as a trend in fashion culture. I also want to consider the ramifications of this enactment with regard to the social circumstances of hybridity as it concerns women of color identity within a diasporic transnational U.S. context. This analysis must be situated within the context of the explicit intentions, objec-tives, and attitudes of the Calvin Klein Cosmetic Company as articu-lated in their press kit, which conveys to the consumer extensive data, facts, and figures. The kit includes everything from ad themes (both photographic and televisual), brand themes, quotes from Klein himself, and the company's political platform, to a priceless "mission statement," all of which beg analysis. Following are the texts of the *cK one* product advertisement and mission statement, respectively:

cK one *Fragrance—Product Advertisement*
If you know who you are. If you'll try anything once. You won't take no for an answer. If you live your own life. If you choose love over stability. If you like to share. If you don't try to be something you're not. If you think conformity is boring. If you're a man or a woman.

cK one *Fragrance—Mission Statement*
We live in a time of enormous change and opportunity. Attitudes and values are shifting, rules are changing. There is an openness to new ideas that hasn't been seen for decades. A new perspective that has permeated everything from fashion to politics to beauty.

As walls come down and boundaries are challenged, the world is getting smaller. People are liberating themselves from restrictions and limitations. Lines between race, sex and age are diminishing. People are focusing on exposing similarities, not disguising differences.

From this fluidity, a whole new vision of style has emerged. Glamour has a different meaning. There is no longer a need to enhance one's gender or conform to a type. Now we are exploring our individuality. Products that put people into specific categories do not make sense anymore. It's all about being real.

We wanted to focus on the intimacy real individuals and true partners experience. People who are so secure that they can share anything. It is a very natural, almost primal state of mind. One that is extremely sexual.

It's not about unisex or androgyny or anything else that neutralizes you as a man or as a woman. It's honest. It's open. It's about being one with yourself and everyone else.

cK one *Fragrance* celebrates the individual. It speaks to a diverse group who identify with this attitude. It is as sexy as the truth. And ultimately, it aims to do what no Fragrance has done before . . . make you free. (Calvin Klein Cosmetics Corporation)

This promotional copy is saturated with postmodern liberalism, with a distinct postmodern focus on alterity, aesthetics, and capitalist individualism as access to freedom. With one bottle of fragrance, the consumer is transformed into a postmodern liberal humanist, existing in eternal hipness, eminently multicultural and one with humankind. If the revolution will not be televised, perhaps it has been bottled; *cK one* will "make you free." Calvin Klein's public relations literature puts forth notions of difference and oneness; it implies that no work needs to be done to create new relationships, to undo social injustices, to redress inequalities, or to end exploitation. Instead, it promotes change on the level of the individual. Success and failure are attributed to individuals—to their actions, or to their failure to act (or to wear fragrance). The construction of alliance in *cK one* is apolitical. Like the photos that comprised its early advertisements, the *cK one* rhetoric both commits and instigates an apolitical embrace of heterogeneity that stands in for the necessary political work—at the level of coalition and solidarity—that brings about social change. In *cK one* ads, racism is a thing of the past; it is acknowledged precisely in the past. The embrace of multicultural, gendered, ethnic, and sexual diversity in *cK one* implies—at least visually— that social equality has been achieved. The "we" invoked through *cK one* is not racist; for this "we" finds racial difference exceedingly hip—so hip, in fact, that it becomes a commodity.

Quintessentially postmodern—where fragmentation and disunity are one—the hybrid/multicultural *cK one* ad campaign adopts postmodern platforms of identity formation in staging photographic images of racial difference, gender ambiguity, and sexual intimation, while actually collapsing these categories of differentiation. Calvin Klein's dissemination of these hybridized images is about surfaces, rather than the content of politics. Yet it is precisely the styles and fashion sensibilities distinctive to a number of specific political contexts (feminisms, queer/of color mobilizing, Civil Rights, and youth culture/gangs) that are co-opted into *cK one*'s surface styling. Subaltern voices are normalized and homogenized into trendsetting potential, and ultimately divested of the counter-hegemonic resistance and political power these movements represent within their specific contexts.

cK one and commoditized hybridity function around the psychic and social ambivalence of their reception; that is, they enact a dual recognition and disavowal of difference. They operate on the ability to hold two contradictory beliefs. This disavowal of difference—*I know very well* that all people are not equal in the United States due to racism, labor exploitation, homophobia, classism, sexism, and so on, *but nevertheless*, I believe that everyone is equal and can be "one"—is structured on the dual recognition of: (1) racial inequality and (2) the multicultural promise that enables the political meanings of these photographs to circulate in the first place. The irreconcilable moments of the postcolonial fantasy are, on the one hand, acknowledging the racial injustices that pervade our histories, and on the other hand, allowing the persistence of hope—hope that we all can live in a society where any subject position is possible—to endure.

In this regard, the *cK one* photos disavow realities of racism, homophobia, sexism, classism, heterosexism, and ethnocentrism. They posture a notion of multiculturalism as the first moment without deconstructing U.S. hegemonic monoculturalisms that give rise to these injustices in the first place. The ads imagine a state of racialized utopia by omitting the bodies (Third World gendered laborers) that produce Calvin Klein clothing and accessories, and the bodies (coalitional solidarities) that give the ads' ersatz multiculturalism their loaded significations. Calvin Klein embodies, therefore, a tremendous power differential as a component of capital, or as Mercer would say, as "an apparatus of power."[9]

But Calvin Klein's force is not omnipotent, and photographic images travel. In this fluid process of consistent dissemination and reception (day after day, month after month, over a period of years), the ads' meanings evolve and redevelop, reconstituting, shifting, rupturing, and reinscribing the photographs' intended purpose—to sell. Specific communities will take these images to their individual locations of culture; they will take their specific experiences, identifications, and alliances and infuse the images with their own consequence and authority.

Enabling alternative and multiple subject positions, the conditions of production and reception surrounding cultural hybridity constitute new forms of associations and identifications. I look at this *cK one* photograph specifically to examine the ways in which commoditization and co-optation are central to capitalism and postmodernism. In focusing on the usages of cultural representation and the production of "multicultural" difference as commodities within economies of fashion in the United States, I am interested in the ways in which concepts of postmodern cultural hybridity—the interstices between and among race, class, gender, and sexuality described by Trinh Minh-ha, Gloria Anzaldua, Homi Bhabha, and others—become *recolonized* by multicultural fashion campaigns in the form of commoditized hybridity. And, more importantly, I am interested in the work that is done to redeem the political value that hybridity signifies within this inevitable transformation. Is recolonization the final step, the last word? For reasons I mention above, I argue that it is not. Certainly menacing appropriations, destructions, and falsifications of crucial political work occur, but the author's intent is never the final word.

*   *   *

A number of issues can be interrogated in these ads in relation to commoditized hybridity—for example, flagrant appropriations of an urban 1980s–1990s queer/ACT UP style/sensibility and "in-your-face" street politics and fashion. While this essay attempts to interrogate an insidious conflation of sexual and racial difference *vis-à-vis* commoditized hybridity, my larger project focuses more markedly on racial difference as commodity. I believe that in these ads race is the primary project, with sexuality, class, and ethnicity manipulated specifically around the provocative 1990s race question. In the *cK one* photographs, "race" is the hegemonic signifier, while sexuality, class, and ethnicity seem secondary or conditional; that is, they seem to be placed in the service of race.[10]

However, race is both foregounded and elided in the photos through a homogenization of gender and sexuality. An effective collapse of gender difference serves as the stage for both centering race as the subversive spectacle of difference, and depleting racial difference of its political import. This process in which hybridity is commoditized   (race = gender = sexuality = unisex = one = *cK   one*) stages race in such a way that difference ceases to matter. This practice of both homogenizing and accentuating race, for effect, is reminiscent of ideological representations of gender in radical/liberal feminism.[11]

The *cK one* photos establish hybrid racial relations through biologistic portrayals of appearance. The staging of the models constructs whiteness as a racial essence cosmetically arranged with "other" racial essences in order to convey an impression of harmony/unity/solidarity. In this respect, *cK one* potentially closes off a space to discuss the different positions whites and people of color occupy in relation to practice, history, and social formations, and structures and relations of power. Through juxtapositions of differently racialized bodies in its ads—which are staged against a homologous black and white backdrop—*cK one* constructs a notion of multiraciality that postures as social diversity. The hybrid figures of 1990s fashion are bodies on which a racialized seamlessness/sameness is inscribed. The models in *cK one* photos are racially diverse, and when they are staged together they signify the currency of a multicultural decade. Their bodies are arranged together and "equalized" in a contrived dynamic through photographic distortion and a deliberate homogeneity of height, weight, pose, style, and expression that invokes a sense of cultural similarity, of oneness. The images are presented in black and white, creating a ground tone of similarity against which difference, as separation, is muted, and heterogeneity is emphasized. The models are always already in contact, integrated, and hybrid. They are aesthetically seductive—extremely cool, hip, and sexy—and they become part of the lure to *cK one*-ness. The models of color appear to be "one" with the white models, creating an illusion of common social and economic positions and cultural identifications. The commoditization of hybridity takes rich heterogeneous spaces of racial and cultural diversity and turns these spaces of promise against their potential, effectively disrupting their ability to spawn real social change. It recolonizes desirable and hopeful formulations of cultural hybridity and transforms them into weapons against the spectator. In short, these ads erase historical memory and social analysis, offering fragrance in return.

The contextlessness of *cK one* characterizes literal and theoretical investments on the part of popular culture in portraying complicated social relations as just another pretty picture. This constitutes an assault on millions of people who strive for the possibility of antiracist coalitions, many of whom have spent their lives fighting uphill battles for social justice. Contrary to their surface imagery, the photos of *cK one* and similar ad campaigns evince a racial crisis in this country that should not go unaddressed.

In an image such as the "Jenny, Kate & Company" prototype, what gap is closed by the fetish of commoditized hybridity? What is papered over? What is solved? What is at stake? How does this image address the problem of the other, or the problem of market multiculturalism? What does "the nation" want, and what does *cK one* offer?

In the United States, "the nation" aspires toward oneness.[12] *cK one* offers one nation in a bottle where people—different, but fundamentally similar—become one. In the melding of bodies, the fetishistic bottling of heterogeneity—wherein the bottle is literalized as the fetish— multiculturalism becomes falsely material. Behind this photograph and its attempt at representing postmodern difference is an absent other: the sweatshop worker who produces the clothes in which the models are dressed (which also bear the Calvin Klein label), and those whose real-life experiences of political violence contradict the utopian muliticul-tural vision that the Calvin Klein Corporation so stylishly offers. What gets fetishistically sutured by commoditized hybridity is an era of racial antagonism, California's propositions 187, 184, 209, 227, and their discontents. *cK one* recolonizes the liminal "Third Space" sweat-shop body, and the liminal space of postmodern hybridity.

What is so compelling about indiscriminate applications of multi-culturalism within advertising is that multiculturalism becomes a bandwagon of opportunity for everyone—it can take anyone anywhere. Politicians—be they Republican or Democrat—can lobby against affirmative action legislation, while radical and liberal feminists can push for universal sisterhood; in each instance, a "multicultural" agenda is evoked. The 1996 passage of anti-affirmative action legislation, the so-called California Civil Rights Initiative (Proposition 209), demonstrates perfectly the strategic possibility for the conservative right to utilize a discourse of multiculturalism to abolish affirmative action.

*   *   *

Hybridity has always been a preexisting reality, and like multiculturalism, the mainstreaming of it gives it a fad-like quality—as if here today, gone tomorrow (or next month at least). Indeed, *cK one* as a multicultural ad campaign is no more. The new wave of *cK one* ads (which premiered in the United States in December 1998) feature individual head shots of a middle-aged White man with stubble, a waifish young white woman with freckles, and a somewhat nondescript young white man with freckles accompanied by the taglines "robert@cKone.com," "anna@cKone.com," and "ian@cKone.com" respectively. It was not until October 1999 that a model of color, "kristy@cKone.com"—a biracial Black/Asian woman—appeared in this subsequent *cK one* campaign. This relative dearth of people of color in the new campaign is a pronounced departure from the hybridized images that once sold *cK one* and a curious commentary on the state of multicultural difference as we enter the new millennium. (It seems that computer/e-mail access are now required if one is to participate in the oneness of *cK one*.)

But hybridity is not temporal. It is a consciousness, a state of being, seeing, and perceiving that defines social and psychic identity and relations. In this work, it is also a beginning, a conceptual instrument to refigure coalition and community. If *cK one* commits an enactment of false community, then what kinds of political community can be enabled by another concept of hybridity; that is, a concept of hybridity where the value of the term is not contingent upon a static and hegemonic order, but rather is reinvented and evolving constantly in and through cross-coalitional dialogue, friction, organization, exchange, and mobilization.

Hybridity stands staunchly against the American melting pot and its teleology of homogenization. The teleology of *cK one* is the *individual*—the American within a hybrid context. One could say, in this regard, that the teleology of multiculturalism is assimilation, while that of hybridity is heterogeneity. *cK one* professes to celebrate a vision of cultural hybridity. Yet *cK one* represents a state of cultural homogeneity by recolonizing racial and cultural perceptions of heterogeneity in the form of commoditized hybridity. *cK one* claims to assert the multicultural diversity so popular in political and social discourses of the 1990s. In reality, it is mere testimony to the facile way in which racial difference is most often regarded. The photographic images presented in *cK one* advertisements are anathema to racial difference. These ads exemplify the co-optation of racial and cultural difference—and the erasure of the urgent political issues that lie therein—by mainstream multiculturalism, via commoditized hybridity.

It is given that the *cK one* ad campaign functions ideologically to support the Calvin Klein Cosmetics Corporation and, by extension, the U.S. economy. The cultural mainstream buys into the image and Calvin Klein's profits are boosted. The political value of the ads is derived from coalitional work that has nothing to do with fashion or fragrance; it accrues through exploitative U.S./Third World labor practices, and Calvin Klein receives the proceeds. That is, economic value is assigned to the Calvin Klein Corporation. But what are the relations between the ad's material exploitation of the work of labor and their appropriation of the material work of coalition? What are the relations between the bodies that produce these kinds of work? The marketing appeal of hybridity is neither directed toward nor absorbed by white consumers exclusively. People of color can be enfranchised—or, more accurately, gain a kind of mainstream cultural currency—through the selling power of hybridity and multiculturalism. At one level, the commoditization of hybridity enfranchises communities of color to participate in cultural performance and American citizenship. Yet, at the same time, the commoditization of hybridity also represses and exploits those communities whose labor produces the goods in question. To assume that coalition happens on one level—that a participant of U.S./Third World coalitional struggles in the academy, for example, who can buy Calvin Klein products protests on the same grounds as an immigrant laborer who (may produce but) cannot afford the same products—further erases the exploitation of U.S./Third World labor within the space of resistance.

While it appears that the *cK one* advertisements represent a level of cultural savvy in staging photographic images of racial heterogeneity and hybridity, they also contain decidedly depoliticized racial representations. These ads present innocuous images of Americanness—of

"community"—that appear both candid and believable. The decon-
textualized and somewhat fantastical photographic representations of
solidarity/coalition between whites and people of color is a misleading
portrayal of the general racial climate in the United States. In particular, these representations mask labor practices that exploit people of
color. For example, in order to maximize high profits, large fashion
corporations that do not move their factories overseas for "cheap"
labor call on subcontractors in the United States to create a number of
small-scale local sewing workshops. These workshops often employ
undocumented immigrant women, or those who have recently emi-
grated to the United States, to work for wages criminally below the
minimum wage. Benetton is a case in point; the company employs subcontractors to perform 40 percent of their knitting and 60 percent of
their garment assembly.[13] Workers in shops like these often are held
captive under the threat of deportation.

While corporate production continues to soar and fashion industry
lobbyists continue to extinguish sweatshop reform bills, conditions for
immigrant women laborers remain dismal. Sewing is often the only
viable employment option for many immigrant women, who become
vulnerable targets of employers seeking cheap labor. According to the
Asian Immigrant Women's Advocates (AIWA) Garment Workers'
Justice Campaign, conditions they observed in sweatshops include
children as young as eight sewing buttons and cutting cloth, elderly
workers paid as little as 50 cents an hour and others—particularly
Vietnamese—earning far below the minimum wage, employees for-
bidden to talk or go the bathroom, bosses keeping phony time cards
and business records to fool labor inspectors, employers forcing workers to pay the fines when inspectors cite their shops.[14]

In her essay, "Colonialism and Modernity," Aihwa Ong describes
the tendency of hegemonic feminisms to construct U.S./Third World
women workers as victims of patriarchy and capitalism, as well as to
treat gender and sexuality outside the specificities of indigenous meanings and lived realities. Ong points to the practice of white feminists
enacting masculinist paradigms and reinstalling notions of cultural
superiority by fixing U.S./Third World women as a universal and
undifferentiated category. This fetishistic commoditization of U.S./Third
World workers elides their agency as laborers who achieve their own
processes of self-actualization through individual and collective
means. In the *cK one* photographs, the Third World subject—and
third space hybridity—is usurped into an economy that either obliter-
ates the racist imagery of the sweatshop worker and replaces it with

something infinitely more politically fashionable (hybridity), or an economy that never recognizes the exploitative histories experienced by Third World laborers in the first place.

This raises rather complicated questions of which histories are read on which bodies by which people. *cK one* obviously does not assume a mass homogenous audience; *cK one* does not even assume a homogenous spectacle in its representation—the spectacle is hybrid. What is so fascinating, then, are the loaded memories/connections *cK one*'s images should evoke with regard to diasporic histories of immigration, migration, and political exile in this country. And what is so problematic about the reception of these ads at the level of the mainstream is that one can never be too certain which historical memories are paid homage to—or, indeed, whether any are. What Ong's work raises for my project is the further complication of precisely what it means to open up a space to engage discursive transnational labor politics, for there is danger as well as promise in this process. While the Asian female transnational laborer is overdetermined within most discourses/ representations regarding market and labor economies within Euro-American feminisms, Calvin Klein effaces her whole existence. She was never exploited; why, she's one of us—*she's cK one.*

The construction of alliance between racial groups in postmodern "multicultural advertising" (friendship, "hanging out," love, sex, etc.) is conveyed through a particular representation of whiteness and its affective identification with communities of color. In the way these ads attempt to construct micro-utopias of oneness—eliding political realities of exploitation, oppression, and inequality in this country—they can be as damaging as blatantly racist images (where the viewer at least knows explicitly what s/he is dealing with). I argue that politics of coalition among—hybridized communities of color—and more pointedly between white communities and communities of color— never can be innocuous or utopian. They are so much more fraught, and their achievements and failures are infinitely more interesting *cK one* is a commodity; it is not coalition. The political reality of sweatshop practices within the U.S. fashion economy and the disproportionate number of women of color who work under abhorrent conditions to clothe the models who appear in *cK one* ads point to a reprehensible disparity between the ersatz citizenship/ oneness *cK one* strives to evoke/create and the economic realities of racial and cultural "difference" in this country. There is real work being done to establish coalition in circuits such as U.S./Third World feminist labor unions in the textile industry, for example, and this work—indeed, the historical conditions that give rise to it—is rendered invisible, in fact unnecessary, by the representations of multicultural bliss proffered by/in *cK one* ads.

The potential for cross-racial and cultural work around labor issues, for example, is fundamental, and the value of this work is undermined by *cK one*, where coalition is falsely and erroneously staged. *cK one* represents a place in time where struggle never preceded the arrival of multiculturalism, thereby denigrating the crucial issues constantly contested in activist arenas for possibilities of real coalition. *cK one* attests to the grim racial/political climate of market multiculturalism and the potential dangers of its tendency toward reckless abandon. Of course, one may argue that *cK one* is "just a product"—read: "just an ad" or "just a photograph"—and it could be just a film, just a text, or just another appalling political candidate. But this does not lessen its power of persuasion; given *cK one*'s transnational advertising scope, with its photographic images sprawling across billboards, magazines, television, buses, and subway stations, its influence is far-reaching.

The traveling of multiculturalism's values and meanings is multidirectional; that is, it moves from the streets to the corporate offices, and back again, making random pitstops along the way. Coalition—individual and collective political mobilization—is too powerful to be evacuated of multiculturalism's transformative political charge by co-optive marketing tactics. Its values and interests can never, in the end, be finally appropriated or co-opted. Calvin Klein Cosmetic Company relinquishes its power over the ads the moment the photos and all of their refracted meanings enter the public sphere and are received, interpreted, and taken up by communities of individuals who reinscribe meanings according to their specifics of home and place.

In this regard, Calvin Klein's depictions of race and sexuality in *cK one* harbor subversive possibilities. These possibilities are imminent for those who identify with the images and feel a sense of cultural acknowledgment in the representations, as well as for those whose racist imaginaries are disrupted by the ad's multicultural nature ("They're hugging!"). At the University of California, Santa Cruz, a *cK one* ad was photocopied onto outreach flyers and wheat-pasted all over the campus in an attempt to organize queer students of color on campus. Regardless of this subversive appropriation of the advertisement, the attention ultimately reflects back onto Calvin Klein, and popularity (read: sales) of the company's products soar. But did these students convene? Yes, they did.

*   *   *

Calvin Klein is a trendsetter, a cultural genius. He constantly redefines what is sexy and what is hot, thereby maintaining his distinguished position at the forefront of global fashion. Part of his seductive appeal—and indeed that of the corporate entity that bears his name—lies in his relentless opposition to the mainstream. From the 1970s eroticization of the neophyte Brook Shields, where "nothing comes between her and her Calvins," to the 1980s pro-sex/nudity/orgy *Obsession* campaign in an era of reclaiming sex and feminism from the clench of antiporn/antisex radical feminists, to the 1990s dialogic of racialized hybrid waifs, "scandalous" prepubescent "pornography" and "heroin-in vogue" in *cK one*, *cK jeans*, and *cK be*, respectively, Calvin Klein has changed the look of fashion. He fixes himself at the cutting edge of culture, constantly reinventing fashion and style, enraging the conservative mainstream and recreating the image(s) of counter culture(s).[15]

The Calvin Klein ads in question are taken up in a variety of different political struggles. Both the photographic images and mainstream notions of multiculturalism operate on disavowal of difference and its ambivalences—is it exploitation? Can it be identification? The disavowal of difference—*I know very well* that people are different . . . *but nevertheless*, I believe that everyone is equal—conflates the multiple vectors of heterogeneous multiculturalisms. This disavowal of the advertisement is at the level of structure of the photograph, and not at the level of intent of power. *cK one* is structured on dual recognition of (1) racial inequality ideologies, and (2) multicultural promise that an Asian dyke can be "equal" to an elderly white woman.[16]

Multiculturalism is structured by the postColonial imaginary and is enabled by a post–Civil Rights fantasy. It operates on the ability to hold two contradictory beliefs at once. They are on one hand, a continuing racial inequity and the persistence of monocultural allegiances in this country, and on the other, a belief in multiculturalism's promise to move beyond facile prescriptions of identity and difference, and to achieve heterogeneous alliances to mobilize for social change.

Through my analysis of *cK one*, I have sought to demonstrate the reductive ways in which people of color become inscribed as signifiers of difference within market multiculturalism or commoditized hybridity, in ways that have less to do with social transformation than with marketing strategies. I am interested in hybridity as more than the mere realization of difference as the point of departure from whiteness, more than mere reaction to the myth of purity, more than the mere reinscription of hybridity as a commodity form, and certainly as more than the sensibly political correct way to be at this late-twentieth-century moment. Hybridity holds so much more promise. Perhaps by theorizing a model for heterogeneous coalitional possibility through hybridity, we can begin to motivate cultural pluralism and relativism in directions that prompt alternative political, emotional, social, intellectual, and physical ways of being and relating. In a world of infinite diversity and multiple contexts, we owe it to ourselves to do this work.

Notes

1. This essay was completed in November 1999.
2. While this essay revolves around the "Jenny, Kate & Company" prototype photograph (which is reproduced herewith), my discussion here applies to the entire series of related photos that comprised the inaugural *cK one* ad campaign. Thus, I refer alternately to the photo(s) and the ad(s), as well as to the campaign itself.
3. My definitions here rely upon an understanding that commoditized hybridity is deployed as a strategy within mainstream multiculturalism. In other words, mainstream multiculturalism is a structure within which commoditized hybridity functions as a vehicle/strategy, specifically for marketing purposes, precluding transformative possibilities that recognize, embrace, and acknowledge the need to negotiate difference.
4. Calvin Klein Cosmetics press packet obtained from the company's New York publicity office (212-759-8888) in 1995.
5. In the Summer of 1996, Calvin Klein released *cK be*, the latest Calvin Klein fragrance on the market, yet *cK one* continues to be simultaneously publicized with *cK be*, and maintains its eminent popularity.
6. *cK one* launched their product in September, 1994 with these ads. In the Calvin Klein Cosmetic press kit the campaign theme is listed as "Jenny, Kate & Company" and "White T-shirt & Company." "Worldwide Fragrance Distribution" includes: Germany, Austria, Switzerland, Italy, The Netherlands, Portugal, Greece, Spain, Sweden, Norway, Denmark, Finland, Argentina, Brazil, Chile, Uruguay, Venezuela, Australia, New Zealand, Hong Kong, Macao, S. Korea, Taiwan, Thailand, U.K., Mexico, Singapore, Malaysia, Indonesia, Philippines, UAE, Bahrain, Oman, Qatar, Kuwait, Panama, Costa Rica, Columbia, 1995. U.S., Canada, Worldwide Military, 1994.
7. There were four ads in the 1994 *cK one* "Jenny, Kate & Company" series, each varying slightly from the others; i.e., the ads sometimes replaced one or

two figures on the right side of the double panel with an image of a *cK one* bottle, or panels were cut and pasted onto separate covers, presenting the figure(s) by themselves, out of context from the original ad.

8. I make reference here to Stuart Hall's essay entitled "The After-life of Frantz Fanon: Why Fanon, Why Now? Why *Black Skin, White Masks?*" in *The Fact of Blackness*, edited by Alan Read (Seattle: Bay Press, 1996).

9. Kobera Mercer, "Busy in the Ruins of Wretched Phantasia" in *Mirage: Enigmas of Race, Difference and Desire*, edited by Ragnar Farr (London: Institute of Contemporary Art, Institute of International Visual Arts, 1995), 52, 15–55.

10. On two occasions, when I presented earlier drafts of this paper, the racial/ ethnic signification of the models took primacy over the signification of sexuality—namely the queering of the ads—in the discussions that followed my presentations. While these instances represent neither an ethnographic citation nor the empirical evidence on which I base the theoretical postulations of my work, they do indicate the predominance of race in the ads' reception. Of course, categories of identity are never separate, and it is not my intention to classify these areas of identification.

11. Difference in the context of radical/liberal feminism is constituted in such a way that racial difference, class difference, nationhood, and ethnicity do not figure specifically into the overall cause of feminist global unity. Yet, it is precisely through the tokenistic inscription of race *vis-à-vis unity* within liberal feminism that notions of collectivity and common identity are invoked.

12. One may say that this aspiration is reflected in President Clinton's "Initiative on Race." It is important to note that these "town hall meetings" on "race relations" have approached the issue at the level of individual relations, as opposed to addressing the larger and far more significant question of historical, institutionalized racism.

13. Enloe, Cynthia, *Bananas, Beaches, and Bases: Making Sense of International Politics* (Berkeley: University of California Press, 1990), 156.

14. *San Jose Mercury News*, Turn-of-century abuses pervade sewing shops, Johnson, Steve; A1; March 28, 1991.

15. In August of 1995, at the outset of the *cK jeans* campaign, the FBI investigated Calvin Klein for possible violations of pornography laws in connection with risqué images of pubescent "teenagers." This scandal swept the mainstream media in the United States from August 1995 to February 1996, when Klein finally pulled the offending images and re-devised the campaign. In February, 1999 a *cK* children's underwear advertisement had to be removed from Times Square one hour after it was mounted due to virulent protest by Mayor Giuliani and his constituents (*New York Post*, February 18, 1999).

16. A lesbian model Jenny Shimizu was one of the principal figures in the original *cK one* ads. One of the many renditions of the *cK one* television campaign included the 1997 version with an elderly white woman saying, "All for one, one for all" in a British accent.

Albita's Queer Nations and U.S. Salsa Culture

Darshan Elena Campos

. . . if the border is the space of a cheek to cheek, it is also a war zone.[1]

Sometimes opting to return to the homeland is like a trip, in the narcotic sense, in the sense of subsistence and love.[2]

What we choose to remember about the past, where we begin and end our retrospective accounts, and who we include and exclude from them—these do a lot to determine how we live and what decisions we make in the present.[3]

Track One

Ripping off the cellophane wrap, forcing open the plastic case, I search for her. She sits, waiting, reclining in a wooden chair. She watches as I read her body. Her unwavering gaze shows an awareness of the ways in which bodies, women's bodies in particular, are read by wandering eyes. Still, my eyes wander, mapping the contours of her body. . . . I purchased Albita's *No se parece a nada* (1995) because her aesthetic spoke to my desire for a lesbian presence in U.S. salsa culture. As her title indicates, *No se parece a nada*, she is like nothing I had ever encountered in hegemonic salsa culture, a field of cultural production and communal gathering that is heteronormative to the point of homophobia. Albita's figuration of butchness on the compact disc's front and back covers provided me—and my femme desire—with a place inside salsa's rigid codes of gender and sexuality. The compact disc's internal imagery revealed feminine markers—high heels and manicured fingernails—that further satisfied my desire for an archive of diverse sexual identities in U.S. salsa culture.

In *Listening to Salsa: Gender, Latin Popular Music, and Puerto Rican Cultures*, Frances Aparicio argues that because women salsa artists exist in a genre of music dominated by male artists, salseras are compelled to engage the dynamics of gender and sexuality.[4] Augusto Puleo offers a similar appraisal of salsa music: "The woman projected in salsa songs is only represented as a source of pain and pleasure, but never as a person in her own right."[5] Puleo and Aparicio interpret the elaborate costumes of salseras such as La India and the late Celia Cruz as a means of feminizing salsa's public male-centered spaces and critiquing the genre's heteronormative masculinism.[6] In the words of Augusto Puleo:

> The visual display of spangled dresses, furs, gold teeth, diamonds, along with all the sumptuous and desirable aspects of their body [sic] help to reclaim female sexuality from being an objectification of male desire to a representation of female desire.[7]

What goes unsaid but underlies Aparicio's and Puleo's reading of elaborate, staged femininities is the notion that women's adorned bodies serve as points of connection between colonized island nations and diasporic subjects; women's bodies in salsa culture, in other words, come to reconstitute the nation and thus strengthen hegemonic discourses of gender and sexuality that imagine women as "symbolic bearers of the nation."[8]

Albita's performance of butchness on her first U.S. release, *No se parece a nada*, departs from the feminine incursions of her peers, La India and Celia Cruz. She refuses to mother the nation.

On the front cover of *No se parece a nada*, Albita is decentered and overexposed. She gazes at her imagined audience with forlorn, almost pleading eyes. Her vintage apparel calls forth memories of displacement from islands whose histories have long been enmeshed, Cuba and Puerto Rico. Though herself Cuban, Albita's longing for her homeland and location in U.S. salsa culture speaks to the concerns of another ethnonational formation whose residence in the U.S. stems from continued colonialism—Puerto Rico—and in this sense, her music and visual design reflect cultural traditions that exceed the geopolitical landscape of the nation. In other words, Albita's erotic body politic comes to signify the historical and immediate concerns of diasporic Caribbean communities who share histories of displacement.

The chromatic technique of the photograph encourages intense feelings of nostalgia; the use of sepia tones historicizes the figure of Albita, while the photograph's background lacks depth and demurs from emphasizing a specific locality. Albita thus appears shrouded in nostalgia—her clothing and downhearted facial expression combine with the photograph's aesthetic qualities to recall 1940s Havana, San Juan, and Spanish Harlem, the time before the communist revolution in Cuba and the launching of operation bootstrap in Puerto Rico. Albita's transhistorical attire also works to challenge that longstanding gendered conventions of U.S. salsa culture—the colorful rumbera dresses of salseras like Celia Cruz and the staid suits of salseros such as Marc Anthony and Gilberto Santa Rosa. Her image thus functions to invoke nostalgic longing for homelands beyond the geopolitical boundaries of the United States while simultaneously providing the semblance of a forthright articulation of lesbian desire in a field that is decidedly heteronormative and masculinist.

Albita's selection of material on *No se parece a nada* reveals the extent of her incursion into salsa's masculinist space. The disc's first track, "Que manera de quererte," first released on the soundtrack for *The Specialist* (1995), engages in a critical dialogue with Gilberto Santa Rosa, a salsero whose music exemplifies salsa rómantica and who released his own version of the song that same year. Albita's interpretation of the song includes cries of explicit sexual desire, while Gilberto Santa Rosa's song is more expressive of sensuality than sex.

Figure 3.1   *Albita: No Se Parce A Nada.*

For example, when Albita calls for "sexo" [sex], Rosa calls for nurturing intimacy, preferring the term, "seno" [breast]. Albita's emphasis on sexual desire and the sex act works to affirm women's desires, while her rendition of the song confronts the genre's central male figures as epitomized by Gilberto Santa Rosa.

"Que manera de quererte" offers a seductive articulation of pleasure. It includes a stream of intensifying, rhetorical questions that address specific body parts. While the song does not state the sex of the body that is being reassembled with each passing stanza, it includes repeated references to lips, blood, and delirium. Albita's deep-throated articulation of *boca, sangre*, and *delirio* suggest lesbian desire. Augusto Puleo relates that accentuation of the mouth "reclaims the female body as a site of power and hope," while Yarbro-Bejarano notes that for women, "the mouth and cunt merge, [as] both [are] represented as organs of speech and sexuality."[9] Albita's compact disc imagery and her rendition of songs such as "*Quien le prohibe* [Who Outlawed It?]" and "*Solo porque vivo* [Just Because I Exist]" combine to accentuate her departure from the genre's rigid gender codes. Albita's "unexpected surges . . . create an effect of excess that disrupts the conventional level of the lyrics, opening the music to other readings, and other pleasures."[10] Albita's erotic body politic—her muscular contralto, her incessant longing for a homeland she cannot access, her fitted suits and manicured fingernails—transgresses salsa's heteronormative masculinism and enable me to claim salsa music as my own.

Track Two

Albita's transgression of normative discourses of gender and sexuality on *No se parece a nada* is as much an example of the corporate management of salsa music as it is an exercise in cultural critique. According to press reports, Albita's image was created by representatives of Double Xxposure's Latino Division.[11] Reflecting upon her new image, Albita stated:

> Eso yo se lo dejo a los expertos, me pongo en manos de los que saben, porque yo a la verdad que no entiendo mucho de esas cosas. Lo unico que te puedo decir es que me gusta la ropa comoda, que me permita mover en escena y que pueda ser yo y punto.

> I left my image to the experts. I put myself in knowing hands because, in truth, I don't understand this stuff. The only thing I can tell

you is that I like comfortable clothing that allows me to move and be myself onstage.[12]

In delving deeper into the compact disc's imagery, it becomes apparent that transnational corporations—Crescent Moon, Epic Records Group, and Sony Music Entertainment—are capitalizing on Albita's transgression. Their logos bisect Albita's body, making her suggestion of lesbianism a means of facilitating transnational capitalism and accessing queer Latino dollars.

Indeed, Albita made her U.S. debut alongside the rise of "lesbian chic" as a marketing gimmick. In the words of Linda Dittmar:

> . . . masculinized attire invokes fantasies of dynamic, autonomous women, even as details feminize their images and compromise this masculinity. Often the images simultaneously float and submerge the women's subcultural signifiers of the unruly. . . . Such systems of checks and balances are essential to the reciprocities of incitement and restraint in which the fashion industry is so deeply invested. The idea of mingling innocence with experience, chastity with desire, exposure with barriers to sight and sound, allure with its prohibition, has always played a major part in defining fashion as a discourse of desire as well as a discourse of class, age, occupation, ethnicity, and other affiliations.[13]

Commercial popular culture, in other words, uses seductive imagery to erase the violence of capitalist economic processes, to "incite desire and invite reverie (en route to consumption)" and maintain class privilege.[14] Albita's figure is emblematic of this trend in fashion and the broader popular culture of the 1990s.

Of course, salsa has long carried the imprint of capitalism—its existence depends upon technologies of reproduction and dissemination. Albita shares this understanding of the recording and marketing of her music: "what is called salsa is just a form of commercialism. But it is clearly música cubana."[15] While the music's origins remain a site of contestation among scholars and aficionados, Albita's comment bespeaks an awareness of the music's dependence on and relation to global economic processes.

Track Three

While Albita's erotic body politic makes a space for the commercialization of racialized lesbian iconography, Albita's aesthetic has the

double-function of normalizing the preferential governmental treatment accorded to educated, upper-class Cubans who "defect" to the
United States—even the term "defection" reveals the enduring success
of anticommunist sentiment and the power of U.S. Cubans to represent themselves as exiles rather than immigrants.[16] Albita came to the
United States after having recorded two albums, produced by the government of Cuba, that became the nation's largest-selling export
albums. It is these albums that enabled Albita y su grupo the "freedom"
to live and work in Columbia and tour the socialist festival circuit in
Eastern Europe.[17] In 1993, after the release of her second record in
Cuba and in the wake of the dissolution of the Soviet Union, Albita y
su grupo decided to defect to the United States. One journalist nar-
rated their defection as follows:

> In 1993 the band secretly began discussing defection. After a musical gig
> abroad in Columbia, they flew to Mexico. The unsuspecting Cuban
> government had obligingly given them exit visas, believing the purpose
> of the trip was to cut a new record there.
>
> The next leg of their flight to freedom would, they hoped, take the
> nine of them to the United States. That assumed an understanding
> American government would consider them political exiles and grant
> them entry visas. Anxious days passed without word from the U.S.
> embassy.
>
> Even when word came that visas were approved and waiting, the
> jittery refugees feared that they might be spotted by Cuban spies if
> they attempted to pick up the visas in Mexico City. They decided to
> cross the border by way of a less conspicuous route. After a dangerous
> trek that included scaled fences, they found themselves on a busy down-
> town El Paso street. Within hours, a smiling entourage winged their
> way to Miami—and to the beginning of a new life.[18]

Another journalist offered this narrative:

> White, black, and Chinese Cuban, with shaved heads and buzz cuts,
> they simply sauntered over the bridge into El Paso, Tex., seemingly
> invisible to the Border Patrol in their ethnic diversity and funkiness.
> They took a taxi to a mall, bought ice cream cones to calm their nerves
> and made a collect call to Miami.
>
> Within hours, a radio station there that calls itself "The Most
> Cuban" had raised the money to pay their way to Florida. At first, they
> lived like genuine refugees, either to a couple of rooms. Miriam Wong,
> Albita's manager, worked construction jobs by day and sewed into the
> night so that Albita would be free to write songs.

But that did not last long. Within a year, Albita, now 34, has been adopted by the glitterati of South Beach, most notably Madonna, and taken under the wing of Emilio Estefan, Gloria Estefan's husband and producer. She was already, in the words of her press agent, Tinga Lopez, "a product."[19]

Having been granted political asylum upon her arrival, Albita y su grupo began performing in small Miami clubs. The group signed onto Emilio Estefan's label, Crescent Moon, several months later and shortened their name to Albita. Shortly after signing the contract with Crescent Moon, Albita reflected upon her exiled status in the United States: "It's all like a happy dream . . . , and I'll take happiness over drama anytime. . . . I've been trying for happiness and to follow my musical aspirations for a long time. Inevitably, I do it because it's in me, like my eyes, my hair, myself."[20] An American Dream, indeed. And, one enabled by crossing the U.S.–Mexico border at El Paso—Juarez.

The celebratory journalistic narrative of Albita's defection to the United States contrasts with the legislative treatment of poorer Cubans. Since the arrival of close to 125,000 Cubans from the port city of Mariel in 1980, several hundred of these refugees have been incarcerated in INS detention facilities, having been denied asylum status in the United States but ineligible for deportation to their homeland.[21] Kevin R. Johnson assesses the preferential treatment of educated, upper-class Cubans in the following passage:

When viewed as white, educated, and middle and upper class, and refugees of communism, Cubans fared well. When the popular construction of the migrants changed around the time of the Mariel Boatlife—as blacker, poorer, and undesirable, the legal treatment became stricter. Similarly, the racialization of Mexicans as dark, poor, uneducated, long has rationalized their harsh treatment under immigration laws. Thus, over time, we see the evolving racialization of Cubans in a way that makes them more resemble Mexican immigrants. Changes in the racialization of Cubans create the potential for future political coalitions challenging immigration law and enforcement.[22]

Albita's treatment, like that of her peers, contrasts with the treatment of other national groups, Mexicans in particular: According to statistics from 1997 to 1998, the U.S. government spends 85 percent of its immigrant deterrent resources on border patrol and migrants caught along the U.S–Mexico border account for 89 percent of deportations.[23] Despite the fact that undocumented immigrants from Mexico

account for 39–54 percent of the undocumented immigrant population, more than 90 percent of the immigrants detailed by the INS are
Mexican nationals.[24]

At the time of Albita's defection to the United States, a series of
anti-immigrant initiatives were coming to dominate the political landscape of the United States, especially the western states of California,
Texas, and Arizona. For example, California's Proposition 187, which
included provisions to ban undocumented immigrants from accessing
social services such as healthcare and education, come to initiate
heated public debates on undocumented immigration in California.
Passed on November 9, 1994 by a three to two margin, the
Proposition was authored by former Immigration and Naturalization
Service officials, Harold Ezell and Alan Nelson, after the failure of
10 similar initiatives introduced to the state assembly by Republican
Richard Mountjoy. The Proposition called for the denial of social services to persons unable to provide the proper identification and granted
border patrol and immigration officials the authority for the immediate deportation of "suspected" immigrants.

Seeking to secure his reelection, Governor Pete Wilson backed the
controversial proposition and developed an advertising campaign that
indulged the xenophobia and racism of California's electorate while
de-emphasizing the state's economic downturn. For example, one
commercial for Proposition 187 juxtaposed footage of immigrants
running across the Tijuana–San Diego border with a still image of
the Ellis Island Statue of Liberty. Against this backdrop, a deep masculine voice intoned, "American citizenship is a treasure beyond
measure . . . but now the rules are being broken . . . There's a right
way and a wrong way . . . Pete Wilson has the courage to say enough
is enough, and to stand up for Californians who work hard, pay taxes,
and obey the laws."[25] The images and voiceover narration of this commercial combine to equate immigrants with criminality and laziness
while simultaneously emphasizing Pete Wilson's commitment to
upholding U.S. policies and fulfilling the nation's promises to its own
citizenry. This campaign included the publishing of a public letter to
President Bill Clinton that implored the President to halt immigration
and replenish state funds depleted from the care of undocumented
immigrants. Pete Wilson's gambit was successful. He was reelected,
and the proposition garnered the support of two-thirds of White exit
poll respondents, a majority of African Americans and Asians, and even
one-third of Latinos.[26] Though overturned in state court, California's
Proposition 187 informed the writing and tenor of the federal policy

on immigration, the Illegal Immigration Reform and Immigrant Responsibility Act of 1996.

Cited as the "the most diverse, divisive, and draconian immigration law enacted since the Chinese Exclusion Act of 1882"[27] the Illegal Immigration Reform and Immigrant Responsibility Act of 1996 revised all previous deportation and exclusion policies. The Act requires the number of border patrol agents to double to 10,000 while investing them with the "authority to order the removal of aliens whom they have determined are inadmissible without providing for further review of such decision, if aliens arrive at U.S. ports of entry either with false documents or with no documents at all."[28] According to David Grable, this provision violates the U.S. Constitution. In his article, "Personhood Under the Due Process Clause: A Constitutional Analysis of the Illegal Immigration Reform and Immigrant Responsibility Act of 1996," Grable uses Supreme Court decisions and congressional legislative history to argue that this rewriting of federal immigration policies denies "aliens' due process" and "flies in the face of Supreme Court precedent establishing aliens' constitutional rights in criminal prosecution."[29] The federal law's language echoes the most contested dimensions of Proposition 187—its attention to "suspect" visual and aural markers of difference and its promise to minimize or altogether halt the delivery of social services such as health care and education to immigrants, legal and undocumented. Cuban immigrants who reach U.S. soil via air transportation, however, are exempt from all the Act's provisions, as are Puerto Ricans whose colonial relationship to the United States grants legal citizenship.[30]

Broad in its scope, the federal government's Illegal Immigration Reform and Immigrant Responsibility Act of 1996 inaugurates several provisions in "defense of women." It "renders deportable any alien convicted, any time after entry, of a crime of domestic violence, stalking, child abuse, child neglect, or child abandonment."[31] Furthermore, the law criminalizes female genital mutilation and forced sterilization and sites these practices as justification for the granting of political asylum.[32] In a sense, the Illegal Immigration Reform and Immigrant Responsibility Act of 1996 signals a new political era where the language and demands of feminism are marshaled to reinscribe state racism and xenophobia.

Albita began the tour for her second U.S. release at the White House, where she sang at President Clinton's second inaugural ball. "It was so bizarre," reflected Albita. "There I was, draped in black velvet, singing 'La Guantanamera' to the President of the United States.

Figure 3.2   *Albita: Una Mujer Como Yo.*

It wasn't even four years since I stood at the border sweating, contemplating a complete break with my past and the possibility of no future whatsoever."[33] Albita's 1997 compact disc, *Una mujer como yo*, erases the logistics of her own migration. On the compact disc itself, Albita's appears desnuda, naked, with her hands raised against an exceedingly black background. The black and white image renders her skin a brilliant, artificial white. On her back, stenciled into exposed flesh, is an aesthetic rendering of the Caribbean that includes Cuba, Puerto Rico, Santo Domingo (which houses Haiti and the Dominican Republic), and Jamaica. Present but peripheral are Central and South America. Texas, and the border between Mexico and the United States at Cuidad Juarez—El Paso, is eliminated from her map.

In Albita's diaspora, the militarized border between the United States and Mexico is disappeared. It is as if the route that enabled Albita y su grupo's illegal border-crossing does not exist. This erasure cements inconsistencies in U.S. immigration legislation and thus sanctions the preferential treatment of educated, upper-class Cubans at the expense of poorer, darker migrants from Mexico, Cuba, and Central Mexico. At the same time, it inscribes a separation between Mexico and Caribbean migrants despite the increasing similarities in their treatment by federal immigration policies.

A critical reading of Albita' queer nations enables an evaluation of the intersection of popular and political cultures. Seductive in terms of its aesthetics but alarming in terms of its politics, Albita's compact disc imagery works to subsume and normalize inconsistencies in immigration legislation and enforcement. This tension between the intertwined discourses of aesthetics and politics reveals that it takes more than seductive aesthetic practices to challenge state violence. It takes what Chela Sandoval calls "differential consciousness" and the creation of "affinities-inside-of-difference" to trespass both the homegrown ideological boundaries of salsa music—its heteronormative masculinism—and the gendered state racisms that motivate federal immigration policies and undergrid the commercialization of minoritarian cultural practices such as salsa.[34] If we wish to actualize social justice, we need to develop an interpretive framework that can critique the dominant political culture that desensitizes the general public to racist immigration policies—the government-authorized registration of immigrants from majority Muslin nations is one current example—and the cultural industries that give them sway.

Notes

1. Sylvia Spitta "Transculturation, the Caribbean, and the Cuban-American Imaginary" in *Tropicalizations: Transcultural Representations of Latinidad*, edited by Frances Aparicio and Susana Chavez-Silverman (Dartmouth: University of New England Press, 1997), 175.
2. Juan Carlos Quintero Herencia, "Notes Toward a Reading of Salsa" in *Everynight Life: Culture and Dance in Latin/o America*, edited by Celeste Fraser Delgado and José Esteban Muñoz (Durham, NC: Duke University Press, 1997), 204.
3. George Lipsitz. *Time Passages* (Bloomington: Indiana University Press, 1990), 34.
4. Frances Aparicio, *Listening to Salsa: Gender, Latin Popular Music, and Puerto Rican Cultures* (Hanover, NH: University of New England Press, 1998).
5. Augusto Puleo. "Una verdadera crónica del Norte: una noche con La India" in *Everynight Life: Culture and Dance in Latin/o America*, edited by Celeste Fraser Delgado and Jose Esteban Munoz (Durham, NC: Duke Unversity Press, 1997), 225.
6. Frances Aparicio, "The Blackness of Sugar: Celia Cruz and the Performance of (Trans)nationalism" in *Cultural Studies* 13(2) (1999): 223–236.
7. Puleo, *Everynight Life*, 231.
8. Anne McClintock, *Imperial Leather: Race, Gender, and Sexuality in the Colonial Context* (New York: Routledge, 1995): 354.
9. Ibid. 225.
10. Yvonne Yarbro-Bejarano, "Crossing the Border with Chabela Vargas: A Chicana Femme's Tribute" in *Sex and Sexuality in Latin America*, edited by Daniel Balderston and Donna Guy (New York: New York University Press, 1995), 41.
11. No author, "Double Xxposure 2: Launching Image Makers for Latino Market," *The New York Beacon*, February 28, 1996.
12. Josue R. Rivas, "Albita Rodriguez: No soy politica, soy artista," *El Diario/La Prensa*, December 6, 1996.
13. Linda Dittmar. "The Straight Goods: Lesbian Chic and Identity Capital on a Not-so-Queer Planet" in *The Passionate Camera: Photography and Bodies of Desire*, edited by Deborah Bright (London: Routledge, 1998), 325–326.

14. Ibid., 320.
15. Phil Roura, "Roll Over, El Duque—Fireballer Albita is Ready to Render her Best Stuff unto Caesar's; Cuban Expatriate's Un-Salsa is Red-Hot," *New York Daily News*, October 25, 1998.
16. The 1966 Cuban Readjustment Act established legal provisions for immigrants from Cuba, granting asylum status and citizenship to Cubans who reach U.S. soil. Following the dissolution of the Soviet Union in 1989, which led to an alarming decrease in the national economy of Cuba and a renewed wave of defection, the United States and Cuba developed a policy whereby Cubans who arrive via plane are granted asylum status while those arriving via foot or boat are denied legal entry into the United States.
17. Deborah Sontag, "Song in Exile," *New York Times*, March 11, 1997.
18. Gigi Anders, "Chantuese on the Loose: Cuban Singer Albita Rumbas from a Miami Supper Club to the Billboard Latin Charts," *Hispanic Magazine*, December 13, 1995, 52.
19. Deborah Sontag, "Song in Exile," *New York Times*, March 11, 1997.
20. Gigi Anders, "Song in Exile," *New York Times*, March 11, 1997.
21. Yvette M. Mastin, "Sentenced to Purgatory: The Indefinite Detention of Mariel Cubans," *St. Mary's Law Review on Minority Issues* 137 (2000): 137–186.
22. Kevin R. Johnson, "Comparative Racialization: Culture and National Origin in the Latina/o Communities," *Denver University Law Review* 78: 654–655.
23. Charles J. Ogletree, Jr., "America's Schizophrenic Immigrant Policy: Race, Class, and Reason," *Boston College Law Review* 41 (2000): 768.
24. Ibid., 768.
25. Michael Peter Smith and Bernadette Tarallo. "Proposition 187: Global Trend or Local Narrative? Examining Anti-Immigration Politics in California, Arizona, and Texas," *International Journal of Urban and Regional Research* 19(2) (1995): 666.
26. Ibid., 668.
27. Dan Danilov quoted in David Grable, "Personhood Under the Due Process Clause: A Constitutional Analysis of the Illegal Immigration Reform And Immigrant Responsibility Act of 1996,"*Cornell Law Review* 83(820) (1998): 821.
28. Austin Fragomen. "The Illegal Immigration and Immigrant Responsibility Act of 1996: An Overview," *International Migration Review* 31(2) (Summer 1997): 445.
29. David Grable, "Personhood under Due Process Clause: A Constitutional Analysis of the Illegal Immigration Reform and Immigrant Responsibility Act of 1996," *Cornell Law Review* 83(820) (1998): 822.
30. Fragomen, 448.
31. Ibid., 443.
32. Ibid., 453.
33. Deborah Sontag, "Song in Exile," *New York Times*, March 11, 1997.
34. Chela Sandoval, "Mestizaje as Method: Feminists-of-Color Challenge the Canon" in *Living Chicana Theory*, edited by Carla Trujillo (Berkeley, CA: Third Woman Press, 1998), 362.

4

Beyond Pocahontas

Joanne Barker

In June 1998, I was reading through my monthly subscriptions to *News From Indian Country* and *Indian Country Today* when I came across an ad soliciting job applications for the U.S. Secret Service.[1] I am going to call this ad Warrior Woman (see figure 4.1). Warrior Woman entreats "young Americans with diverse skills and backgrounds who are interested in a challenging career in federal law enforcement." Centered at the top of the ad in bold-faced print, the ad seeks *"a new kind of* WARRIOR.*"* Below, an American Indian woman stands direct in a black suit and white buttoned-up dress shirt. Behind her left arm there is a detail of the Secret Service's badge, shadowing her in gray outline. In her right hand, she holds a spear garnered with feathers and wrapped in cloth (you almost forget to notice her polished nails, matching lipstick, and silver ring). Around her left ear, dangling down into the inside of her jacket's lapel, is an almost transparent ear-piece. On her lapel, there is a small silver pin in the shape and colors of the U.S. flag. The first button on her jacket is large and silver, bearing a design of four arrows pointing out. Framing the bottom of the ad is the main text, overlaid another U.S. flag. The badge centers the "Secret Service." Below the image appears the following text:

> Everyday the U.S. Secret Service battles to protect our nation's leaders and financial systems. We are looking for young Americans with diverse skills and backgrounds who are interested in a challenging career in federal law enforcement. To find out more, give us a call.
>
> (202) 435–5800 www.treas.gov/treasury/bureaus/usss

Figure 4.1   "A New Kind of Warrior," U.S. Secret Service Advertisement.

It is a stunning ad. The image is bold; the textures and lines are sharp; the woman is proud and powerful. For one quick moment, you actually consider a career in federal law enforcement. And for any woman of indigenous citizenship, that is one very long, richly complex moment. In this essay, I would like to think about why that is so. I begin with my own crass investigation.

To Find out More, Give Us a Call

After seeing Warrior Woman, I ask around. According to family, friends, and colleagues, she seems to circulate for a couple of months in various newspapers, magazines, and journals. Tribal colleges receive her in full poster form with no accompanying explanation or information about the kinds of jobs that the posters are advertising. Many end up in the trash. Meanwhile, I make some phone calls. My first round is to the public relations department at the Secret Service. I want to know the name of the advertising agency, photographer, model, and any other details about the campaign and about who put the Warrior Woman together. I also ask for a list of the specific presses that the ad has appeared within. But I am unable to obtain any kind of information. The Secret Service is hardly forthcoming. So, I take a different approach. A friend in Los Angeles works as a researcher for a Japanese production firm that makes commercials and print ads for U.S. companies to be shown in Japan. He tells me of a company in the Midwest that, upon payment of $150, will track down all of the details about a specific ad that you want. Apparently, advertisers often use this type of service to secure information on photographers and models they are interested in working with. So, I call the company. They can find out nothing. Nothing at all.

So, I take another track. I call the Secret Service at the *to find out more* number but the receptionist is more than flustered. Apparently, Secret Service ads for jobs usually have reference numbers and when you call for information you are sent a packet for the corresponding job that includes detailed guidelines regarding qualifications, application procedures, and test dates (for some jobs, there is an intensive two-year security background check). I tell the receptionist that the ad I am looking at does not mention a specific job or include any reference numbers and that I am making a more general inquiry into the kinds of opportunities for Indian women that the ad is announcing. To say that I confused her would not say enough. "What job is it that you want to apply for?" "Do you have any unique skills or interests?" "Do you have secretarial skills, for example?" Like typing or short-hand. "Accounting skills, perhaps?" No. "Janitorial skills? Something like that?" Not exactly the kind of stuff that I had in mind this *new kind of* WARRIOR Woman was doing nor that the ad wanted me to emulate.

After trying to explain that I just wanted to know what kinds of opportunities that the Service had for Indians, the receptionist became suspicious and belligerent. She demanded to know my name and from where I was calling. When I told her I was a student at the University of California, Santa Cruz, her tone relaxed somewhat but I could tell that she still found me suspect. After several minutes, she relented and promised to send me a brochure—which I never received—and that I could call back if I had any further questions after reading it. She also referred me to the website and said that I could learn more about what the Service had to offer there. (Truly a waste of time. The page is an internet version of a glossy brochure—telling you everything and nothing all at the same time.)

After my pedestrian investigation, it was confirmed for me that the ad did not really want Indian women to apply at all. It had not anticipated soliciting referrals, it merely wanted to reinvent its image among Indian communities, or perhaps more generally, to confirm the Service's commitment to antiracism and antisexism in the context of recent debates about Affirmative Action policies. (Like Chevron's environmental awareness TV ads in the wake of its own destruction of U.S. reserves.) Maybe the Service was hoping to instill reassurance among Indian communities that any Indian person working for a U.S. federal law enforcement agency is trustworthy, proud, and deserving of respect? Maybe they hoped for more cooperation given their affirmation of all of the "skills and backgrounds" Indian people have to offer? In either or any case, the ad is most decidedly *not* a solicitation for applications. So, what is it advertising?

A "*new kind of* WARRIOR" Woman?

There are as many versions of the story of Pocahontas as there are representations of her in U.S. popular culture. It would be impossible to sort through all of these images and the ensuing questions about their factuality and significance here. Were she and John Smith in love? Did she save Smith from her father? Why did Smith only write of the scene in his draft of the *Generall Historie of Virginie* (1624) after Pocahontas had gained notoriety in England as the famed "Indian Princess"? Why did Pocahontas spend all of her time at the fort? Why did she marry John Rolfe, convert to Christianity, change her name to Rebecca, leave for England? Why was she returning home? (And, why did Thomas Rolfe later lead U.S. troops against his mother's people?)

All of these questions are very compelling and I do not mean to minimize the importance of having them adequately addressed. In fact, several scholars have pointed out the necessity of understanding the historical and cultural context from which Pocahontas came and that would have informed the political agendas and actions of her father, Powhatan, with regards to Smith and the colony. Indian women have cared very deeply about what Pocahontas's story tells us about the history of Indian women's roles generally and Pocahontas's role as a Powhatan woman specifically. Was the famed salvation scene actually an enactment of a Powhatan adoption ceremony that would have brought Smith under the authority of Powhatan? Is there a possibility that Pocahontas spent so much time at the fort because of an estrangement from her own community following an alleged rape? Was she spying for her father and carrying out an elaborate scheme to obtain intelligence on the colonists and their plans?

My efforts are not to recover "the facts" in answer to the questions engendered by Pocahontas and her story. Rather, I want to try to understand how the narrative works. It is a different strategy that cares about the way "the facts" are put to use rather than, say, deconstructing the plausibility of particular fact-claims in understanding what histories still need to get told.

In "The Pocahontas Perplex: The Image of Indian Women in American Culture," Cherokee scholar Rayna Green suggests that the persistence of Pocahontas's story has been its utility within the mythic structures of U.S. nationalism, particularly in (re)enacting the inferiority of Pocahontas's culture and the dominion of Smith's in what was to be figured as America. Pocahontas's alleged defiance of her father, her choice to save Smith, her attention to Smith and the other colonists' survival, her marriage and conversion, her Christian renaming, and her move to England are all made evidence that she knew her own culture lacked the qualities valued by Smith's and the New World (Berkhofer 1979). In the end, Pocahontas is made to speak to that New World, to that America, as heroine and ancestor. She is thereby stripped of any vestiges of her own political agenda and her own cultural affiliation and identity.[2]

What is so insidious about the interpretative practices that transfigure Pocahontas into a quintessential American hero is the way such inventions render her insignificant outside of her heterosexualized relationships to men and how they erase her identity and affiliation as a Powhatan. Dispossessing Pocahontas of her sovereign identity, culture, and history—and so the possibility for political concerns and agendas other than those serving U.S. colonial men and interests—makes it impossible to consider that she might have spoken for or to other issues, such as those addressing her father's powerful position, her people's autonomy and survival, and the treatment of Indians by the colonists. Instead, Pocahontas becomes merely everybody's great-great grandmother, resolving conflicted problems of dispossession and genocide that characterized her and her nation's history with an all too easy and hypocritical "affirmation of relationship" (Green 1990, 20).

Warrior Woman is more than coincidentally (in)formed by the representational practices of Indian women's figuring as icons of U.S. nationalism. These practices are registered in the very moment that Warrior Woman is both dispossessed from her own history, culture, and identity and invites Indian people to identify with and emulate that dispossession.

At the bottom of the ad, the Secret Service tells us that it "battles to protect our nation's leaders and financial systems"—"everyday," no less—and solicits applications from "young Americans with diverse skills and backgrounds who are interested in a challenging career in federal law enforcement." This call for recruits is juxtaposed with the text at the top of the ad which solicits "*a new kind of* WARRIOR." But what exactly does the ad mean by "new"?

Given the timing and location of its appearance, the ad anticipates applications from recent high school and college graduates. The first response to the ad, then, is to conflate the "new" with the "young" American Indian students it seeks as applicants. I think a more purposeful reading is to understand the way that the "new" works in junction with "diverse skills and backgrounds." There, the ad implies that there are Indian Warriors with culturally unique abilities and understandings that could employ those "skills and backgrounds" to the more "challenging" ends of the Secret Service. So, just what is "new" about the Warrior the Secret Service is soliciting?

The feather-adorned spear is a generic ornament, a too-easy signifier for the warrior in the Warrior but without any of the stuff that would mark it culturally relevant (indicating, e.g., that it is used in fishing or in conflict or identifying which specific culture it is employed within [not all Indian nation's using spears of that kind, etc.]). In other words, while the ad offers its recognition of the "diverse skills and backgrounds" of Indian Warriors, it does not make reference to any specific kind of culturally relevant skill or background that Indian Warriors might have to offer or any specific kind of culturally defined Warrior, such as members of Lakota Warrior societies or Cherokee "red town" councils. Neither does it make reference to Indian Warriors who have already proven their service to other kinds of acts of "federal law enforcement," such as the Diné Code Talkers of World War II or the thousands of Indian persons who are and have served in military and police forces throughout the United States and around the world ever since (Nielsen and Silverman 1996). Instead, the ad makes an Affirmative Action-sounding acknowledgment of the "diversity" of Indian "skills and backgrounds" in reference to the other kinds of warriors already in its legions.

Given the kind of nonexclusive reference to the relevance of Indian cultural knowledge to the Secret Service, the "new" is more in concert with the reference to the particular needs of the Secret Service in its search for applicants. Since the ad specifically announces that it "battles" "everyday" to protect U.S. national leaders and financial systems from outside threat and corruption, perhaps it is asserting that there is something about Indian Warrior's "skills and backgrounds" that would serve those ends in a "new" way. Perhaps the ad means to suggest that what "diversity" the Indian Warrior could bring to the Service is the skill and background in defending as opposed to threatening those leaders and systems. In its very celebration of this possibility, the adornment of the Indian Warrior with a spear implies that this emblem is somehow a remnant of a past when the Indian Warrior was successfully trained in fighting against the very U.S. military and economic structures that the Service is now firmly situated within maintaining. In other words, what would be "new" would be using those skills and backgrounds in service *to* the United States. If this is the case, then the Indian Warrior's "skills and backgrounds" are being understood as going unchallenged in the contemporary world of Indian people. What is "new" is the opportunity the Secret Service provides to Indian Warriors to remember and reemploy their otherwise seemingly outdated abilities in a challenging and meaningful way.

That the Indian Warrior is a woman is central to how the ad carries out its signifying chain from the old to the new to the old again. The Warrior Woman wants us to believe that what would be "new" is neither the idea of Indians in the Service nor of the relevancy of their "skills and backgrounds" to the Secret Service but rather the very notion that the Warrior would be a woman. The *"new kind of* WARRIOR" *is a Woman* is the jingle that I believe the ad invites its audiences to sing. The Secret Service wants to foreground its acknowledgment of "diversity" by extending it from Indian to woman—from race to gender—in one sweeping Affirmative Action gesture. It wants us to believe that the Secret Service counters the often hypermasculinized and racist notions of U.S. patriotism, particularly those associated with the growing incidence of Euro-American militia activities in the United States, with the very radical idea that the Secret Service already recognizes and reveres the qualities of heroic loyalty that Indian women possess. In circuitry, of course, that quality is an invention of the very U.S. nationalism on which the Secret Service stands.

The "new" erases a multitude of historical and cultural sins from the pages of U.S. history that the ad so desperately wants to rewrite, or rather, show that the Secret Service has already rewritten. Beginning with the fact that Indians had to continually transform their "skills and backgrounds" in order to defend themselves against U.S. military, economic, and cultural aggression, that as anywhere from 60 to 95 percent of the Indian population in the United States died by disease and armed-conflict in the 1800s alone (Stiffarm and Lane 1992), that Indian people have been systematically removed from their lands, communities, beliefs, and languages in efforts to eradicate Indians from everything Indian—and that U.S. national leaders and economic systems have had an instrumental hand in directing and implementing these policies in practice—is all shaken from the ad's apparent affirmations of antiracism and antisexism like Indian–U.S. history were an Etch-A-Sketch drawing that could be turned upside down and started anew when the lines got too messy.

The Warrior Woman suggests that what is "new" about herself is that a woman could be a warrior (like there weren't ever any Indian women warriors!) or that the service of Indian women as a whole in the Secret Service has been unnoticed until now. But I believe that she is fooling herself. That the Warrior is a Woman is as much a precondition of the erasure of the history of the role of U.S. national leaders and economic systems in carrying out U.S. imperialism as it is a reconfiguration of it. The Warrior Woman simultaneously constructs an Indian woman who is removed from her own histories and cultures as a warrior for the Secret Service, as a detribalized Indian generically adorned, as a deterritorialized warrior without a nation of her own "to protect and to serve," as she constructs those erasures to be lived within. The cost of her ability to serve the secret intents of federal policy and economic intent is displaced from the very scene that celebrates the possibility of that service.

Enough Is Enough

In "Thoughts on Indian Feminism," Assiniboine scholar Kathryn Shanley argues that American Indian women have too often been made into "tokens" for a "white feminist movement" which has ignored the historical and cultural specificities of their own particular struggles and beliefs (Shanley 1984, 213–215). Shanley posits that the concerns characteristic of the "white women's movement" over the economic and social oppression of the mainstream workforce and "nuclear family" has little translation into contemporary Indian women's lives and concerns. For Shanley, sovereignty and cultural autonomy are the basis for any reformulation or understanding of Indian women's epistemologies and politics, informing the range of their activism with regard to environmental, resource, and land rights, domestic violence, language retention, education, health care, and a myriad of other issues.

Drawing from Shanley's and other Native women's works on the politics of hermeneutics,[3] I suggest that an oppositional reading strategy for the Warrior Woman ad would be to start from an understanding that Indian women are first and foremost situated within and concerned about the struggles of their own unique nations for sovereignty and cultural autonomy as well as that of all indigenous people in the Américas—North and South. This methodological perspective takes sovereignty and cultural autonomy as the primary frames of reference for understanding the politics of representation for/of/about/by American Indian women.

This is not to suggest that all Indian women have experienced histories of relocation, dispossession, and genocide in the same way, nor that their ideas and goals about how to accomplish the repatriation of their histories, cultures, and identities are the same. Rather, by insisting on sovereignty and autonomy as the primary frames of reference for a hermeneutics of Indian women's representations, the strategy emphasizes the embeddedness of Indian histories, cultures, and identities in systems of meaning that are discrete *and* related. Issues of national and cultural survivance, concepts of membership and belonging, and socially defined roles and political agendas provide the context from which to interpret representational practices of/by Indian women (Kauanui 1999).

In the case of Pocahontas, this approach would fundamentally impact not only understandings of her significance, but also the possibilities of her use as an iconographic reference for U.S. nationalism. Her representational significance would be understood in the context of how she has been made not only receptive to but solicitous of the colonizing man/colonial project, continually being made over as giving herself, her people, and her lands to him/it. Her role within her nation as Powhatan's daughter, what motives Powhatan and Pocahontas might have had for her spending so much time with the colonists and marrying into their community, what kinds of cultural traditions informed her seizure of the alleged execution attempt are all issues that resituate the analysis of her representational significance within her own historical and cultural experiences. The point would not be to romanticize her as an antihero—maybe she was a sellout, maybe she did give up, give in, but maybe not. (An analysis beyond the scope of this essay but certainly worth fuller consideration.)

In the case of the Warrior Woman, insisting on sovereignty and autonomy as the frames of reference impact the possibilities of reading her significance. Unlike Pocahontas, Warrior Woman is not a historical figure per se. Believing that agency is something you do and not something you are or are not given, I suggest that Warrior Woman's political and cultural agency is located within her self-determining history, culture, and identity. The challenge, of course, is that the image does not identify her Indian national affiliation; the codes provided by the term "warrior" and the emblematic spear are far too tribally generic as to be helpful. So, I'll have to look elsewhere to enact the reading.

In "Rosebuds of the Plateau," Green suggests a story for the two Indian women lounging on Japanese American photographer Frank Matsura's fainting couch (*Two Girls on Couch* 1910; Green 1992). Though I would never presume to speak for Warrior Woman, I would like to take my cue from Green and make up a story that might fill in her confused dress, proud stance, and role in the Secret Service. Because at some level I can not quite explain away, I like her. I am transfixed by her. I am deeply troubled by her. From the moment that I ran across this ad, I wanted to cut it out, frame it, hang it on the wall. I mean, there she is with her matching polished nails and lipstick, her MIB (WIB!) suit and silver adornments, her spear, and that wonderfully suggestive earpiece. I don't know, maybe I've watched too much of *The X-Files*, but I like this woman.

So, I have decided that the story I like best for her is that she is a double agent. Perhaps I am informed by the readings of Pocahontas's role and historical significance that suggest her hanging out at the fort and salvation of Smith from execution as part of some wider political strategy by Powhatan to take in the colonists like he had taken in so many Indian villages in the building of his empire. Or perhaps I am informed by Joy Harjo's remembrance in her collection of poetry, *In Mad Love and War*, of Anna Mae Pictou Aquash, the Indian activist assassinated in the 1970s by, most likely, people doing the bidding of the FBI and then dismembered by the FBI for fingerprint identification

(Mattiessen 1983; Churchill and Vander Wall 1988; Harjo 1990). Or perhaps I am still waiting for that "great American novel" or weekly TV drama starring an older Indian woman like Tantoo Cardinal as a PI solving mystery after mystery without one tired old reference to Indian tracking skills or night vision. In any case, the story I like best for Warrior Woman is that she is a double agent—that the *secret* in her *service* is that she is an informant *to* and not *of* federal law enforcement activities. How delicious is that?

From the seemingly endless reserve of data banks, filing cabinets, and musty ill-numbered boxes in Pentagon basements and Nebraska warehouses, Warrior Woman is passing on information to her people that she has finally been made privy to after years of loyal and quiet service. So loyal and quiet, in fact, that she is almost unnoticed. Almost invisible. Even now. And who could doubt the likelihood of that scenario? A woman too dark, too smart, too competent to be seen by the sexist structures in which she works; appearing in conference rooms and department meetings only on year-end personnel review and employment statistic forms that get filed before they're really read; seen only as a satisfaction of a quotient for "race" and "gender" diversity, as if that were what Affirmative Action was about.

So, she decides to take advantage of her invisibility—of her being seen only as a statistic. Unbeknownst to any of her colleagues in one of the world's most infamous intelligence agencies, the dust-ridden secrets hidden away in encryption codes and storehouses are brought out of their hiding places and passed on to those who can decipher their significance, break their codes, and unseal their overdue warnings for "confidentiality" and "national security" to assist them in their struggles for sovereignty.

On the day that this picture was taken, Warrior Woman had scheduled a rendezvous with one of her contacts. She has discovered a password for www.treas.gov/treasury/bureaus/usss that allows the user to enter all *usss* files at will and she is anxious to pass it on.

She has been well-placed at the front of the President's caravan in a parade for some misconstrued national holiday down NYC's main street—the perfect Kodak moment. She resisted carrying the spear, arguing that it would get in the way if there were trouble, but her superior had had it specially dug out of a box of supplies in the oldest part of a Nebraska warehouse. As she marches on through the heat, stopping occasionally to pose for pictures, she imagines the spear's history.

She has decided that the spear was used in the special "citizenship ceremonies" developed by Secretary of the Interior Franklin Lane in

1916. Lane had decided to make the delivery of land patents and the commensurate status of U.S. citizenship under the provisions of the General Allotment Act of 1887 a ceremonial event, probably because he thought he knew how important rituals were to Indian people. In the ceremony, Indians were to solemnly step out of a teepee and shoot an arrow across an assembly in order to signify that they were leaving their Indian way of life behind for the responsibilities of U.S. citizenship. (Possibly the presiding official, for those tribes who did not use bows and arrows, carried around a supply like so many Edward Curtis props. On one day, perhaps, his supply got left behind and the Indians had to use their own spears, confiscated by the agent in the confusion that followed. So that, instead of shooting an arrow, the Indians had to fling their spears across center stage. I am sure, at any rate, that it could have happened that way.)

Moving slowly away from their teepees, the Indians were supposed to place their hands on a plow to demonstrate that they had chosen the responsibilities and demands of a farming, tax-paying life. The reasoning was that by being given their allotment and citizenship, they would have to earn a living for their families by "making use" of the lands that they were being "given." With hands on plow, Indians were handed a purse by the presiding official to remind them to save what they earned that they might fulfill their new responsibilities. At the close of the ceremony, the Indians were presented with an American flag and directed to repeat the following phrase: "Forasmuch as the President has said that I am worthy to be a citizen of the United States, I now promise this flag that I will give my hands, my head, and my heart to the doing of all that will make me a true American citizen" (McDonnell 1991, 95).

To conclude the ceremony, the presiding official pinned a badge decorated with an American eagle and the national colors on the recipient to remind the Indian to act in a way that would honor the flag and the privileges of U.S. citizenship that had been afforded to him/her that day. (These ceremonies were first performed on the Yankton reservation in South Dakota in 1916, and were conducted by Lane himself [McDonnell 1991, 95–96].)

As Warrior Woman carried the spear down Main Street, she wondered about those that participated in the citizenship ceremonies. She is sure that many of them went through the ceremony half-heartedly, even mockingly, but that probably many more were interpellated into the life it enacted (Althusser 1971). Participation didn't have to mean compliance but it would be hard for a spectator to tell the difference.

Like those who watched her march down Main Street like an emblem of the President's Affirmative Action prowess, like a symbol of Secret Service loyalty and patriotism, they would probably believe her a modern day Pocahontas—a hero, a traitor, depending. They wouldn't know that she had switched the frequency of her radio over to a station playing Buffy St. Marie's "The Universal Soldier." That she had flipped over the pin on her lapel so that the flag was upside-down. That she was waiting for her contact to bump into her through the crowds so that she could pass on the small notepad hiding in her left coat pocket with a secret password scribbled on it to provide access to the mysteries of the Secret Service. But that's all okay, she thought. She knew.

When All Things Old Are New Again . . .

American Indian women, while sharing experiences with other "women of color" in the context of ongoing histories of U.S. nationalism, are not another "ethnicity" in the rainbow of American cultural difference. For identifying as Indian is not quite the same thing as identifying, for instance, as "Black" or "Chinese-American." To identify or mark indigeneity is to claim oneself as a member of a people—a "collective non-state entity" (Wilmer 1993, 164)—with internationally recognized legal rights to political and cultural sovereignty and autonomy. This is why so many Indian people insist on their national or tribal identities in opposition to being identified as Indian. In fact, the very processes of racialization of Indian people in the United States as *Indians* has been an integral part of the political processes that have sought to undermine Indian sovereignty and autonomy. To the extent that Indians have been counted as "minorities," "under-represented," and/or as making up an "ethnic group" within the larger U.S. polity, the notion that they are citizens of their own unique nations has been undermined, displaced. This has important and immediate consequences to self-government, land and resource rights, juridical autonomy, and cultural survivance. In other words, the *ethnicization* of Indians and the representational practices that employ it have been extremely useful in the systematic negation of Indian people's sovereignty and autonomy (Barker 1995, 2000).

Of course, issues of dual citizenship and the more slippery concepts of membership and belonging for mixed-race and mixed-tribal Indians complicates matters even further. There are Indians who want to be recognized as U.S. citizens and consider themselves patriots; there are those who have not recognized themselves as citizens of Indian nations at all; and, there are those who believe themselves to be citizens of two countries. Further, the identities and memberships of "mixed-bloods"—those of mixed racial and/or mixed tribal descent—make it impossible to render a simple notion of what it means to identify or be identified as Indian within the context of representational practices. I do not mean to dismiss these complexities but rather to suggest that for Indian people in the United States the erasure of the sovereign from the Indian has been a particularly strategic goal of dispossession, genocide, and assimilation. This goal is encapsulated by the Warrior Woman: denationalized, detribalized, an emblem of diversity within the "our" of U.S. politics and economics.

The issues that Warrior Woman embodies are foregrounded by the way the ad sets up a tension between the hegemonic knowledge practices of U.S. nationalism and the oppositional strategies of American Indian women. It is not a natural tension. It is very much a construction of the kinds of power imagined within colonialism, capitalism, and patriarchalism. Pocahontas as an historical figure is enigmatic of these troubles, her dispossession and death the precondition of her usefulness in maintaining the mythic structures of U.S. nationalist discourses. Warrior Woman indicates that these troubles have been carried forward in the continued possibilities for making Indians speak to/for the very political and economic agendas that have undermined their struggles for sovereignty and autonomy. It follows that the precondition of her service is the simultaneous erasure of her own unique history, culture, and identity and the erasure of the diversity of Indian histories, cultures, and identities in the Americas. I have tried to show how it might be otherwise.

Acknowledgments   •

I am indebted to Jennifer Gonzales, Valerie Soe, and Theresa Harlan for their feedback on the version of this essay that I presented at the 1999 workshop. I would also like to acknowledge the original editorial board of *Beyond the Frame*—Victoria Banales, Luz Calvo, Ceclia Cruz, J. Kehaulani Kauanui, and Keta Miranda—who conceived of and directed the project as well as the members of the Women of Color in Collaboration and Conflict Research Cluster at UC Santa Cruz who planned the workshop. A warm thank you to Luana Ross for providing me with a copy of the ad in color.

Notes

Previously published as "Looking for Warrior Woman (Beyond Pocahontas)" in *This Bridge We Call Home: Radical Visions for Transformation*. AnaLouise Keating and Gloria Anzaldúa, eds. (New York: Routledge Press, 2002).

1. See inserts, *News From Indian Country* (XII:11 June 1998: 9A) and *Indian Country Today* (June 8–15, 1998: B8). Apparently, the Secret Service is one of the main subscribers to NFIC and ICT (according to an editor with ICT).
2. As Green shows in "The Pocahontas Perplex," the image of Pocahontas is troubled further by her twin, the squaw/whore, who shares her one-dimensional referentiality to colonial men and colonial processes.
3. See also Patricia Monture-Angus' *Thunder in My Soul: A Mohawk Woman Speaks* (1995) and Lee Maracle's *I am Woman: A Native Perspective on Sociology and Feminism* (1996).

References

Althusser, Louis. "Ideology and Ideological State Apparatuses." *Lenin and Philosophy and Other Essays*. New York: Monthly Review Press, 1971, 127–188.

Barker, Joanne. "Indian Made." Qualifying Essay. History of Consciousness. University of California, Santa Cruz, 1995.

———. "Indian™ U.S.A." *Wicazo Sa Review: A Native American Studies Journal* [University of Minnesota Press] 18:1 (Spring 2003).

Baudrillard, Jean. "Simulacra and Simulations." In *Selected Writings*. Mark Poster, ed. Stanford: Stanford University Press, 1988, 166–184.

Berkhofer, Robert F. Berkhofer, *The White Man's Indian: Images of the American Indian from Columbus to the Present*. New York: Vintage Books, 1979.

Churchill, Ward and Jim Vander Wall. *Agents of Repression: The FBI's Secret Wars Against the Black Panther Party and the American Indian Movement*. Boston, MA: South End Press, 1988.

Green, Rayna. "Rosebuds of the Plateau: Frank Matsura and the Fainting Couch Aesthetic." In *Partial Recall: With Essays On Photographs of Native North Americans*. Lucy R. Lippard, ed. New York: The New Press, 1992, 47–53.

———. "The Pocahontas Perplex: The Image of Indian Women in American Culture." In *Unequal Sisters: A Multicultural Reader in U.S. Women's History*. Ellen Carol DuBois and Vicki L. Ruiz, eds. NY: Routledge, 1990, 15–21.

Harjo, Joy *In Mad Love and War*. Hanover, New England: Wesleyan University Press, 1990.

Kauanui, J. Kehaulani. "A Fraction of National Belonging: Anatomy of One 'Hybrid Hawaiian' in 1930s Racial Classificatory Schema." In this volume.

Maracle, Lee. *I Am Woman: A Native Perspective on Sociology and Feminism*. New York: Press Gang Publishers, 1996.

Monture-Angus, Patricia. *Thunder In My Soul: A Mohawk Woman Speaks*. Nova Scotia: Fernwood Publishing, 1995.

Mattiessen, Peter. *In the Spirit of Crazy Horse*. New York: Viking Press, 1983.

McDonnell, Janet A. *The Dispossession of the American Indian 1887–1934*. Bloomington: Indiana University Press, 1991.

Nielson, Marianne O. and Robert A. Silverman, eds. *Native Americans, Crime, and Justice*. Boulder, Colorado: Westview Press, 1996.

Rich, Adrienne Rich. "Compulsory Heterosexuality and Lesbian Existence." *Signs: Journal of Women in Culture and Society* 5:4 (1980), 631–660.

Rountree, Helen C. *"Pocahontas's People" The Powhatan Indians of Virginia Through Four Centuries*. Norman: University of Oklahoma Press, 1990.

Shanley, Kathryn. "Thoughts on Indian Feminism." In *A Gathering of Spirit: A Collection by North American Indian Women*. Beth Brant, ed. Ithaca, NY: Firebrand Books, 1984, 213–215.

Stiffarm, Lenore A. and Phil Lane, Jr., "The Demography of Native North America: A Question of Indian Survival." In *The State of Native America: Genocide, Colonization, and Resistance*. M. Annette Jaimes, ed. Boston, MA: South End Press, 1992, 23–54.

Wilmer, Franke. *The Indigenous Voice in World Politics*. Newbury Park, CA: Sage Publications, 1993.

5

"Come Up to the Kool Taste": Race and the Semiotics of Smoking

Sarah S. Jain

Although most often paired with alcohol in policy and culture debates, tobacco more readily compares to sugar or coffee in its ubiquitous and continual availability (and until recently, acceptability) to all classes. The intimate pleasures of the cigarette—from the flip-top box to the perfected flick of an ash or the excuse to ask a stranger for a light—should not be understated. The cigarette and the social rituals it has motivated made it truly iconic of popular culture through the mid-twentieth century. Consider, for example, its adaptability: readily slipped into a pocket or behind an ear, a means to a private or a social moment, a lift or a sedative. The cigarette acts as a snack, prop, drug, or coping mechanism. The cheapness and efficiency with which it satisfies, and the only short-lived gratification it bestows, the cigarette takes the commodity to its most refined, profitable, and complete incarnation. While consumed nearly completely, literally disappearing into a puff of smoke (the butt easily disposed of under a shoe), the cigarette's solitary blemish lies in the fact that, over time, the cumulative effect of its debris slowly and irrevocably sickens and kills its consuming host, preventing it from procuring anew.

In the legal framing of capitalism in the United States, this one flaw should have been enough to have the cigarette—as a manufactured, designed, advertised, and sold product—not only regulated, but banned outright. Despite its vicissitudes and varied theories, product liability law has arisen in the United States as the infrastructure through which Americans can claim their right not to be injured by the products that they buy and use as intended. But only recently have people been able to consider themselves injured in a legal sense by cigarettes, as a third wave of lawsuits has made claims against tobacco corporations ranging from false advertising and defective design to knowingly selling an addictive product. One of the most interesting of these recent suits was an attempt to highlight the economic racism of cigarette marketing through a Civil Rights claim. Brought in Pennsylvania in 1998 on behalf of Black smokers by the Reverend Jesse Brown, it raised the issue of niche marketing, discrimination, and the "staggering loss of life, premature disability, disease, illness, and economic loss" resulting from "the Tobacco Companies' intentional and racially discriminating fraudulent course of misconduct."[1]

The *Brown* complaint had many aspects, but it basically contended "that Defendants have for many years targeted African Americans and their communities with specific advertising to lure them into using mentholated tobacco products..."[2] As a result of the increased danger of mentholated cigarettes and "a conspiracy of deception and misrepresentation against the African American public," it argued that African Americans have disproportionately suffered the injury, disability, and death that invariably follow from smoking menthols. In arguing the enhanced dangers of menthols (both menthol as an ingredient as well as other design factors—such as tobacco engineered for increased nicotine content—that have attended mentholated cigarettes), *Brown* pointed out that first, menthol contains carcinogenic compounds such as benzopyrene. Second, mentholated cigarettes contain higher nicotine and "tar" levels than non-mentholated versions. Third, menthol encourages deeper and longer inhalation of tobacco smoke. Menthols account for between 60 percent and 75 percent of cigarettes smoked by African Americans, and thus puts these smokers under increased risks.[3]

The fact that this suit was brought under the Civil Rights Act of 1866 provides a radical departure from products liability approaches to legal retribution for defective products. By claiming transgression of the Civil Rights Act, originally written to protect recently freed slaves from a variety of discriminatory practices, the complainants of the *Brown* class action suit sought to show the unconstitutionality of targeting African Americans with defective products. This strategy sidestepped the problematic way in which product liability law seeks to reestablish the *status quo* through compensation (and thus tends to under-compensate women and minorities) as well as address the structural issue of race targeting by attempting to have advertising directed toward African Americans banned. But complainants had to assert their claims very narrowly. For example, under section 1982, they needed to show intentional discrimination on the part of the defendants that would impair the plaintiff's ability to "make contractual arrangements for the sale and purchase of tobacco products." The court, in dismissing *Brown*, set aside the issue of targeting because plaintiffs were unable to show that they were offered less favorable contractual terms than Whites were. Essentially, the court noted that plaintiffs were free to buy any type of cigarettes, and the mentholated products that many did smoke were "just as defective and dangerous as the mentholated products" that were sold to Whites with equal terms of sale.[4] Thus *Brown* was dismissed by a federal District Court in 1999 on a set of narrow but important legal grounds, and the key charges of targeting a dangerous product were not considered by the court.

Nevertheless, the case—as one in a series of attempts by various groups to mobilize against extreme cultural and economic target marketing—raises sets of crucial issues both about the ways in which individuals and communities are socially and physically constituted by products and consumption decisions and about the place of rights in consumer culture. Despite the issues of targeting, racism, and consumption raised by *Brown*, the significant media attention it garnered tended to fissure along the same lines as a product liability case would. One view, seemingly allied with tobacco corporations, claimed that African Americans are as capable of making choices as anyone—and everyone makes choices they regret. The other view consolidated generally around the position that tobacco corporations have behaved reprehensibly, and unquestionably should be held responsible for resulting injuries. In neither of these sides are African Americans portrayed as naïve dupes or hapless victims, but rather, each carries assumptions about human, non-human, and institutional accountability. Elaine Scarry would frame this problem in the terms of "object-responsibility": manufacturers ought to ensure that their products embody a "material registration of the awareness" of end users.[5] Given adequate product design human users will be able to make responsible choices.

Framing the issue of defective products as one of Civil Rights rather than product liability forces an added dimension to assumptions about reasonable products and reasonable users: Should the product, and its manufacturers, have "known" that it would be more appealing and more lethal to a specific disenfranchised group of Americans, or did it truly offer itself to all takers on an equal basis? Where do economics and culture intersect in this question? Through these questions, the mentholated cigarette and the *Brown* case offer a view into the broader framework of capitalism and the always already unequal terms of consumption. Here I investigate this by situating cigarette target marketing within the context of a developing African American consumerism, and then, in the second part of the paper, to the particular way that mentholated cigarettes were paired with African American smokers.

This essay, as a small part of a book project investigating the politics of social and physical injury, focuses on a short but crucial period of smoking history: the 1950s and 1960s. Several reasons collude to make this a period of key importance. Legal suits necessarily spotlight this era, as people who began smoking before health warnings on packages and advertisements appeared have met considerably more success in soliciting the empathy of jurors. Furthermore, African Americans were "discovered," or constituted, as a market, represented in various ways, and targeted in uniquely new ways for a slew of new products. Cigarette companies had led target market campaigns since the early century, and, already well aware of the dangers of their product, used marketing with particular abandon. This requires investigation, since the fact that Brown and Williamson (B&W) advertised proportionately more to Blacks than Whites throughout the 1960s (while 10 percent of the population is Black, B&W spent 17 percent of Kool's advertising budget on "black advertising"[6]) does not build a strong case for the significance of targeting Blacks during the 1960s, though this statistic was strongly claimed in the *Brown* suit. I suggest that other factors contributed to the sway of this campaign.[7]

Marketing in the 1950s and 1960s also coincided with the Civil Rights movement and boycotts protesting discrimination in hiring practices as well as the later generational and philosophical rifts in the goals for the movement. During this period, as Michael Omi and Howard Winant argue, the "black movement redefined the meaning of racial identity, and consequently of race itself, in American society."[8] With an analysis of the ways that "race" circulated and was contested during this period my hope is to come to a clearer understanding of how the *Brown* suit throws into relief the poverty of our ways of thinking about physical injury, and in particular the slippery links between physical and social injuries and their categorization—and furthermore, their relations to consumption more generally. Finally, the number of Black smokers increased dramatically during this 20-year period, and smoking by everyone was at its twentieth-century peak: 52.5 percent of Americans were smokers by 1966.[9]

As good a place as any to start this story is the August 1967 special issue of *Ebony*. In this issue, publisher and founding editor, John H. Johnson, explores "the challenging and bewilderingly complex world of the more than eleven million Negroes who are below the age of twenty-five."[10] Although Johnson stresses his concern about youth and their identity crises, the issue is also about Civil Rights, featuring articles on activist movements, the dearth of educational opportunities, Jessie Jackson (whom Johnson claims as a close friend) on economics, unemployment, Vietnam, as well as a proto-feminist piece on the successes of an Iowa coed pool player. As befits the predominant readership of the magazine, the preponderance of its advertisements are woman-oriented.

This content generally fits into the human interest, celebrity, bootstrap rubric under which Johnson had founded *Ebony*. While in the early- to mid-1960s *Ebony* readers were better educated, held more white-collar jobs, had a much higher mean income, and were 10 years older than the general Black population, 31 percent of readers earned an annual income of less than $5,000 and 41 percent did not complete high school.[11] Through the 1960s the magazine covered Civil Rights issues, though its coverage waned as the movement became increasingly radical. By the late 1960s the magazine reverted again to a self-help rather than protest orientation.[12]

Looking back to August 1967, one notes that unlike the women featured by the magazine's articles who stand in lines, have meetings, and work day jobs, the advertisements parade the summer of 1967 as one filled with women overcome with ecstasy over sporting tampax, visiting the manicurist, procuring straight hair, quaffing Pepsi, lathering down in the shower, and ironing clothes while a child bangs pot-lids (thanks to Bayer aspirin's cure for his mother's resulting headache).

In the midst of the confusion and crisis of identity and youth and fervent women, one turns from the front cover of *Ebony*, on which is pictured a wildly graffitied broken-down brick wall, "Negro Youth in America Anxious Angry and Aware," to find an invitation to "Come up to the KOOL Taste." The moment of calm on the cover's flip-side transports the reader to a stream babbling through a woody area as the blurred background to a couple relaxing on a quixotic wooden bridge. Although the couple seem to be about the same age as the "youth" featured in the magazine, they are certainly of a different generation (see figure 5.1).

In this formally dressed down leisurely pose in the woods, the woman in her kool turquoise-green mint dress with matching shoes and bracelet seems to emerge, genie-like, from the box of cigarettes. Even the twist of her body highlighted by the folds of her frock echoes the magical children's story version of Aladdin, who emerges from a genie lamp in a curl of smoke. But if this is so, it is the only suggestion

Figure 5.1   Cover (L) and Inside Cover of *Ebony*, August 1967.

of smoke, for these white-toothed nonsmokers do not even have their cigarettes lit. The couple is confidently heterosexual, overlapping if not touching—he, dark and handsome and she straight-haired and gorgeous, while a wedding ring is conspicuously absent. Perhaps they are courting; they are certainly wealthy and upwardly mobile. These charming people wait, curiously, invitingly, genuinely, for some sign from the observer, and the cigarette box below reflects this offer. The invitation of this scene is as unabashed as the class and assimilationist aspirations. If the appellation "KOOL" plays on a real or imagined Black vernacular, the enticement is to a middle class. The Kool brand was hailed by *Advertising Age* as a success for its call to upward mobility and the well-dressed couple in an outdoors scene was reflected in the advertisements for Newport and Salem menthols throughout the mid- to late-1960s menthols.[13]

Though marginally interesting in its details, this ad promises a prosaic menu of success, achievement, and pleasure—the standard fare of advertisers everywhere. Nevertheless, it is emblazoned with the struggles of *Ebony* founder and editor-in-chief, John H. Johnson. Johnson's 1989 autobiography, *Succeeding Against the Odds*, is one diffracted through the lens of a foundational belief in equal opportunity capitalism. Born in 1918, Johnson completed the eighth grade twice, the last grade available to Blacks in Arkansas, while his mother earned the money to move with her son and daughter to Chicago so that he could attend high school. Johnson epitomizes the American Dream, and his autobiography is largely a story of overcoming, though perhaps not as much as he would have liked. He writes, "if I hadn't operated with the handicap of racial barriers, I could have made billions, instead of millions."[14] To be sure, compelling evidence buoys this observation.

Johnson's initial success with *Negro Digest* (1942), initiated with a $500 loan that used his mother's furniture as collateral, led him to found *Ebony* (1945), *Tan* (1950), and *Jet* (1951). *Ebony*'s first issue, launched with nary a subscriber as an oversized monthly of "Negro news and pictures," had by 1966 reached a circulation of close to a million.[15] One of Johnson's main obstacles, after having overcome so many to have *Ebony* published at all, was to find advertisers for the magazine. Even after it reached a staggering circulation of 400,000, Johnson struggled against racism in his efforts to gain advertisers; Johnson wanted "the big four color ads that were the staple of white magazines" rather than the inferior black and white small-scale ads typical of Black publications.[16] Johnson shares several anecdotes in his autobiography—in a paternal "you can too" guise—of how he was able to reach the offices of a significant number of CEOs and finally convince them to advertise.

One of his broader-range strategies involved a two-pronged operation to convince White corporations of the size and profitability of the Negro market, and ultimately, to teach them how to coddle this market. Publishing in the early 1950s, Johnson spearheaded a burgeoning industry of market consultants involved in a similar venture.[17] Johnson's goal was clear: "To increase the profits of corporate America and, incidentally, the profits of Johnson Publishing Company, we have to change the perceptions of corporate America."[18] By 1967 *Ebony* had the lion's share of the annual $8 million spent on Black-oriented magazine advertising.[19]

The strength of the African American market and the community's positive response to respect in advertising had been demonstrated as early as the mid-1930s. Kellogg Company was among the first U.S. food corporations to pursue this market by broadly advertising Cornflakes in a non-derogatory manner in the Black press.[20] This invitation to consume must have been powerfully evident. Grace Elizabeth Hale shows, for example, how in that period southern segregation enforced systems of consumption that involved violently suppressing the "uppity" Negro who emulated the White middle class and selling only poor quality goods to Blacks. Thus, even wealthy Blacks could not access goods and other signifiers of class, and when they could, they found that the symbols of oppression went far beyond second class service and goods. They were met at the county store with not only staggeringly racist advertising and product labels but sales counters that sold souvenirs of the latest lynching—including postcards and Black fingers and toes. As they became available though, brand name products were relied on by northern and southern Blacks to avoid discriminations such as short weights and poor quality goods. Similarly, the growth of supermarkets and standardized services saved the Black shopper from continually being bumped to the back of the line.[21] Nevertheless, the egregiously elementary tutorials offered by Johnson and others reflected advertisers' continued racism: "Don't exaggerate Negro characters, with flat noses, thick lips, kinky hair, and owl eyes . . . Always avoid the word 'Pickaninny,' or lampooning illustrations of Negro children. They are as dear to their parents as are other children, irrespective of race."[22] The secondary effects of racism needed pointing out: "Don't set up contest prizes that a Negro winner could not enjoy, such as a free trip to Miami Beach, or a new suburban house in an area where the Negro might not want to live."[23] Changing the perceptions of corporate America meant refiguring popular representations of race in the media.

As the White market represented more than 10 times that of the African American market, many corporations claimed that integration in advertising may offend a large portion of White consumers. African American market advisors took several tacks against this fear. They began by noting the sheer size of the market. By the mid-1960s, the advertising community generally concurred that "Negroes, as a group, represent a purchasing power of around $20 billion, approximately as large as the markets of Belgium, Sweden, Denmark, and Norway combined."[24] Size by population was not in itself the crucial factor, so self-conscious attempts were made to diminish the notion that African Americans were poor. Johnson, for example, commissioned a survey on the brand preferences of Black families to discredit the "general assumption that this is simply a market for low cost goods."[25]

Other advisors tried to put a positive spin on the particular experiences of African Americans. One claimed that hired domestics "exert a direct influence on the purchase of several commodities in the home"[26] Johnson focused on the fact that they had "become acquainted with expensive merchandise through working with wealthy White people—as butlers, valets, maids, housekeepers. . . ."[27] Racism provided for other marketing opportunities as well: since African Americans had far less opportunity for recreation and housing, it was argued that they tended to spend their money on commodities, thus matching and exceeding White disposable income in several categories. The categories that were most often mentioned had to do with looks and "prestige items," such as scotch. This example illustrates a point that is not uncommon in the literature of this period: "The Negro . . . will spend much more money on food, clothing, appliances, automobiles, and other items in order to help overcome his insecurity neurosis. The result has been that Negro standards of living in many categories of goods are a match to white standards."[28] The "insecurity neurosis" and "inferiority complexes"[29] that African Americans purportedly suffered provided an opportunity for advertisers to offer what Jackson Lears has since called the "therapeutic ethos" of consumption.[30]

Other consultants studied the ways that race exceeded the problems of class and the accessibility of products. For example, African American sociologist Henry Allen Bullock's 1961 two-part study in the *Harvard Business Review* was based on a survey of nearly 2,000 people, and in-depth interviews with a further 300. Bullock's most interesting data have to do with Blacks' and Whites' approaches to consumer choices, which detail varying moral codes of consumption. In the first category, consider the example of credit, the use of which Black people "felt obliged to display an elaborate system of rationalization" to justify. For Whites, credit tended to be used more liberally for products that they wanted, rather than what they "needed."[31] Overall Whites tended to be more accepting, and even envious of higher consumption levels, whereas Blacks held a more traditionally protestant view of consumption above and beyond financial liberty. In considering air conditioners, for example, a White person said, "They [owners] are spoiled, but I think it's wonderful. I wish I could afford to do it."[32] African Americans tended to feel that air conditioning was an unnecessary luxury. These examples indicate a different approach to class privilege and consumerism that goes beyond a simple ability to buy more; they indicate the ways in which class transformation also required a resocialization about consumption and entitlement.[33] This ambivalence between race and class in consumer decisions was also noted slightly differently by Dave Berkman in his 1963 study of advertising in *Ebony* and *Life*. He concluded that, what the Black man "does want is to be a *middle-class Negro*; but for right now, and for as long as the two are, to a large degree, essentially contradictions in terms, he will find most appealing those items whose consumption most clearly say 'white'—*but only because they also say 'middle-class.'* "[34]Freedom in consumption might by seen as a way out of the restrictions of segregation.

Many of the market consultants genuinely believed in the integrity of their work. One 1961 article claims, "Children, for example, do hear and learn the advertising message. They, too, are destinators [*sic*]. What kind of people they become is determined, at least in part, by the tonal quality of the advertisers' message. When sellers turn communicators, they inevitably become educators."[35] Another African American consultant wrote, "As the Negro becomes freer, he becomes more race conscious. There would be no Negro market in the United States if it weren't for the racial tension."[36] This evidence suggests that consultants believed that the eradication of racism in marketing and advertising would offer a clear path away from the vicious racism of the early century.

The work of African American marketers, however, was not universally celebrated as progressive. Sociologist E. Franklin Frazier, for example, cited statistics in his 1957 study of the "black bourgeoisie" indicating that by 1938 Blacks *already* spent about 90 percent of their incomes in White owned businesses.[37] Frazier wrote that, "The myth that Negroes were spending $15 billion in 1951 [nearly 3-times what could be demonstrated using available statistics] was widely circulated by Whites as well as Negroes in the United States and whet the appetites of the Black bourgeoisie, both Negro businessmen and Negroes employed by American corporations in their efforts to reap benefits from the increased earnings of Negroes."[38] Indeed, *Sponsor* reported, "The growing awareness that understanding is the key to effective advertising has created a boom for 15 or 20 Negro public relations firms. Billings for D. Parke Gibson, for example, are up 40 percent over a year ago. . . ."[39] Thus, it is not at all clear that target marketing brought overall more money to White companies, though it seemed to provide [limited] job opportunities for Black consultants and magazine editors. Frazier argues that this misrepresentation of the size of the market served a tripartite purpose. First, it gave an exaggerated sense of worth to bourgeois Blacks; second, it strengthened the false notion that the accumulation of wealth could solve African Americans' problems; and third, it posed that integration was a possibility for African Americans (an idea he disagreed with).

Though later in the 1960s Civil Rights strategies became more radical, early Civil Rights activists employed boycotts against White

corporations. But for African Americans with stakes in these companies, boycotts were perilous. Therefore, Johnson outspokenly opposed
a Christmas boycott that had been suggested by James Baldwin, Louis
Lomax, and Ossie Davis in the wake of the 1963 Birmingham church
bombing.[40] But several marketing campaigns addressed these boycotts. One article, describing Black women's purchasing habits,
reports: "Further, she is militant in her pursuit of economic and civil
rights, and will cross off her shopping list the name of any company
she believes or suspects practices discrimination."[41] By 1964 when this
article had appeared, companies had ample opportunity to experience
the effects of boycotts; the previous year *Advertising Age* had puzzled
over the fine line among placating, fearing, and bribing angry Black
boycotters.[42]

At least to some extent, advertising to Blacks was understood, even
as it targeted race, in relation to desegregation. It would not be impossible to suggest that some corporations were willing to capitulate, at
least rhetorically, to some civil rights demands. After the lunch counter
boycotts in 1963, for example, Woolworth's decided to "really get a
very strong, positive program—one which includes employment opportunities and perhaps scholarships—to overcome the bad reputation it
acquired."[43] Other corporations, such as Greyhound, acted on African
American marketing advice and installed a "total marketing" approach
that included hiring Black executives and drivers, and picturing
Whites and Blacks seated together in commercials.[44] On the other
hand, companies were also quick to co-opt Black culture—by making
short films depicting "the Negro in education, entertainment, agricul-
ture, national affairs, and medicine," for example, and illustrating ads
with cultural icons such as jazz bands, sports idols and Civil Rights
activists. One *Advertising Age* article describes a contemporary
Liggett and Myers campaign to its overwhelmingly White readership:
" 'Super bad' actually means especially good or super excellent in the
current black lexicon."[45]

Cigarette companies were on the leading edge of post–World War II
segmented marketing; one of the four first advertisements that graced
the pages of *Ebony* in 1947 was for Chesterfield cigarettes. They had
already been advertising in target presses to Jews and Germans in the
early century, and starting in the early 1950s featured Black models in
Black magazines and White models in White magazines, often with the
same copy. Quantitative evidence has suggested that targeted cigarette
advertising has "worked,"[46] while tobacco documents have linked the
high sales of Kools in the 1960s to the nicotine and sugar content of

the cigarette. Perhaps for both those reasons and others, the percentage of smoking African Americans increased significantly between 1955 and the mid-1960s.[47]

The rise of the lifestyle magazine as a form of popular culture post–World War I also fomented a consolidation of a middle class.[48] The uneasy position of all people identified as and with Black Americans in the middle class is clear as the Ebony reader in August 1967 turned from the cover image of the graffitied wall to the Kool advertisement on its backside. The cover hints at the violence of the era. Martin Luther King and Malcolm X, who surely frightened Black conservatives—readers of Ebony—as much as Whites, had been shot. The Black Panthers and other political groups were being infiltrated by the FBI as young Black men were being drafted for Vietnam. Perhaps readers of Ebony, having grown up in the era of Jim Crow when "talking back" could be a capital crime, were terrified for children who had tired of what they saw as their parents' inaction.[49] The Kool advertisement offered other fantasies, ones based in the history of a Civil Rights movement that had used law to open new possibilities in education and employment. In this way the ad reflects not only Johnson's own struggles, but the way that they exemplified a long tradition of Black conservatism, whose roots in Booker T. Washington's reliance on hard work and self-improvement found voice through twentieth-century women's clubs, Black churches, and appeals to the Supreme Court.[50] The magazine's readership and the products advertised in Ebony were reflected in each other. Professor and activist Angela Y. Davis, for example, smoked unfiltered Pall Malls in the mid-1960s rather than mentholated cigarettes precisely because of the sorts of middle-class assimilationist African American identity that attended the menthol image.[51]

If the ambivalence evoked by the magazine was one of class and aspiration, it also needs contextualization against the direct information management strategies of tobacco corporations. It is no secret that tobacco companies have been tireless in their tentacular struggle to erase tobacco's traces. For example, the advertisement-free Reader's Digest, the nation's then largest circulating magazine, had published the first widely read popular article on the health effects of smoking in 1952, bringing information of the health risks that had long been known in medical communities to the general public.[52] In 1957 American Tobacco's public relations employee J. T. Ross pressured its own and Reader's Digest's ad agency—Batten, Barton, Durstine & Osborn—to drop the magazine's advertising account. Since American

Tobacco billed about $30 million annually, compared to *Reader's Digest*'s $2 million, the agency dropped *Reader's Digest*.[53] This small example stands in here for hundreds of such cases where tobacco corporations have stultified the press by any means necessary. *Ebony* magazine has received a steady 10 percent of its ad revenue from cigarettes since 1947 and as many as one in three color advertisements in some issues is for cigarettes. Studies find that "in its more than 40-year history, it has never published a major article on the leading cause of death among Black Americans: tobacco."[54] The cigarette and its effects joined in the making of culture not only through its hastening of the deaths of various cultural producers (and arguably through the increased production-effect of nicotine) and through the changed economies spurred by the industry, but also through the assurance of strategic ignorances in the population at large, a point to which I shall return in the next section.

Thus, while it may be true, as Thomas Laqueur argues, that "Addiction is not only an attachment to a substance, it is also an attachment to a passion of great spiritual and cultural thickness,"[55] one must be wary to historicize the terms of that cultural thickness. Discrimination pervaded the rise of U.S. consumerism in the 1950s and 1960s. Key tensions arise in this period of intensifying popular and corporate activity in the ways that the most prominent images in American culture—advertisements—were finally including groups of minority people in seemingly respectful ways. These embodied promises of the contemporary Civil Rights struggles—for education, jobs, and housing—not only through the fantasies that they portrayed, but also through the economic channels of supporting African American market consultants, publishers, magazines, models, and writers. As many of the civil legal and regulatory promises were thwarted, the stakes in systematic racism for cigarette companies were few. Thus, cigarette companies (unlike housing developers[56]) were free to interpellate people of any race, class, gender without fearing the loss of their other customers. This liberty enabled them to ally themselves with any cause—from Civil Rights to Billie Jean King's demand for an equal tennis purse.

Thus we catch a glimpse of a few of the many actors and institutions on the supply-side of the cigarette equation in the 1950s and 1960s. The agentive moments of advertisers, consultants, editors, consumers, and commentators were as many as they were complicated—and through these, a group called "African Americans" was identified in various and contradictory ways. While on the one hand, equality in advertising posed a way out of the racist portrayals of African Americans, on the other a movement that defined liberation in terms of cultural expression (and struggled to determine what that would mean) rather than the freedom to consume sundry Americana was already taking hold. Yet, as with other subcultures, various groups of African Americans took the cigarette into their modes of expression, and tobacco companies seemed to know exactly how to make this happen.

Regardless of how questions of agency and choice are framed, there is simply no way around the fact that cigarettes have had a devastating impact on the African American community: tobacco smoking is the number one killer and disabler of African Americans. It results in more deaths among Black Americans than homicide, car accidents, drug abuse, and AIDS combined. It intensifies serious health problems that disproportionately affect Black Americans: hypertension, diabetes, low birth weight, infant mortality, and hazardous occupational exposures.[57] The incidence of tobacco-related cancers including that of the lung, esophagus, oral cavity, and larynx; heart disease; and cerebrovascular disease all have a higher incidence in Blacks than in Whites. Lung cancer accounts for 25 percent of all cancer cases in Black males (as opposed to 14 percent for White males) and increased 220 percent between 1950 and 1985 (compared to an increase of 86 percent in White men).[58] In 1992 lung cancer became the leading cause of cancer mortality among African American women aged 55–74 years.[59] Blacks also tend to be diagnosed when diseases are at a later stage than Whites and have a significantly lower survival rate after diagnosis.[60]

A further crucial point to make here is that not only do socioeconomic differences account for smoking's exacerbation of other health problems, but also education is a primary indicator of who will smoke. It is well established that smoking rates are about twice as high for adults with less than a high school diploma when compared with those with four or more years of college.[61] Smoking is related to education in another key way—the children of smokers suffer from a significantly higher incidence of low birth weight, lower IQ, higher incidence of learning disorders, more sick days, and a higher rate of asthma and other respiratory disorders. Thus, smokers' kins' physical injuries constitute them as less able to share in social goods—material and cultural—at the same time as they require more access to medical, educational, and financial resources.

While *Brown* cites the cause of the attraction of menthols to African Americans as the focused and deceptive advertising for a highly addictive product, tobacco companies claim a simple supply–demand curve. Meanwhile, a few medical studies cite the excess injury in an African American body more susceptible to the harms of tobacco smoke. Still, that a preference for menthols has existed among certain African Americans is uncontested. Given the wreckage of this product, what are we to make of the particularity of this hybrid?

Tobacco and mint leaves have likely been mixed together and smoked for thousands of years, and menthol crystals have been added to snuff (tobacco powder) for hundreds of years. In the age of the contemporary cigarette, however, mentholation—which acts as a mild anesthetic that numbs the throat to the harsh elements of tobacco smoke and thus allows a deeper and longer inhalation—was introduce by Axton-Fisher with a cigarette called "Spud." Brown and Williamson (B&W), formed in 1894, launched the mentholated "Kool" in 1933 and priced it at 15 cents, 25 percent cheaper than Spud, and swiftly outsold it.[62] The first ads featured a penguin and inaugurated the 70-year bid to associate menthol cigarettes with refreshment and the outdoors. "Like a week by the sea, this smoke. . . . is a tonic to hot, tired throats."[63] The award-winning 1946 ad focuses on the pharmaceutical value of Kools, "Head stopped up? Got the Sneezes? Switch to Kools . . . the flavor pleases!"[64]

Notwithstanding recent taxes, cigarettes have traditionally provided a cheap and accessible indulgence to all classes, and gaining momentum throughout the century, cigarette companies have ensured that smoking has been introduced to literally hundreds of cross-referenced niche markets. Sometime in the 1950s or 1960s, mentholated cigarettes came to be identified—at least by Blacks (a fact that was noted in contemporary industry documents[65])—as a Black product, though the contentious issue here is which came first, the targeting or the preference. Industry attorney Jeffrey G. Weil claimed, "The targeting is not because they're African-American—it's because they like menthol cigarettes."[66] Various reasons for this seeming tautology have been offered by sociologists, marketers, and smokers. Charyn Sutton, for example, a plaintiff in the *Brown* class action suit and president of Onyx Group, Philadelphia, said that B&W "put extra effort into promoting menthol cigarettes to Blacks," and discusses how "when I was in high school they [B&W] made the penguin into a person, and we really thought he was a stand in for African Americans because at that time African Americans really couldn't be portrayed in ads in the general market. . . . The class took that penguin and made him the class mascot—that's how intense the identification was by that kind of advertising."[67]

African American's preference for menthols has also been explained as a cultural preference, or as identification with the vernacular roots of "cool." But it is highly possible that the mentholation of cigarettes also resonates with menthol's roots in folk medicine and over-the-counter drugs. Oil of peppermint, from which menthol is steam distilled, has been used as an ingredient of medicinal mixtures for thousands of years. Its popularity with the lay public stemmed from its use, combined with sodium bicarbonate or powdered rhubarb, as a treatment for a wide range of conditions, including as an antacid, appetite stimulant, and purgative. Mentholated commercial products, such as lozenges, inhalers, and chest rubs, were common in Britain and North America by the mid-nineteenth century.[68] Reports that African Americans have spent 2–4 times as much as White Americans on over the counter medications,[69] likely as a result of their disenfranchisement from medical institutions, indicate a possible identification with mentholated products and coincides particularly with the way that Kools were advertised for their purported medicinal properties.[70]

Whichever came first, targeting or taste, market studies attest to a strong preference for menthols among African Americans—both for the qualities of the cigarette as well as for its image. For example, in 1980, as Philip Morris, planning its own niche advertising strategy for the cigarette "Merit," had a 166 page document prepared on ethnic marketing.[71] Several pages are dedicated to analyzing the success of Kool cigarettes, and the document quotes African American smokers who focus on taste, style, and loyalty. Kools were considered by smokers to be "so smooth and mild you can smoke them all the time," and they work "like an anesthetic." Smokers described the experience of smoking Kools as "relaxing," a means of "escape," and as a way to meditate. Kool style was considered to be the crucial element to Kool's success. Kool was "heavily" associated with a very positive, often glamorous self-image: "to be cool you smoke kool"; "smoking a kool? Like riding a Rolls Royce." The study concluded that "Kool smokers see themselves as very stylish and apart from other smokers who haven't made it to Kools"; they were, as the 1967 advertisement reflects, separate from the crowd. These reactions to the Kool advertisements were reflected by one Black smoker's reminiscences in 2000: "I don't know if I smoked because I saw the ads. I do know that they made me feel a certain way, like I was part of that whole glamour thing."[72]

Though the smokers' testimony collected by Philip Morris may seem too simple in its reiteration of advertising's promises, it also makes clear the extent to which the identity of the Kools smoker was wrapped up in the expression of taste as a measure of class and good breeding. Like other highly advertised products, such as Coca-Cola, that are taken into the body in a pleasurable way, or like other intimate personal embellishments such as purses, pocket knives, or Mustangs that are exhibited, cigarettes express, through consumption and display, an identity, style, fashion, self. This versatility in expressing a variety of identities is a distinguishing feature of the cigarette: the consumer believes it to express what he or she wants it to. Thus, in the early century, advertising virtuoso Edward Bernays (perhaps not incidentally Freud's double nephew) allied cigarettes with women's liberation as "torches of freedom" and thus began the long history of identifying smoking with nearly every market niche's evolving desires—from patriotism, liberation, weight loss, sexuality, stress relief, daring, hipness. More recently, other campaigns have more or less successfully attempted to expand this image set to include filth, tackiness, dependence, and uncool.

The facility with which cigarettes can be consumed is not mirrored in their renunciation. The abysmal rates of success of quitting for all Americans demonstrate the severity of nicotine addiction, as well as the high resource intensity of the project. Antismoking is a multibillion dollar industry that includes counseling, nicotine patches, gum, and Zyban.[73] Of those who quit cold turkey on their own, only 3–4 percent succeed, while with stop-smoking drugs the rate rises to 10 percent.[74] A combination of the drugs with counseling increases the rate to 20 percent. For African Americans, statistics reveal poorer results. While on average African Americans attempt to quit more often than White Americans, studies have shown their attempts to be 34 percent less successful.[75]

Different studies have highlighted varying reasons for these racially disparate statistics, focusing on class access to medical care, genetic reasons for susceptibility to the poisons in smoke, cultural aspects of smoking, and the purported characteristics of the Black body. For example, minority smokers are both less likely to participate in smoking cessation programs (which can be expensive) than the general population, and less likely to receive cessation advice from health care providers.[76] It has also been suggested that African Americans metabolize carcinogens and nicotine more slowly than White Americans.[77] Recent studies suggests that menthol smokers have greater addiction rates since a higher inhalation of smoke (because of the anesthetic effect of menthol) leads to higher nicotine and carbon monoxide levels. Thus, African Americans, who tend to smoke menthols, would be more at risk, though they average fewer cigarettes (15 versus 19) per day. Richard Pollay's research also finds that tobacco companies advertised fewer products in the African American press, and that "filters were offered by ads to Blacks years after being promoted to White consumers."[78] While filters have not been found to defray the health effects of cigarettes, this fact seems to indicate that tobacco companies believed these customers to be less health conscious and/or less well educated.

Further evidence considers the design of menthol cigarettes. By the 1960s, tobacco companies understood the cigarette as a drug delivery device, monitoring and managing the quantity of nicotine in the product. For example, in 1964 the legal counsel for B&W advised the initiation of a search for a cigarette that would remove the "unattractive side effects of smoking [cancer]," while still upholding a "challenge [to] those charges [of the Surgeon General that cigarette smoking is extremely dangerous]" and still deliver "a nice jolt of nicotine."[79] A Philip Morris scientist, Al Udow, contended in 1972 that Kool had the highest nicotine delivery of any king-size cigarette on the market. He wrote that this was its secret to success, and recommended that PM also "pursue this . . . in developing a menthol entry."[80] Although it would still be difficult to argue that the industry had a clear intent to market a more dangerous product to African Americans, certainly by 1972 B&W was well aware Blacks were particularly attracted to mentholated brands. In 1994, B&W admitted—after initially denying that it bred plants for specific nicotine levels—that it had developed and imported (from Brazil) a tobacco plant that contained twice the amount of nicotine that was in regular American tobaccos.[81] These facts indicate that smokers of menthols, particularly the B&W brand Kool, will have a significantly higher level of addiction than smokers of other cigarettes.

Unraveling these moments of how the smoking institution has fixed race as a category—by calculation or elision—and thus giving it meaning, has been the key point of this essay. Advertisers interpreted African Americans as an always already psychologically injured group that needed and responded to respect in the creation of desires. While they did this to suit their own ends, the appalling caricatures of African Americans in advertising may have made the penguin appealing to Black (would-be) smokers, as plaintiff Charyn Sutton pointed out. The distribution of educational and medical services based on financial means has disproportionately affected African Americans, and at once indicates the possible attraction of menthol as well as the fact that African Americans are less likely to receive cessation advice and that their diseases are treated at a later stage. For John H. Johnson, his race kept him from earning the billions that he could have earned, and it proscribed how he defined what African Americans needed, desired, and aspired to—in his magazine and in his selling of the community to advertisers. Genetic studies of African Americans attempt to show that Black people metabolize carcinogens differently. For a social group that had, for historical reasons, a particularly small gene pool (such as Ashkenazi Jews) this conclusion may make sense. But a pool as diverse as that which has been socially consolidated as "African American," presents difficulties to this type of genetic research, and biologists such as Joseph Graves and Stephen Jay Gould have shown that race has no biological validity.[82] On the other hand, research—based in social, cultural, or ethnic practices—such as that on smoking cessation, "has been conducted almost exclusively in White, middle-class populations."[83] Thus, race is constituted through—and only becomes meaningful through—the shifting corroborations of these economic and cultural interests. Tobacco corporations have attempted to manipulate these but they are by no means the only actors.

Conclusion

Not only the injury caused by smoking itself, but also the turning to injured status through law "on behalf of Black smokers," collaborates in creating an injured and racialized group. And here is where the example of cigarettes both reflects consumer culture more generally and zeros in the specificity of the cigarette, for the right being claimed is also a right to have the cultural respect and self-esteem to what? Not to have started smoking in the first place? Not to have culturally or racially specific advertising? The specificity of the danger of mentholation over and above other tobacco flavorings surely does not override the clear indication that the right being claimed to nondiscriminatory consumption is not only to be free from physical injury, but also from the preceding cultural and economic injuries that have to do with many decisions about smoking, not only of mentholated cigarettes and not only by African Americans. Thus the claim for rights to equal opportunities in consumption cuts deeply into the socioeconomics of U.S. culture. *Brown* is a symptom of the broader inability of U.S. institutions to both structure the most physically dangerous aspects of capitalist production and to deeply comprehend and eradicate racism.

Another way to look at race, might be through the relation of African Americans to injury: through an injured groups' turn to law and very specific self-definition as those injured through use of a particular product, through the consequences of the use of a more dangerous product and its access to fewer medical resources, and through ads that both portrayed and took advantage of the real and assumed "psychological injuries" of centuries of racism. The discrimination at stake in the *Brown* case and others like it includes not only the right to not be targeted with more dangerous products and to be treated with respect where they spend their money (as the 1964 Civil Rights Acts claims), they ineluctably also include having the education to know about products that are not advertised directly to them or the consequences of which are not written about in their magazines.[84] They necessarily include having access to medical resources and scientific research that has included responsible race specific research— even as many self-identified African Americans support the interests of tobacco companies. In this way, the structure of racialized injury goes far beyond consumption by choice. The particular issue that *Brown* presents is not only the racialized claim for rights to equality in consumption, but also an expression that is echoed in all tobacco litigation: of regret. I shall only briefly address each of these here.

Claiming a right from the state conceals the ways in which African Americans were produced as a racialized group through the interacting forces, some of which I have elucidated here, of corporations, marketers, activists, governments, and so on. Thus, as Wendy Brown has so magnificently argued, that developing "a righteous critique of power from the perspective of the injured . . . delimits a specific cite of blame for suffering by constituting sovereign subjects and events as responsible for the 'injury' of social subordination." Such claims, she contends, cast "the law in particular and the state more generally as neutral arbiters of injury rather than as themselves invested with the power to injure."[85] This point is particularly poignant given the multiple factors of education, medical access, and class that determine smoking practice and its effects. Furthermore, it is uniquely illustrated by the way that cigarette companies could provide African Americans the freedom to consume in a new way in the 1950s and the 1960s while also providing means for cultural expression by sponsoring programs of all kinds.

Finally, tobacco cases more generally, and this one in particular, raises a key anthropological predicament of injury law, and one that is at the heart of the moralism that has tended to pervade both the pro- and anti-smoking debates. Which are we to privilege: the agent with its series of knowledges about the cigarette, the corporation, the law, and the body that decided to smoke and kept smoking for years? Or the agent that, with a different set of knowledges and a new diseased body, takes on a different subcultural identity—that of the injured—and decides to sue? The morality play that sees the legal contest as one between (self-righteous or innocent) smoker, and (greedy or paternal) corporation misses the key way in which these agentive moments can be understood in some sense as the shifting identity of what Ulrich Beck calls the "biographic solution to systematic contradictions" where both consumption and injury are built in to economic environments.[86]

To take this argument one step further is to begin to understand how the cigarette is both unique among products in its injuring potential, but also how it is symptomatic of the place of physical injury in capitalism. Consider that the importance of the tobacco industry to the U.S. economy has for decades been used to argue against its regulation, even though it is considered unique among products for its capacity to injure when used as intended.[87] Thus, we might understand the injury caused by [cigarette] consumption as a sort of collateral damage—an unavoidable but regrettable side affect of consumer capitalism and the health of the economy, at the same time as it involves (requires?) the destruction of the presumed reason for the economy in the first place—the citizenry. The *Brown* suit emerges—as does other tobacco litigation—as a symptom of deeply serious political fissures that cut across, as they consolidate, both race and class, but they also demonstrate how injury categories fissure in ways that cannot solely be reduced to only these analytic categories.

Put most simply, the two linked arguments I develop here are as follows. First, that the language of rights—the right to consume on an equal basis, or the right not to be injured in consumption, blots out an understanding of the ways that mentholated cigarettes, in particular, circulate in economies that cannot be satisfactorily traced solely to an evil (as in aberrant) corporation and a neutral government. Second, in the agentive moments separated by time (the liberal chooser and the injured litigant), race is mutually produced in the actions of human and nonhuman actors: scientists, advertising agencies, farmers, popular magazines, government agencies, nonsmoking lobbies, cells, trains, facts about smoking, cessation programs, product liability laws, civil rights claims. To return, then, to the problem of "object-responsibility" is to note that the continuing fascination of the cigarette lies precisely in the way that it has so completely flaunted any question of responsibility or accountability to anything but itself. In that sense at least, the cigarette has been a true American icon.

Notes

Hearty thanks are due to my friends, colleagues, and relatives who have contributed to this essay through discussion, reading drafts, and inviting me to present this work-in-progress: Genevieve Bell, Susan Boyd, Ruth Buchanan, Evelyn Jain, Matthew Kohrman, Jake Kosek, Samara Marion, Catherine Newman, Richard Pollay, Matt Price, Robert Rabin, Derek Simons, Ann Stoler, Lucy Suchman, Victoria Vesna, Robert Weems, Sylvia Yanagasako, Claire Young and the participants of the HRI seminar at UCSC, including Deborah Bright, Angela Y. Davis, Gina Dent, Laura Kuo, and Neferti Tadiar. I also would like to acknowledge the able research assistance of Colleen Pearl. This essay was written with support from the Social Science and Humanities Research Council of Canada and from the Killam Foundation, and is dedicated in gratitude to my dissertation advisor and mentor Donna J. Haraway. Please direct correspondence to sarjain@stanford.edu.

1. Second Amended Class Action Complaint, Section A.5.
2. Rev. Jesse Brown et al. versus Philip Morris, Inc., et al., 1999 WL 783712 (E.D.Pa.). September 22, 1999.
3. Michael Bail, Caroline Scooler, David G. Altman, Michael Slater et al., "How Cigarettes Are Advertised in Magazines: Special Messages for Special Markets" *Health Communication*, 3(2), 75–91. Menthol has only very recently been studied for potential carcinogenic compounds, and the issue is still controversial.
4. Claims of breach of warranty or fraud and misrepresentation were state law claims, not Civil Rights claims, and therefore dismissed by the Pennsylvania U.S. District Court. *Brown*'s other claims, brought under section 1983 were dismissed since *Brown* was unable to show that tobacco companies should be understood as "state actors." Similarly, charges brought under section 1985(3) were dismissed on statutory grounds.
5. Elaine Scarry, *The Body in Pain: The Making and Unmaking of the World* (New York: Oxford University Press, 1985), 295.
6. B&W document cited in New York Times News Service, "Tobacco Industry's Ad Assault on Blacks is Detailed in Records Newly released," Sunday February 8, 1998.
7. In 1974 B&W sold 56.1 billion units of KOOL after spending $15 million for advertising the cigarette in 1973. "Brown & Williamson Tobacco Co." *Advertising Age*, August 26, 1974. RJR introduced Salem in 1956, the first filter-tip menthol, which by 1960 outsold Kool 3–1. By the late 1960s, however, B&W's Kool was again the largest selling mentholated brand—thanks to a much touted and emulated advertising campaign.
8. Michael Omi and Howard Winant, *Racial Formation in the United States: From the 1960s to the 1990s*, 2nd edn (New York, London: Routledge, 1994), 99.

9. Cited in "Tobacco Timeline," available at: <http://www.tobacco.org/History/Tobacco_History.html> (Copyright 1993–2001 Gene Borio).
10. Editor's introduction, *Ebony*, August 1967.
11. Paul M. Hirsch, "An Analysis of *Ebony*: The Magazine and Its Readers," *Journalism Quarterly*, 45: 261–270 and 292 (1968).
12. Ibid., pp. 267–268. In 1966, circulation was 926,644. *The Negro* Handbook (Chicago: Johnson Publishing Company, Inc., 1966), 384.
13. K.A. Wall. "Positioning your brand in the Black market." *Advertising Age*, 44 (25), 1973: 71–76. Other 1960s ads for mentholated cigarettes collected in the Archive of Cigarette Advertising at the University of British Columbia.
14. John H. Johnson with Leone Bennett, Jr., *Succeeding Against the Odds: The Inspiring Autobiography of One of America's Wealthiest Entrepreneurs* (New York: Warner Books, 1989), 90.
15. As described in *The Negro Handbook*, compiled by the Editors of *Ebony*, Johnson Publishing Company, Inc., Chicago, 1966. This compilation of facts and statistics on the African American community, was, suggests Robert Weems, possibly a guide to the Black community for White corporations—with a distinct bias against Black-owned businesses. Robert E. Weems, *Desegregating the Dollar: African American Consumerism in the Twentieth Century* (New York and London: New York University Press, 1998).
16. John H. Johnson and Leone Bennett, Jr., *Succeeding Against the Odds*, 161. In 1967, a full-page black and white ad cost $5,870 for a one-time printing, while a four-color cost $9,075—the guaranteed circulation was one million. "Admans' Guide to Negro Media," *Sponsor* (*Negro Market Supplement*), 21, July 1967: 42–45, 48–51.
17. In addition to a number of publications, Johnson produced two films, "There's Gold in Your Backyard" and "The Secret of Selling to the Negro."
18. John H. Johnson and Leone Bennett, Jr., *Succeeding Against the Odds*, 230.
19. No author noted, "Admans' Guide to Negro Media," *Sponsor* (*Negro Market Supplement*), 21, July 1967: 42–45, 48–51.
20. Weems, *Desegregating the Dollar*, p. 46
21. Ibid., 26.
22. David J. Sullivan, "Don't do This—If You Want to Sell Your Products to Negroes!" *Sales Management* 52 (March 1, 1943): 46–51.
23. In a 1952 article in *Advertising Age*, Johnson advised would-be advertisers not to "use the term 'nigger,' 'negress,' 'darky' or 'boy.' John H. Johnson, "Does Your Sales Force Know How to Sell the Negro Trade? Some Do's and Don'ts," *Advertising Age*, March 17, 1952.
24. Arnold M. Barban and Edward W. Cundiff, "Negro and White Responses to Advertising Stimuli," *Journal of Marketing Research* 1964: 53–56.
25. "*Ebony* Survey Reveals Negro Buying Habits," *Advertising Age*, 21, July 29, 1950: 16–17.
26. Marcus Alexis, "Pathways to the Negro Market," *Journal of Negro Education*, 28(2), Spring 1959: 115 (pp. 114–127).
27. Johnson, *Advertising Age*, 1952.
28. "The Forgotten 15,000,000 . . . Three Years Later," *Sponsor*, 6, July 28, 1952: 76–77.

29. "Because of the psychological considerations involved, Negros are extremely desirous of being identified as customers 'who recognize and demand quality merchandise.'" "*Ebony* Survey Reveals Negro Buying Habits," *Advertising Age*, 21, August 1950: 17.

30. T.J. Jackson Lears, "From Salvation to Self-Realization: Advertising and the Therapeutic Roots of Consumer Culture, 1880–1930" in *The Culture of Consumption: Critical Essays in American History, 1880–1980*, edited by Richard Wightman Fox and T.J. Jackson Lears (New York: Pantheon Books), 1–38.

31. Henry Allen Bullock, "Consumer Motivations *in Black and White—I*," *Harvard Business Review*, 38, May/June 1961: 99.

32. Ibid., 102.

33. Leiss discusses how in consumer culture "class" is about learning to consume at a particular level. William Leiss, *The Limits to Satisfaction: An Essay on the Problem of Needs and Commodities* (Toronto: University of Toronto Press, 1976).

34. Dave Berkman, *Journalism Quarterly*, 40, 1963: 43–64.

35. Bullock, "Consumer Motivations—*II*," 113.

36. "Admans Guide" quoting Moss H. Kendrix, African American owner of a Washington consulting firm, on p. 42. Italicized in original. The article goes on to note that, "although the Negro no longer wants to be white, he most certainly wants to have the same things and do the same things as white people" (42).

37. E. Franklin Frazier, *Black Bourgeoisie* (Glencoe, *II*: The Free Press, 1957), 56.

38. Ibid., p. 173.

39. No author given, "Clients Seek Advice on Negro Market," *Sponsor* (*Negro Market Supplement*), vol. 20, July 25, 1966, 40–43. The article notes that R.J. Reynolds Tobacco ranks first and Liggett & Myers seventh for advertisers providing the most business on "Negro-appeal" radio stations.

40. No author given, "Yule Boycott is Senseless, Johnson Says," *Advertising Age*, October 21, 1963, 3; "No Christmas Boycott," *The Crisis*, vol. 70, November, 1963, 555–556, "Will Negroes back Christmas Boycott?" *Advertising Week*, October 4, 1963.

41. Ramona Bechtos, "Ads in Negro-Market Media do Double Duty with Negro Buyers, Zimmer Says," *Advertising Age*, January 13, 1964, 72. No author, "Be Sure Negroes Featured in Ads are Identified with Civil Rights Effort: Robinson," *Advertising Age*, April 10, 1967, 12. This article reports Jackie Robinson advocating the use of prominent African Americans who are affiliated with the Civil Rights movement in advertising.

42. No author given, "Ads Alone Won't Win Negro Market: Russell," *Advertising Age*, October 21, 1963, 3, 130.

43. Ibid.

44. No author given, "Clients Seek Advice," 43.

45. "L&M Cigarettes Pitched to Blacks as 'Superbad'" *Advertising Age*.

46. See, e.g., John H. Pierce, Ph.D.; Lora Lee, M.A.; Elizabeth Gilpin, M.S., "Smoking Initiation by Adolescent Girls, 1944 Through 1988: An Association

with Targeted Advertising." *Journal of the American Medical Association* 271(8), February 23, 1994: 608–611.

47. Tomas E. Novotny, Kenneth E. Warner, Juliette S. Kendrick, Patrick L. Remington, "Smoking By Blacks and Whites: Socioeconomic and Demographic Differences." *AJPH*, 79(9), September 1988: 1187–1189.

48. Stuart Ewen, PR!: *A Social History of Spin*, Basic Books, 1996.

49. Hirsch reports that by 1966, "CORE, SNCC, and the Southern Christian Leadership Conference Were out of Favor with *Ebony* and its Readers." "An Analysis of *Ebony*," 267.

50. Many thanks to Deborah Bright, who offered me substantial written feedback on a very early draft.

51. Personal communication, December 2000.

52. Roy Norr, "Cancer by the Carton," *Reader's Digest*, December, 1952: 7–10. See also R.C. Smith, "The Magazines' Smoking Habit: Magazines that have Accepted Growing Amounts of Cigarette Advertising have Failed to Cover Tobacco's Threat to Health," *Columbia Journalism Review*, January/February 1978.

53. "Advertising; RJR Flap Not the First in Ad History," Philip H. Dougherty, *New York Times*, April 7, 1988. Cited in "Tobacco Timeline," Copyright 1993–2001 Gene Borio, available at: <http://www.tobacco.org/History/Tobacco_History.html>.

54. "Nor did *Ebony* editors express any interest in covering the historic conference on the Realities of Cancer in Minority Communities." Alan Blum, "The Targeting of Minority Group by the Tobacco Industry," edited by L.A. Jones *Minorities and Cancer*, New York: Springer Verlag, 1989: 153–162.

55. Thomas Laqweur, "Smoking and Nothingness," *The New Republic*, 47, 48.

56. Ironically, the growth of a White middle class and its attendant White flight enabled the high-density inner-city neighborhoods to became crucibles for high-density advertising (billboards, buses, bus stops).

57. Karen Ahijevych and Mary Ellen Wewers, "Factors Associated with Nicotine Dependence among African American Women Cigarette Smokers," *Research in Nursing and Health*, 16, 1993: 283–292.

58. Henry Weinstein and Alissa J. Rubin, "Tobacco Firms Targeted Blacks, Documents Show," *Los Angeles Times*, February 6, 1998.

59. Laurie Hoffman-Goetz, Karen K. Gerlach, Christina Marino, Sherry L. Mills, "Cancer Coverage and Tobacco Advertising in African-American's Popular Magazines," *Journal of Community Health*, 22(4), August 1997: 261–271. This study was done on adult women, and supports the observation that women read popular magazines in order to acquire information rather than from habit.

60. United States Department of Health and Human Services, "Health Status of Minorities and Low-Income Groups," 17 (1990).

61. David Koepke, Brian R. Flay, C. Anderson Johnson, "Health Behaviors in minority families: The case of cigarette Smoking." *Family and Community Health*, May 1990, 35–43. See also Gilbert J. Botvin, Eli Baker, Catherine J. Goldberg, Linda Dusenbury, and Elizabeth M. Botvin, "Correlates and

Predictors of Smoking Among Black Adolescents," *Addictive Behaviors*, 17, 1992: 97–103.

62. Kluger, *Ashes to Ashes*, 93.
63. Ibid.
64. Ad on file at The History of Advertising Archives, University of British Columbia, curated by Richard Pollay.
65. See, e.g., "A Pilot Look at the Attitudes of Negro Smokers Toward Menthol Cigarettes," Submitted to Philip Morris Inc., New York, Submitted By: Tibor Koeves Associates, Sag Harbor, N.Y. September, 1968. Available at <http://www.pmdocs.com/>. This study concludes that "here was a product [menthols] which by some virtue was especially suited to the needs, desires, and tastes of Negro consumers," 2–3.
66. Quoted in "Court Urged to Dismiss Menthol Cigarette Class Action," *Law News Network*, Thursday, April 8, 1999.
67. Quoted from National Public Radio, "As it Happens," November 2, 1998.
68. R. Eccles, "Menthol and Related Cooling Compounds," *Journal of Pharmacy and Pharmacology*, 46, 1994: 46, 618–630. Menthol can also be extracted or synthesized from other essential oils such as citronella, eucalyptus, and Indian turpentine oils. Eccles cites a number of studies that demonstrate that menthol inhalation causes "a subjective nasal decongestant effect without any objective decongestant action" (622). Thanks to Stuart Anderson of the London School of Hygiene and Tropical Medicine, Katie Eagleton assistant curator of the London Science Museum, and George Twigg for e-mail communication on this issue.
69. Weems, *Desegregating the Dollar*, 34. In 1963 Dave Berkman found 49 ads for patent medicines and other health aids in *Ebony* compared to only 14 in *Life*. He notes that this "was not an unexpected finding in a magazine whose readership contains such a high proportion of people engaged in work demanding heavy physical exertion (and a race whose memberships' deaths occur, on the average, about eight years earlier than among the White population)" (Berkman, "Advertising in 'Ebony' and 'Life,' " 54–55).
70. "Documents about the Kool brand showed that the company sought to 'capitalize upon the erroneous consumer perception that their [*sic*] is a health benefit to smoking mentholated cigarettes.' Richard Pollay, "Getting Good and Being Super Bad: Chapters in the Promotion of Cigarettes to Blacks," Working Paper, The History of Advertising Archives, University of British Columbia, 1993, 18. The Philip Morris document "A Pilot Look at the Attitudes" also quotes several smokers who believe that menthols are better for ones health (7).
71. See the "secret tobacco documents" posted on <www.tobacco.org>, "Merit Ethnic Research," prepared for Philip Morris, February 1, 1980, 166 pages scanned into the site. All quotes in this paragraph are from 101–106.
72. Warren Mitchell quoted in Tracey Reeves, "A Targeted Payback; Black Communities in Md. Want More Tobacco Money," *Washington Post*, Wednesday, February 16, 2000.
73. Zyban is the trade name for the antidepressant drug bupropion hydrochloride for which there is not yet a generic form. Extrapolating from Canadian figures (since I have been unable to find complete U.S. figures), Americans would

spend about $10 billion per year on drugs and counseling (Canadian Broadcasting Corporation, "Marketplace," February 16, 2000). This extrapolation is based on population only, it does not account for the vastly inflated cost of healthcare in the U.S. or for the aggressive governmental anti-smoking campaign in Canada.

74. Mayo Clinic web site.

75. Fiore M.C., Novotny T.E., Pierce J.P., Hatziandreu E.J., Patel K.M., Davis R.M. Trends in cigarette smoking in the US: the changing influence of gender and race. *JAMA*, 261, 1989: 49–55.

76. Department of Health and Human Services, Centers for Disease Control and Prevention, National Center for Chronic Disease Prevention and Health Promotion, Office on Smoking and Health, 1998. U.S. Department of Health and Human Services. *Tobacco Use Among U.S. Racial/Ethnic Minority Groups African Americans, American Indians and Alaska Natives, Asian Americans and Pacific Islanders, and Hispanics: A Report of the Surgeon General.* Atlanta, Georgia: U.S. "Appendix: A Brief History of Tobacco advertising Targeting African Americans."

77. For studies that show a possible genetic difference between African Americans and Whites in the metabolization of nicotine, indicating that Black smokers have a higher exposure to cigarette's carcinogenic components even when they smoke fewer cigarettes, see "Editorial, "Pharmacogenics and Ethnoracial Differences in Smoking," *JAMA*, 280(2), July 8, 1998: 170–180; Ralph S. Caraballo et al., "Racial and Ethnic Differences in Serum Cotinine Levels of Cigarette Smokers," *JAMA*, 280(2), July 8, 1998: 135–139; Eliseo J. Perez-Stable, MD et al., "Nicotine Metabolism and Intake in Black and White Smokers," *JAMA*, 280(2), July 8, 1998: 152–156; Karen Ahijevych and Lea Ann Parsley, "Smoke Constituent Exposure and Stage of Change in Black and White Women Cigarette Smokers," *Addictive Behaviors*, 24(1), 1999: 115–120. None of these studies questions a generic use of genetic categories as "black" or "white." William Feigelman and Bernard Gorman found that class and stress differences, rather than race, account for variations in smoking behavior and that race is primarily a correlate of other demographic features. See "Toward Explaining the Higher Incidence of Cigarette Smoking Among Black Americans," *Journal of Psychoactive Drugs*, 21(3), July–September 1989: 299–305. For the importance of "cultural" as opposed to "socioeconomic" factors, see Geoffrey C. Kabat, Alfredo Morabia, and Ernst L. Wyner, "Comparison of Smoking Habits of Blacks and Whites in a Case-Control Study," *American Journal of Public Health*, 81(11), November 1991: 1483–1486.

78. Pollay, "Separate but Equal," 52.

79. Addison Yeaman cited in *Cigarette Papers*, 54. Nicotine was always known to be the central ingredient to cigarettes. A senior scientist for PM wrote this in a confidential document released in a 1988 trial, "Think of the cigarette as a storage container for a day's supply of nicotine." Reported in Jerry Carroll, "Killing Us Softly: Women, a prime target of cigarette advertisers, are about to overtake men as the tobacco industry's best customer," *San Francisco Chronicle*, September 1, 1996: 4. Smoke is considered the optimal vehicle for nicotine absorption.

80. Cited in "Tobacco Timeline," Copyright 1993–2001 Gene Borio, available at: <http://www.tobacco.org/History/Tobacco_History.html>.

81. Cited in *Brown*, section 170. At that time, four million pounds of the high nicotine imported tobacco, used in five brands, were found in B&W's warehouses. Tobacco companies also add several ammonia compounds to cigarettes in order to increase the nicotine transfer efficiency.

82. Joseph L. Graves, Jr. *The Emperor's New Clothes: Biological Theories of Race at the Millennium* (New Brunswick, NJ: Rutgers University Press, 2001).

83. Kolawole S. Okuyemi, M.D., M.P.H.; Jasjit S. Ahluwalia, M.D., M.P.H., M.S.; Kari J. Harris, Ph.D., M.P.H. "Pharmacotherapy of Smoking Cessation," *Family Medicine*, 9(3), March 2000.

84. This suit could be linked to accident law and race in the nineteenth century. Nan Goodman, e.g., shows how "the law of the Good Samaritan helped significantly to designate African Americans as a class of expendable accident victims—a class defined by its existing marginality and by its actual or imagined incompetence, whose purpose was to have the accidents and bear the injuries the middle classes would then be fit to avoid." *Shifting the Blame: Literature, Law, and the Theory of Accidents in Nineteenth Century America* (New York: Routledge, 1999), 119.

85. Wendy Brown, *States of Injury: Power and Freedom in Late Modernity* (NJ: Princeton University Press, 1995), 27.

86. Ulich Beck, *Risk Society: Towards a New Modernity* (London; Newbury Park, Claif: Sage, Publications 1992), 137.

87. A provision in the United States Code put it this way: "the marketing of tobacco constitutes one of the greatest basic industries of the United States with ramifying interests which directly affect interstate and foreign commerce at every point, and stable conditions are necessary, therefore, to the general welfare." 7 U.S.C. section 1311(a), cited in FDA versus Brown & Williamson in the majority opinion to support the argument that Congress never intended that the FDA regulate tobacco products.

Part II

Self/Identity, Memory/History

6

Conjuring up Traces of Historical Violence: Grandpa, Who is Not in the Photo

Naono Akiko

So that the terrible evil that brought so much suffering to Hiroshima may never happen again, let us remember—works of love and prayer are works of peace.

—Mother Teresa, 1984

It would be sufficient for my present purpose to say that if any indiscriminate destruction of civilian life and property is still illegitimate in warfare, then, in the Pacific war, this decision to use the atom bomb is the only near approach to the directives of the German Emperor during the first world war and of the Nazi leaders during the second world war.

*—Judge Radhabinod Pal of India, International Military Tribunal
for the Far East, 1946*

Whereas the role of the Enola Gay during World War II was momentous in helping to bring World War II to a merciful end, which resulted in saving the lives of Americans and Japanese. . . . Now, therefore, be it Resolved, that it is the sense of the Senate that any exhibit displayed by the National Air and Space Museum with respect to the Enola Gay should reflect appropriate sensitivity toward the men and women who faithfully and selflessly served the United States during World War II and should avoid impugning the memory of those who gave their lives for freedom.

—United States Senate Resolution 257, 1994

It was good that the United States dropped the atomic bombs on Japan, because it hastened our independence [from Japan]. I think Japan [was atom-bombed] as a result of invading Asian countries, including Korea.

—Chang Pyŏng-hyŏn, 1987[1]

We refer to the extraordinary experience of horror as "a nightmare"; but what happened that day is far more horrifying than a "nightmare." ... One day, I was describing [what I witnessed on that day] just as requested. My friend was drawn into my tale. I was just about to move onto the scene inside a streetcar—passengers were charred to death sitting on the two rows of seats. Suddenly, I found myself taking pleasure in talking fluently [about that day] and drawing the listener into my tale. "No, I ought not to talk about that day like this. It cannot be talked smoothly." I tasted bitterness in my throat—I was at loss of words. Since then until today, I have never spoken of that day.
—Hachiya Kazuye 1993: 116–117

Shadow in the Photo

On the day of my *omiya mairi* [a shrine visit of a newborn baby], Grandma and her sister visited us from Hiroshima. Grandpa could not make it, so he is not in the photo (see figure 6.1).

*   *   *

When I was about four or five years old, I expressed to Mom my uneasiness about the absence of one grandpa: I had seen two grandmas but only one grandpa.

"*Ojiichan* [Grandpa] and *Obaachan* [Grandma] are in Niihama. Why only *Obaachan* in Hiroshima? Where is *Ojiichan*?"

"Your *ojiichan* in Hiroshima died because of the atomic bombing."

*   *   *

"Hiroshima" evokes various memories in the minds of people across the globe. On the one hand, it is remembered by some as one of the greatest tragedies of the twentieth century. Such remembrance celebrates the "Spirit of Hiroshima," an unwavering hope for the abolition of nuclear weapons and the realization of lasting world peace. On the other hand, "Hiroshima" reminds some of Japanese aggression in the Asia-Pacific region during World War II, such as the surprise attack on Pearl Harbor and the Nanking Massacre. In fact, many Americans justify the dropping of atomic bombs on Hiroshima and Nagasaki by arguing that the bombs hastened the end of the war, saving thousands of lives as a result. Moreover, many Asians and Pacific islanders who lived under Japanese colonial and military rule often claim that the atomic bombs liberated them from Japanese aggression.

Re-membered within the space of the Hiroshima memoryscape, which is filled with contention over the meaning of the atomic bombing,

Figure 6.1 Late Spring 1972; from top left (clockwise): Grandma's elder sister, Grandma, Dad, my brother, myself, Mom.

those who were killed by the bombing become "martyrs for peace," "Japanese *higaisha* [victims]," or "Japanese *kagaisha* [aggressors]." Torn into these subjects, *jiichan* [my grandpa], who was killed by the bombing, disappears from the space of "the beloved."

*   *   *

Jiichan died about one month after the atomic bomb was dropped on Hiroshima. He survived "damages from heat rays, shock wave and blast, and high-temperature fires" caused by the atomic bombing, but did not survive "the acute radiation damage." He is one of "approximately 140,000 (error of ±10,000)" who were killed in Hiroshima by the end of December 1945.[2] He died of what later came to be known as radiation sickness.

I do not recall when, but I learned that Mom, Auntie, and Grandma are all *hibakusha*, survivors of the atomic bombing, and that I am a *hibaku-nisei*, a second-generation atomic bomb survivor. As I read stories about the children who died from leukemia, which was believed to be symptomatic of the "radiation sickness" caused by the bombing, I became afraid that I might develop such sickness myself.

At an early age, I became grateful that I was alive and healthy, although I could never eliminate completely concerns about developing some unknown radiation sickness in the future. My feeling of gratefulness, combined with a naïve sense of justice, led me to decide that I would dedicate myself to work for peace. This "commitment" had long dictated how I talked to *jiichan*.

Because he was killed by the atomic bombing 27 years prior to my birth, *jiichan* appeared to me as an absent figure. Initially, learning about the source of his absence through familial stories told by Mom seemed to offer me a safe and warm space to talk to *jiichan*. As I searched for him, however, I began to bump into the uncanny forces on my way: *jiichan* no longer appeared as a beloved figure.

Being drawn by some unknown forces, I found myself inside the Hiroshima memoryscape. And my search for *jiichan* turned into a journey through the memoryscape, without knowing exactly when this journey had begun. Retrospectively, my first encounter with *genbaku* [the atomic bomb], through recognizing *jiichan*'s absence, marked an entry into the Hiroshima memoryscape. But this encounter was not completely or deliberately my own choice. I was merely searching for *jiichan*. I am not sure why I bothered to look for *jiichan* whom I have never even met. Could it be that the spirits of those killed by the bombing drove me to this? A local journalist in Hiroshima, only half jokingly, once told me, "Ms. Naono, you are possessed by *hibakusha*'s spirits."

Practicing sociological imagination, this essay draws out how my memory of *jiichan* came to be covered by the shadow of "the bomb"— a sign of the violent forces that took him away from me—and how I desperately try to rescue him from that shadow, albeit unsuccessfully, by taking a journey through Hiroshima's memoryscape.[3] This is not a story about *jiichan*, but it cannot be told without his absence. This is a story about how I remember him; how I have talked to him; how my talks to him have been shadowed by the lasting effects of "the bomb"; and how I long for his loving presence back in the photo.

My story evolves around what is *not* seen and barely sensed, so it might be called a "ghost story." In her analysis of ghostly matters and haunting, Avery Gordon proposes that, rather than being simply a missing or a dead person, a ghost is a sign of unresolved violence or injury that appears to be the things of the past, "but is nonetheless alive, operating in the present, even if obliquely, even if barely visible" (Gordon 1997: 66).[4] Once encountered, Gordon further argues, a ghost forces us to recognize "the living effects, seething and lingering, of what seems over and done with, the endings that are not over" (Gordon 1997: 195).

The theoretical approaches I use in this essay derive from Gordon's careful and politically enabling analysis of ghostly matters in relation to the presence of sociohistorical violence. At the same time, I have serious reservations about identifying *jiichan*'s presence as a ghost, for the word "ghost," or a Japanese translation of it, "*yūrei*" or "*obake*," seems to reduce him to an objectified and impersonal figure. For me, *jiichan* is my grandpa, whether he is alive or not. Part of my reservation is connected to the very way his presence became ghostly, as I later delineate. Moreover, those who survived the unprecedented atomic horror use a metaphor of "*yūrei*," which often appears in pictures of Buddhist hell, to describe the thousands of terribly burnt and disfigured fleeing from ground zero, for they looked "out-of-this-world." If I employed "*yūrei*" to signify *jiichan*'s presence, that would subject him again to the cruel death brought upon him by the bomb, which reduced humans to inorganic creatures. As a granddaughter, I want to rescue him from being made into "objects" and keep his warm presence *alive*. But precisely because the source of his absence cannot be separated from a troubling past, which has not passed yet, *jiichan*'s presence became ghostly.

Ghost's presence is never clearly visible, so we might wonder if it is our imaginary creation. But a ghost is never simply a product of our imagination or representation: it produces material effects on those who are haunted. An encounter with a ghost, therefore, is uncomfortable at the least and can even be dangerous. Once being haunted, we might be "grasped and hurtled into the maelstrom of the powerful and material forces that lay claim to [us] whether [we] claim them as [ours] or not" (Gordon 1997: 166). Yet we are haunted not simply to be drawn into the world of ghosts. Gordon helps us recognize, with

Benjamin's historical materialism, a utopian possibility in the presence of a ghost:

> The monad or the ghost presents itself as a sign to the thinker that there is a *chance in the fight for the oppressed past*, by which I take Benjamin to mean that the past is alive enough in the present. . . . Benjamin goes even further, calling on us to protect the dead from the dangers of the present as if they were proximate enough for such loving embrace. (Gordon 1997: 65, emphasis in the original)

In order to fight for the oppressed past, Gordon urges us that we must endeavor to "obliterat[e] the sources and conditions that link the violence of what seems finished with the present" (Gordon 1997: 66). The ghost appears to you because "the dead or the disappeared or the lost or the invisible are demanding their due" (Gordon 1997: 182).

In some cases, a response to the ghosts demanding their due might take a form of revenge. Many of those who were killed by the bomb, indeed, asked for revenge on "America," as they took their last breath. Sometimes, I cannot withhold my anger toward the United States for willfully killing hundreds of thousands of civilians, including *jiichan*, and bringing so much suffering and lasting terror of radiation to those who survived and their offspring. Worse still, the United States continues to justify its act in its righteous claim of having "saved lives" and insists on the power and necessity of nuclear weapons. As it will become clear in this essay, however, the "Enemy" takes many forms, which makes it almost impossible to seize it and carry out my revenge. As I try to avenge for *jiichan*'s death, I become more and more confused about what I am fighting against—who the "Enemy" is.

Because I want to find "my beloved grandpa," I follow the ghostly presence of *jiichan*. By following his presence, though not always willingly, I journey through the Hiroshima memoryscape, under the shadow of "the bomb."

Talking to *Jiichan*

"Dad was working in the house that morning. I was with Mom in a shelter-house in Yamate, further northwest of our house [in relation to the hypocenter]. I was in the living room after eating breakfast. There suddenly was a big flash. Windows were shattered into pieces. And I was thrown up in the air and then against the floor. The next thing

I remember is I was being held by Mom in an air raid shelter with the neighbors. Dad came back to Yamate around 4 in the afternoon that day. The back of his head was injured, with a piece of glass sticking in it. It took Dad a long time to get home because he didn't know alternative routes to get around the rivers. He just waited for the water to get low enough to cross the rivers. He was such a hardworking man and never played around, so he didn't know the way around. He was the oldest of 11 siblings, and after he graduated from elementary school, he began working for his father. He worked hard so that he could send all his siblings to college. He did not look badly injured. But he got really sick. He suffered so much that he begged to be killed. One day, we were all called beside his futon. Dad held my hand and told me to study hard and be a good girl. But I quickly pulled my hand away. His body was filled with purple spots. He was a very kind and warm father. He was the only one in the family who died because of the bomb."

Mom told me the story again and again, every time I asked her about *jiichan* (Grandpa). *Jiichan* died on September 3, 1945, due to acute radiation sickness. He was exposed to the bombing a mere 800 meters from ground zero.[5] With his body covered in purple spots, a typical symptom of radiation sickness, *jiichan* must have looked horrifying. But at least he died under the care of his family; many died without being reunited with their loved ones.

I am not sure how much of Mom's story I understood when I first heard it, given how young I was then, but by the time I finished elementary school, I had already decided to work for peace. I believed that, as a granddaughter of a man who was killed cruelly by a nuclear bomb, I had been assigned such a mission. As I grew up, I read many accounts and stories about the atomic bombing. These were in accordance with the master narrative of the bombing in Japan that had been fully developed by the late 1970s.

In the 1980s, when I did most of my initial learning about the bombing, the "Spirit of Hiroshima" was firmly in place.

The damage done by the A-bomb was so catastrophic that this conviction was deeply rooted in the minds of the people of Hiroshima; humanity cannot coexist with nuclear weapons and their use must not be allowed. Based on this conviction—the Spirit of Hiroshima, an unwavering hope for the abolition of nuclear weapons and the realization of lasting world peace, the city of Hiroshima turned toward the world and began its journey on a path to peace. (Hiroshima Peace Memorial Museum, Panel A6001 "Path to Peace")

"The Spirit of Hiroshima" is, though, now widely criticized as the master narrative of Japanese victimhood, which positions the "Japanese" as "*higaisha* [victims]" of the war while concealing Japan's colonial past and its aggression in neighboring Asia Pacific Islands (Dower 1997; Hein and Selden 1997; Yoneyama 1999). I cherished this Spirit, with its concealing effect of Japan's colonial past, as my memory of Hiroshima. And this Spirit had long dictated the way I talked to *jiichan*.

The primary way I talked to *jiichan* was through the prayer held on every August 6—the anniversary of the bombing. At Dad's insistence, it had become my family's ritual to gather in front of TV about 8:00 A.M. every August 6 to watch broadcasting of the peace memorial ceremony. As part of the ceremony, one-minute of prayer is dedicated to the victims of the bombing at 8:15 A.M., the time the bomb was dropped on Hiroshima. At 8:15 A.M., my family sat in front of the TV and prayed for one minute. I talked to *jiichan* for one minute every August 6, although it is not the anniversary of his death. "How are you, *jiichan*? I will work for the abolition of nuclear weapons and the realization of lasting world peace. So, watch over me from where you are."

My *jiichan*, whom I talked to every August 6, must have wished for the abolition of nuclear weapons and lasting world peace, so that the tragedy of Hiroshima would never be repeated. In my talks to *jiichan*, colonial inequality among the victims of the atomic bombing was erased under the "Spirit of Hiroshima." In my talks to him, the United States never appeared in my consciousness, although it did in Mom's story. "In the air raid shelter [after the bombing], I remember this boy, about 10-year-old, with a badly injured father. The father said to the boy, 'I'm not going to make it. You take revenge on America.' 'I will,' the boy promised his father. I think the boy died, though."

My ritual of talking to *jiichan* was never separated from the national ritual of commemorating Japanese victims under the guise of "universal aspirations for peace," but I always imagined him in my consciousness as my grandpa, not a "Japanese victim," a "national martyr," or a "martyr for world peace." As I went further in my search for him, however, my talks to *jiichan* began to be covered by "the bomb's shadow"—the living effects of violent historical forces that appear to be the things of the past. And he began to appear as a ghostly figure.

Colonial Memories

Just out of high school in the summer of 1990, I volunteered as an interpreter for the World Conference for the Ban on A- and H-bombs in Hiroshima, which was organized by *Gensuikin* [Japan National Congress against A- and H-Bombs]. I had developed "political consciousness" and wanted to make the pilgrimage to the "mecca for peace" to participate in the celebration for world peace, not necessarily to console the soul of *jiichan* or the souls of others who were killed by the bombing.

At a preparatory meeting, I met a retiring junior-high school teacher. He was *hibakusha*. Meeting this man would mark my encounter with colonial memories in Hiroshima's memoryscape. To initiate a conversation, he asked me where I was from.

"I am from Nishinomiya [about 300 kilometers east of Hiroshima]."
"What made you come all the way and volunteer for this conference?"
"My mom is a *hibaku-nisei* from Hiroshima. And, I guess, because I am hibaku-nisei and want to contribute to the cause of peace and anti-nuclear activism."
"Your mother told you that? She is very brave. Usually, if you live away from Hiroshima or Nagasaki, you do not tell that you are *hibakusha*, even to your family, especially to the children, because we fear discrimination."

For a long time after the bombing, many *hibakusha* were subjected to various forms of social discrimination, especially upon their employment and marriage. The nature of the radiation aftereffects was unknown, and many feared that *hibakusha* had been infected with some kind of contagious disease by inhaling "poisonous gas."[6] Many of those exposed to high levels of radiation suffered from acute radiation sickness, the symptoms of which included hair loss, bleeding, nausea, diarrhea, and lowered counts of white blood cells. Like *jiichan*, even those who did not look seriously injured by the bombing began to die in significant numbers as the fall of 1945 approached. A rumor spread throughout Hiroshima: "Once you start bleeding and losing hair, you are finished." Many died because of the delayed effects caused by the bomb's radiation. Moreover, some *nisei* developed, and even died of, leukemia.[7]

Had it not been the nuclear bomb, *jiichan* would have had a much greater chance of surviving and those seeking loved ones or giving aid to the injured and dying in the immediate aftermath of the bombing would not have had to live in fear. Many came into the city to search for their family members. Others came in as members of the rescue and relief teams. There was no way of knowing, then, that they would be exposed to deadly radiation. Even those who were engaged in cremating the countless corpses were exposed to high levels of radiation. Had it not been the nuclear bomb, those "children" who were in the wombs of mothers who were near the hypocenter at the time of the bombing would not have developed "A-bomb microcephaly." I despised the bomb and its cruel lasting effects, but soon I would find out that many hailed it for saving lives.

When I read a report regarding a citizens' conference on Japan's military aggression in Asia, which was published in 1990, I encountered the "Asian" narrative of the atomic bombing—"The bomb liberated Asia from Japan's colonial aggression." For those who suffered under Japan's military occupation, the bomb ended the war and, thus, liberated them from Japan's aggression. The bomb killed *jiichan*, but it "saved" the lives of many Asians and Pacific Islanders who might have been killed by the Japanese troops.

Soon after this first encounter with colonial memories, I learned about Korean *hibakusha* in a conversation with the junior-high school teacher—*hibakusha* I met at the World Conference. He was in the ninth grade at the time of the bombing. One hot afternoon in late August 1990, he and I walked through the Hiroshima Peace Park. As we walked, he described to me how he escaped from the devastation, leaving behind his friend, who was begging for help. He guided me to a specific place. We stood before the Memorial for the Korean Atomic Bomb Victims, which was then located outside the Peace Park.[8] This teacher said that those most victimized by the atomic bombing were the Korean people and that he considered himself to be their *kagaisha* [victimizer]. Glancing at a visible scar left on his face by the atomic bombing, I could not compose a single response. Until then, I had never met any *hibakusha* who considered him- or herself a *kagaisha*. Over the course of several conversations during the early 1990s, he told me how he came to see himself that way.

He had received wartime imperial education. This education resulted in his belief that a holy war was being fought to liberate Asia from Western imperial powers. At that time, many Koreans worked at the factory to which he had been mobilized to work as a student.

Those Koreans were made to be exposed to the atomic bombing. Had they stayed in Korea, they would not have been killed by the bomb.

They were brought by the Japanese. For Asian neighbors, all Japanese are *kagaisha* [aggressors]. And I am Japanese. It was hard to acknowledge my role as a *kagaisha* after suffering from the bombing. About thirty years ago, I spoke about [my/Japan's] victimizing role publicly and met with much resistance. But after thirty years of hard work, not many would dismiss or oppose my opinion any longer.

The Korean Association for Assistance to Victims of the Atomic Bomb estimated that about 30,000 of the 50,000 Koreans who were exposed to the atomic bombing in Hiroshima and 10,000 of the 20,000 Koreans exposed to it in Nagasaki died as a result of the bombing (cited in Ichiba 2000: 27). After the colonization of the Korean peninsula by Japan in 1910, many Koreans crossed the sea to come to Japan.[9] Many of them worked in the military industrial sector during the war for very low wages under severe conditions. At the factories of the Mitsubishi Heavy Industries in Hiroshima, for example, about 2,800 Korean men were brought as forced labor in 1944 and were subsequently exposed to the atomic bombing (Yamada 2000: 107). In addition to being subjected to dangerous working conditions and discrimination, these Korean workers were not paid their full, stipulated share; at the time of "recruitment," they were promised by Mitsubishi that half of their wages would be sent to their families in Korea, but that portion of their wages was never sent to the families nor paid directly to those men (Yamada 2000: 111).[10]

Employing legal, economic, and cultural means, such as citizenship laws, family registration laws, and assimilation policies, colonial inequalities between the Japanese imperial subjects and the Korean colonial subjects were produced and maintained. These inequalities coalesced in the immediate aftermath of the dropping of the atomic bomb on Hiroshima. In the midst of the devastation, some Japanese refused to give medical treatment to badly injured Koreans. Moreover, since they lacked familial and neighborhood support networks, many Koreans remained in the radiation-contaminated city, having nowhere to go (Ichiba 2000: 326). According to a survey conducted by the Korean Church Women's Alliance in 1979, only 10 percent of the Koreans who were exposed to the bombing took refugee in the shelters, mountains, and outskirts of Hiroshima (cited in Iwadare and Nakajima 1999, vol. 3: 229).

After Japan's defeat, many Korean *hibakusha* went back to the peninsula. According to several testimonies of those Korean *hibakusha* who returned home, there was a rumor after the war that Koreans remaining in Japan would be killed. Many feared a recurrence of the

mass murder of Koreans after the Great Kanto Earthquake. It is estimated that of the surviving 30,000 Korean *hibakusha*, 23,000 went
back while 7,000 remained in Japan (The Korean Association for
Assistance to Victims of the Atomic Bomb, cited in Ichiba 2000: 27).

Many of those who returned to the peninsula had no livelihood or
family on whom to depend. It is unknown how many of these
returnees were killed during the Korean War, but certainly their lives
were further devastated (see Ichiba 2000; The Association of Citizens
for Supporting South Korean Atomic Bomb Victims 1987, 1996).
Most of them have been silent about their experiences with the
bombing, partly because of a lack of understanding in Korea about
the aftereffects of the atomic bombing and partly due to a fear of
being labeled as "returnees from Japan," that is, "traitors." Upon
returning to Korea, those children who grew up in Japan during the
wartime did not understand the language and were often bullied. Even
after acquiring the language, they continued to be subjected to harsh
statements, such as "You are not Korean nor Japanese!" Many
Korean *hibakusha* in the peninsula died without receiving any official
support from the Korean, American, nor the Japanese government. In
1986, it was estimated that approximately 15,000 *hibakusha* were living in South Korea and 2,000 in North Korea (Weiner 1997: 95–96).
The number declined significantly in the following 15 years: only
2,204 were identified in South Korea in 2000 and 928 in North Korea
in 2001.[11]

Colonial inequality continues today. Despite the fact that neither of
Hibakusha Medical Law of 1957 nor the *Hibakusha* Special Measures
Law of 1968 includes any restriction on citizenship or residency, the
vast majority of *hibakusha* residing in the Korean peninsula, North
and South Americas, and other parts of the world have not benefited
from these measures. The Supreme Court ruling in the "Son Chintu
trial" in 1978 seemed to have opened a venue for non-Japanese
hibakusha to be eligible for medical and other relief benefits granted to
Japanese *hibakusha*.[12] Yet, the Ministry of Health and Welfare has
refused, until the very recent court ruling, to extend these benefits to
those who reside outside Japan, citing a notification issued by the chief
of the Division of Hygiene in 1974 that the Special Measures Law
would be applicable to only those *hibakusha* who reside inside the
territory of Japan (cited in Tamura 1999: 511). In order to receive
the free medical care and related benefits guaranteed under the new
relief measure legislated in 1994, one must be physically present in

Japan, which is too expensive and physically taxing for most aged *hibakusha* living abroad.[13]

The recent ruling at a Japanese court first appeared to make possible the extension of the relief measures to oversea *hibakusha*. After years of struggles, in December 2002, the Osaka High Court ruled in the "Kwak Kifun trial" that the *Hibakusha* Relief Law of 1994 must be extended to those *hibakusha* who reside outside of Japan. Stormed by requests not to appeal to the Supreme Court by associations that support Korean and other overseas *hibakusha* and concerned citizens, the Japanese government finally gave up on appealing to the higher court, as it always did in prior cases. The Ministry of Health, Labor and Welfare released a statement on December 18 that the government's decision not to appeal to the Supreme Court is made out of a "humanitarian" concern and this decision was not delivered as a form of state compensation. To prove its point, the government expressed its unwillingness to extend the relief measures to those overseas *hibakusha* who received the health benefit prior to 1997 or those who have never received the *hibakusha* health certificate. The health certificate and related benefits can be issued only inside Japan and only those who are granted the benefits in Japan are eligible to keep receiving the benefits after returning to their respective country of residence.[14] Therefore, given the present position of the national government, it is unlikely that the court decision will benefit most of the aged *hibakusha* living outside of Japan.

*   *   *

When I bumped into colonial memories of Asia-Pacific, I also began to wonder whether *jiichan* had been a "*kagaisha* [aggressor]." *Jiichan* was an owner of a local tin factory. His factory, like those in other war-related industries, was assigned the role of munitions plant by the Japanese military-government. He, then, actively participated in Japan's war efforts. As an active participant in the war efforts, he was in complicity with Japan's aggression in the Asia Pacific region.

> *Jiichan* was a "*kagaisha*" . . .
> But he is my *jiichan*.
> I am confused. I don't know who he is anymore . . .

Lost in the Memoryscape, the Enemy (Dis)appears in the Shadow

As I searched for him, I lost *jiichan* (Grandpa) in the Hiroshima memoryscape or, perhaps, I got lost. After bumping into colonial memories in the memoryscape, I soon came to face that there are many others who celebrate the bomb. Immediately after my arrival in the United States in January 1991, the Gulf War broke out. For the first time in my life, I met people who viewed the dropping of a nuclear bomb on living humans with enthusiasm. It was painful for me to learn that many people there, too, justify the dropping of the atomic bomb—the bomb that took away *jiichan* from me.

The most recent public manifestation of U.S. celebration of the bomb occurred during the 1994–1995 controversy over the *Enola Gay* exhibit at the Smithsonian National Air and Space Museum. In the midst of the storm of criticism leveled at the Smithsonian, the U.S. Senate, in the fall of 1994, unanimously voted in favor of a resolution that characterized the atomic bombing as a force that "mercifully" ended the brutal war. The resolution even went so far as to suggest that the bombs, by shortening the war, saved not only American but also Japanese lives. The atomic bombs the United States dropped on Hiroshima and Nagasaki *killed* 210,000 (error of ±20,000) human beings by the end of December 1945. The dead included not only *jiichan* and other "Japanese" civilians, but also Japan's colonial subjects and even American citizens.[15] Tremendous deaths caused by the bomb, however, remains almost invisible in the public discourse in the United States of the bombing. Moreover, the acts of aggression conducted by the United States in its century-long imperial project in the Asia Pacific region, which were both in competition and complicit with Japanese imperialism, are absent in the U.S. narratives concerning the bomb. To achieve its imperialist expansion in the Philippines, for example, the United States supported Japan's annexation of Korea. Given this complicity, then, Korean *hibakusha* are victims not only of Japanese colonialism, but also of the U.S. act of dropping the bomb and its imperial project.

Q: "Who should bear the responsibility for the atomic bombing?"

In Seoul
42 out of 113 (37%) responded: "The Japanese government."
68 out of 113 (60%) responded: "Both the Japanese and U.S. governments."

In the Kyongsang-Bukdo region
90 out of 151 (60%) responded: "The Japanese government."
29 out of 151 (19%) responded: "Both the Japanese and U.S.
governments."

"If Japan had not colonized Korea, we would have never been exposed to
the atomic bombing in Hiroshima and Nagasaki as 'the Japanese.' "
(Report of the State of *Hibakusha* in Korea[16])

As a part of the benefits granted by the *Hibakusha* Relief Law
passed in 1994, a 100,000-yen bond was sent to Mom. The government
bonds were issued to those *hibakusha* who lost family members to the
atomic bombing before March 31, 1969. The purpose of these bonds
was to offset the cost of funerals. Mom received a bond in 1994 to offset the cost of the funeral of *jiichan*, who died in 1945.

I was exposed to the atomic bombing as military personnel of the
Japanese army and have suffered from keloid on my arms, chest, and the
abdomen throughout my life. I strongly believe that I should be granted
the same rights as the Japanese *hibakusha*. . . . I am 76 and there is not
much time left in my life. Please extend the same benefits [granted to the
Japanese *hibakusha*] so that I can lead the remaining life in peace.
(A statement delivered at the Trial for the *Hibakusha* Relief Law by Kwak
Kifun, a Korean *hibakusha*, July 14, 2000[17])

Bumping into the memories of those who suffered under Japan's
colonial rule, I have encountered the living effects of Japanese imperialism and military aggression, materialized in the willful neglect of
Korean *hibakusha* by the Japanese government. Given the continued
presence of colonial inequality, I have to confront the historical forces
that position *jiichan* and me as the "Japanese" vis-à-vis Korean
hibakusha. This partly entails acknowledging *jiichan*'s role as
kagaisha [aggressor] and examining the way my privilege is afforded
by the continued presence of Japanese imperialism in Asia-Pacific. But
I still cannot call *jiichan* "*kagaisha*." Unable to call him this, I am
likely to be criticized by the Japanese leftist peace activists as lacking
"critical consciousness."[18] Even with such criticism, I still refuse to
reduce *jiichan* to "Japanese *kagaisha*," because I want to claim him
back from the shadow of "the bomb" and offer him a hospitable space
where he can be embraced by my loving arms.

I was trying to criticize U.S. celebration of the bomb and its imperial
project in Asia-Pacific, not Japan's colonial aggression. Why can't I
ever solely engage in a critique of the United States, which publicly

expresses its aspiration to maintain and strengthen its unilateral hegemony in the world by building up arsenals and attacks other states that are suspicious of developing weapons of mass destruction? Why can't I solely express my rage toward U.S. military aggression and its continued justification of the use of the bomb, a weapon of mass destruction, against a civilian population? In my condemnation of the violent force that brought such a cruel death to *jiichan*, why do I constantly feel extremely uneasy about *jiichan*'s position in Japanese imperialist aggression? I was supposedly fighting against the living effects of the violence brought by the United States. Why is it that I always fight against that of Japan in the end? In my fight to reclaim *jiichan* to the space of the beloved, the "Enemy" changes its face. If the violence Japan inflicted in its name was the "Enemy," is *jiichan* also included in the "Enemy" because he participated in Japan's war efforts? What does it mean, then, for me to take revenge for *jiichan*'s death?

End of the Story but not the Exit of the Memoryscape

On the fifty-sixth anniversary of the atomic bombing, I was standing at a gas station in Hiroshima, where *jiichan*'s house used to stand. At 8:15 A.M., I was at a spot where *jiichan* supposedly was at the time of the bombing. I did not know what to say to him anymore. I could no longer tell him, "Please rest in peace," or "I will work for peace." I desperately wanted to hear *jiichan* speak to me, but I heard nothing. I went there looking for something, but I could not find anything.

*   *   *

In my journey through the Hiroshima memoryscape to find *jiichan*, he appears to me as a ghostly figure. If I were to claim *jiichan* back as my beloved grandpa, I must exorcise the ghost from his presence. An act of exorcism, however, is not the same as silencing and domesticating the ghost, as Avery Gordon cautions (see Gordon 1997: 205–206). If we tried to reduce the ghost to intelligible or manageable language, such as dichotomy between "*higai* [victimhood] and *kagai* [aggression]," it will return to haunt us and *jiichan*'s presence will continue to remain ghostly.

A ghost appears to notify us that the violence that made our loved ones disappear is still operating in the present. Therefore, exorcising a ghost entails the labor of identifying and transforming the sociohistorical forces that produced it, so that we can create a different future (see

Gordon 1997: 182–183). Unless we recognize what the ghost is signaling to us by "reckoning with it" (Gordon 1997: 64), it remains as a specter, wandering in the same violent conditions that made it appear in the first place.

To claim *jiichan* back as my beloved grandpa, I fight the forces that brought cruel death to him and continue to keep him in the "state of death" by naming and claiming him as an objectified and impersonal figure, such as "national martyr," "precious sacrifice for peace," "Japanese *higaisha* [victim]," and "Japanese *kagaisha* [aggressor]." By turning him into those objects, and thus stripping away his social relations with the living, these forces both silence *jiichan* and ensure that he remains dead. They even condition my relationship to *jiichan* by subsuming me, as the remembering subject, and *jiichan*, as the remembered subject, under the position of "Japanese." But these forces cannot determine who he is or my relationship to him; *jiichan* is my grandpa whom I wish to keep alive and present.

The work of rescuing those killed by the bombing from the realm of death is becoming increasingly urgent, as a force of the "Enemy" is gaining power across the Pacific. At both ends of the Pacific, chauvinistic nationalisms are on the rise, such as the Japanese Society for History Textbook Reform and the American Council of Trustees and Alumni. These call for the promotion of heroic accounts of national history so that "our children can be proud of being Japanese" or "our children can be proud of being American." The war dead, including those killed by the atomic bombing, play an important role in this history as "national martyrs" who sacrificed their lives for the creation or the defense of peace or freedom. Turned into "silent national objects" (see Tomiyama 1995: 91–93), the war dead in both countries are made to serve their respective nations even in their deaths.

Chauvinistic nationalisms in Japan and the United States greatly contribute to the execution and concealment of state violence, such as imperialism and war. By positioning "Japanese" and "American" war dead as "enemies," for example, chauvinistic nationalisms conceal the complicity between Japanese and American imperial projects in the Asia-Pacific region and their collaboration in the postwar period under the Cold War system. In so doing, these nationalisms erase from the Hiroshima memoryscape Korean atomic bomb victims who suffered under the collaboration between Japanese and American imperialisms and military aggression. Furthermore, together with other forces of the "Enemy," they attempt to lock "Japan" and "the United States" or "Asia" into the positions of "the former enemies" and "new allies and partners," while concealing complicities, alliances, and oppositions that exceed the relations and boundaries of the nation-state and the empire.

Even after dropping the atomic bomb and killing hundreds of thousands and brutally injuring even more, the American state continues to kill again "the dead of August" and wound *hibakusha* by developing and maintaining highly sophisticated nuclear weapons. Furthermore, the U.S. government remains committed to using nuclear weapons, if necessary. The March 9, 2002 edition of the *Los Angeles Times* revealed secret Pentagon contingency plans to use nuclear weapons against China, Russia, Iraq, Iran, North Korea, Libya, and Syria. Launching military attack on Iraq, the White House refused to exclude an option of using nuclear weapons.

The Japanese government consistently went along with Washington and collaborated with U.S. state violence since the end of the war. Regardless of its pledge for peace and nuclear disarmament made public annually at the peace ceremonies of Hiroshima and Nagasaki, the national government of Japan has never, since the end of the war, accused the United States of violating international law for using weapons of mass destruction against civilian populations. Moreover, even after the secret Pentagon contingency plans were revealed, Tokyo issued no protest against Washington (see *Chugoku Shimbun* 2002). Rather, Tokyo continues to ally with Washington in ensuring U.S. military dominance in the world and rely on the "American nuclear umbrella" for the "security" of Japan and the Asia-Pacific region.

In order to claim back *jiichan* as a beloved figure, I must fight nationalism, state violence, and even *jiichan*'s and my complicity in them. Fighting the "Enemy" on these fronts, however, turns out to be very difficult. The overshadowing power of the nation-state to structure and condition our memories and emotions remains prevailing, even in its critique, as my story demonstrates. Furthermore, my acts of exorcism are filled with ambivalence and contradictions.

As a powerful counterblow to the "Enemy," leftist activists and intellectuals in Japan have identified forces of nationalism and state violence that operate in the Hiroshima memoryscape. Moreover, they have gone so far as to locate individuals who are responsible for nationalism and state violence. In their identification of the responsible parties, however, leftist activists and intellectuals, in the process, have judged Japanese dead, like *jiichan*, and *hibakusha* guilty of the crime committed by the state; thus they name these guilty "Japanese *kagaisha.*"[19] I feel very sympathetic to leftists' politics and ally myself politically with them in many cases, out of a concern for social justice, particularly in relation to those who were formerly colonized by Japan. In spite of my alliance, though, I cannot call *jiichan* "*kagaisha*" or judge him guilty of the crime committed by the Japanese state, even in my awareness that he contributed to Japanese state violence. I want him to be solely my grandpa. But he should not have to be completely innocent for me to embrace him. Perhaps the work of exorcism can be completed only when I can accept and love him the way he was, without condemning him as "*kagaisha*" or idealizing him as innocent. Making *jiichan* innocent would keep him in the state of death by making him an ideal object of my love. Not knowing him firsthand, however, makes it even more difficult for me not to idealize him. Moreover, I sometimes hesitate to practice the act of exorcism, for if the "ghost" disappeared, I am afraid that *jiichan*'s presence, even though seen as absence, would not be as strongly near to me anymore. As troubling and even unnerving as it seems, I want to remain haunted by his ghostly *presence*.

> *Jiichan*, I feel you.
> But I can't hear you.
> Why did I bother to look for you?
> I have never even met you.
> I can't even imagine how you sound.
> How come do I want you to be my beloved, if I have
>   never even known you?
>
> *Jiichan*, am I disturbing you?
> Were you resting in peace until I started talking to you?
> Am I the one who is haunting you?
> Do you wanna be left alone?
>
> Can I keep searching for you?
> To offer you a hospitable memory.
>
> Talk to me, *jiichan*.

Notes

I thank Neferti Tadiar and Avery Gordon for giving me critical and encouraging feedback on the first and later drafts of this essay.

1. Chang, cited in The Association of Citizens for Supporting South Korean Atomic Bomb Victims (1987: 147). Cited quote is my translation from

a Japanese text. All translation from Japanese to English in this essay is mine. I received assistance from Jin-hee Lee for romanization of Korean name.

2. For official descriptions of the damage caused by the atomic bombing, see City of Hiroshima–City of Nagasaki (1995).

3. I distinguish between "the bomb" with and without the quotation marks—the former being a sign of both the nuclear weapon itself and the historical forces, such as racism, fascism, and war, that made possible its use on civilians, and the latter being the actual weapon that was used on Hiroshima and Nagasaki.

4. Gordon's theory is largely based on textual analysis of Luisa Valenzuela's *He Who Searches* and Toni Morrison's *Beloved*.

5. The statistics of casualty in the Nishihikimido-cho neighborhood, where *jiichan* was the morning of the bombing, were the following: about 80 percent of the residents were killed instantly; about 14 percent were injured; only 6 percent were spared from injury (Hiroshima-shi 1971: 721).

6. Since they did not know that they were irradiated by the nuclear weapons, many *hibakusha* referred to the effects of the radiation as caused by "(poisonous) gas."

7. While medical studies have concluded that there is no significant effect of radiation caused by the atomic bombing on the second-generation survivors, there have been speculations that parents exposed to radiation would transmit its effects to the second-generation survivors genetically. It was suspected that the bomb's delayed effects might have something to do with these *nisei*'s death.

8. For a detailed analysis of the Memorial for the Korean Atomic Bomb Victims, see Yoneyama (1999).

9. Many came to Japan because colonial administration's industrial and economic policies, which recruited "cheap" Korean labor for work in Japan. Further, these policies displaced farmers in the countryside, thus driving displaced Korean farmers and their family members to Japan, where they saw better economic opportunities. Yet others were brought to Japan because of the program of forced labor beginning in 1939 (Weiner 1997; Ichiba 2000: 199–201). For a detailed study of the migration of Koreans under the Japanese colonial rule, see Weiner (1994).

10. In December 1995, six Koreans who worked for Mitsubishi as "forced labor" and were subsequently exposed to the bombing filed an action in the Hiroshima Regional Court against Mitsubishi and the Japanese national government. In following August, 40 more joined the suit. In March 1999, the Court judged the Japanese government and Mitsubishi not guilty; subsequently, the plaintiffs appealed against a decision to the Hiroshima High Court in April 1999. Between the filing of the suit in 1995 and the delivery of the decision in 1999, six of the plaintiffs passed away.

11. <http://www.chugoku-np.co.jp/abom/02abom/zaigai/index.html>.

12. Son, a Korean *hibakusha*, illegally entered Japan in 1970 and demanded that he should be issued a *hibakusha* health certificate. After being denied the heath certificate, Son brought the case before the Fukuoka Regional Court in 1972 and fought until the victory at the Supreme Court in 1978. See The Korean Association for Assistance to Victims of the Atomic Bomb (2000).

13. Even those Korean *hibakusha* who remained in Japan have mostly been neglected as "second-class citizens." Although Koreans were forced to become "Japanese imperial subjects" under Japan's colonial rule and to fight as "the Japanese" during the war, they were stripped of Japanese citizenship and legally positioned as resident aliens in 1952. Even those who are born in Japan are given legal status of "resident aliens" and subjected to oppressive legal and administrative practices as well social discrimination.

14. The 1957 Medical Law defined *hibakusha* as those who fell under any of the following four categories: (1) those directly exposed to the explosion of the atomic bomb in the areas of Hiroshima city and its specified outskirts; (2) those who entered into the specified areas in the city and its outskirts from the time of the bombing to August 20, 1945; (3) those irradiated by engaging in rescue operations, cremating corpses, and other activities; and (4) fetuses of those who fall under categories (1) through (3). In order to obtain a *hibakusha* health certificate, an applicant must submit documentation, which proves that the applicant falls under one of the four categories set under the law. If no documentation is available, an applicant can submit the witness accounts by two people besides his or her immediate family. If two witness accounts are not available, an applicant can submit his or her own testimony detailing the circumstance after the atomic bombing. In actual practice, however, if an applicant only provides his or her own testimonial account, a certificate is usually denied. After 60 years since the time of the bombing, it is extremely difficult to find two witnesses; therefore, it is getting harder and harder to obtain the health certificate.

15. There were several American POWs in Hiroshima and Nagasaki, but most Americans who were killed or wounded by the bombing were Japanese Americans. For a memoir of a pilot of the B-24 plane Lonesome Lady, who was captured and brought to Hiroshima as POW, but spared from the bombing because he was sent to Tokyo a few days prior to the attack on Hiroshima, see Cartwright (2002). For accounts of those Japanese American *hibakusha* who came back to the United States after the war, see Sodei (1997).

16. Cited in Ichiba (2000: 115).

17. As described in the text, the Osaka High Court ruled in December 2002 that the benefit granted under the *Hibakusha* Relief Law must be extended to Mr. Kwak.

18. During my fieldwork for my master's paper and dissertation in the late 1990s and early 2000s, I have met several peace activists who hailed those *hibakusha* who can face their role of aggression during the war, but condemned those others who "are unable to go beyond their own suffering" for having developed "little critical consciousness."

19. It should be stressed that these leftist activists and intellectuals make a firm distinction, in terms of the degree of war responsibility, between those who were in the high positions of the military-government and the civilians and the rank-and-file soldiers.

References

The Association of Citizens for Supporting South Korean Atomic Bomb Victims 韓国の原爆被害者を支援する市民の会. *To Hiroshima* ヒロシマへ, Hiroshima: The Association of Citizens for Supporting South Korean Atomic Bomb Victims 韓国の原爆被害者を支援する市民の会, 1987.

The Association of Citizens for Supporting South Korean Atomic Bomb Victims 韓国の原爆被害者を支援する市民の会. *50 Years of the Korean Atomic Bomb Survivors* 在韓被爆者が語る被爆50年, Hiroshima: The Association of Citizens for Supporting South Korean Atomic Bomb Victims 韓国の原爆被害者を支援する市民の会, 1996.

The Association of Citizens for Supporting South Korean Atomic Bomb Victims 韓国の原爆被害者を支援する市民の会;. *When Hibakusha are not Recognized as Hibakusha* 被爆者が被爆者でなくなるとき, Hiroshima: The Association of Citizens for Supporting South Korean Atomic Bomb Victims 韓国の原爆被害者を支援する市民の会, 2000.

Cartwright, T.C. *A Date with the Lonesome Lady: A Hiroshima POW Returns*, Austin: Eakin Press, 2002.

Chugoku Shimbun. 中国新聞 Editorial, March 22, 2002.

City of Hiroshima–the City of Nagasaki. *Outline of Atomic Bombing Damage of Hiroshima and Nagasaki*, 1995.

Dower, John. "Triumphal and Tragic Narratives of the War in Asia." In Laura Hein and Mark Selden, eds., *Living with the Bomb: American and Japanese Cultural Conflicts in the Nuclear Age*, Armonk, NY: M.E. Sharpe, 1997, 37–51.

Gordon, Avery. *Ghostly Matters: Haunting and the Sociological Imagination*, Minneapolis: University of Minnesota Press, 1997.

Hachiya Kazuye 八谷嘉壽枝. "Iro no nai kioku" 色の無い記憶. In Hiroshima Joshi Kotoshihan Gakko Fuzoku Yamanaka Koto Jyogakko Genbaku Shibotsusha Tsuito Bunshu Henshu Iinkai, ed., 広島女子高等師範学校附属山中高等女学校原爆死没者追悼文集編集委員 会 *Tribute: Enlarged Edition: The Wishes of Hiroshima* 追悼記・増補 ヒロシマの願い, Hiroshima: Hiroshima Joshi Kotoshihan Gakko Fuzoku Yamanaka Koto Jyogakko Genbaku Shibotsusha Tsuito Bunshu Henshu Iinkai 広島女子高等師範学校附属山中高等女学校原爆死没者追悼文集編集委員, 1993, 116–118.

Hein, Laura and Mark Selden. "Commemoration and Silence: Fifty Years of Remembering the Bomb in America and Japan." In Laura Hein and Mark Selden, eds., *Living with the Bomb: American and Japanese Cultural Conflicts in the Nuclear Age*, Armonk, NY: M.E. Sharpe, 1997, 3–36.

Hiroshima-shi 広島市. *The Damage of Hiroshima Caused by the Atomic Bombing* 広島原爆戦災史 (5 volumes) 全5巻, Hiroshima: Hiroshima-shi 広島市, 1971. <http://www.chugoku-np.co.jp/abom/02abom/zaigai/index.html>.

Ichiba Junko 市場淳子. *Bringing Hiroshima Back to Their Homeland* ヒロシマを持ちかえった人々, Tokyo: Gaifu Sha 凱風社, 2000.

Iwadare, Hiroshi and Nakajima Tatsumi, eds. 岩垂弘、中島竜美 *Anthology of Japanese Atomic Bomb Theories* 日本原爆論体系 (7 Volumes) 全7巻, Tokyo: Nihon Tosho Senta 日本図書センター, 1999.

Sodei, Rinjiro. "Were We the Enemy? American Hibakusha." In Laura Hein and Mark Selden eds., *Living with the Bomb: American and Japanese Cultural Conflicts in the Nuclear Age*, Armonk, NY: M.E. Sharpe, 1997, 232–259.

Tamura Kazuyuki 田村和之. "Korean Hibakusha and the Application of the Hibakusha Relief Law" 在韓被爆者への被爆者法の適応. In Iwadare Hiroshi and Nakajima Tatsumi, eds., 岩垂弘、中島竜美 *Anthology of Japanese Atomic Bomb Theories* 日本原爆論体系 (Vol. 3), Tokyo: Nihon Tosho Senta 日本図書センター, 1999, 511–523.

Tomiyama Ichiro 冨山一郎. *Memory of the Battlefield* 戦場の記憶, Tokyo: Nihon Keizai Hyoron Sha 日本経済評論社, 1995.

Weiner, Michael. *Race and Migration in Imperial Japan*, New York: Routledge 1994.

———. "The Representation of Absence and the Absence of Representation: Korean Victims of the Atomic Bomb." In Michael Weiner, ed., *Japan's Minorities: The Illusion of Homogeneity*, New York: Routledge, 1997, 79–107.

Yamada Tadafumi 山田忠文. "Forced labor: Exposure to the Atomic Bombing and the Sufferings in the Following 50 Years" 強制連行・被爆そして苦しみの半世紀. In Kosho Tadashi, Tanaka Hiroshi, and Sato Takeo, eds., 古庄正 田中宏 佐藤健生. *War Crimes Committed by Japanese Companies* 日本企業の戦争犯罪, Tokyo: Soshi Sha 創史社, 2000, 107–114.

Yoneyama, Lisa. *Hiroshima Traces: Time, Space and the Dialectics of Memory*. Berkeley, CA: University of California Press, 1999.

7

"The Face Value of Dreams": Gender, Race, Class, and the Politics of Cosmetic Surgery

Victoria M. Bañales

Why is the woman in the photograph covering three-quarters of her face? Only parts of her eyes, eyebrows, and forehead are visible (figure 7.1). At first glance, it seems as though she is guarding against hazardous fumes, covering her nose and mouth. Her overall countenance is one of pain, and one suspects that she is perhaps crying. In fact, the person in the photo, 26-year-old Ana Ponce, is covering her face because she has just received a nose job for the "bargain-basement" price of $300. The photograph appeared in a 1998 *San Jose Mercury News* article entitled "The Face Value of Dreams: Bogus Plastic Surgeons Lure Peru's Poor With Cheap Promise of Better Life," authored by *Associated Press* journalist David Koop. According to the article, like Ponce, 22-year-old Maria Espichan (not pictured) awaits her turn to "straighten her curved nose" while Patricia Lira, 33 (also not pictured), expresses her desire for a fifth operation even after a series of surgically related nasal complications.

With high hopes of altering or erasing the racial/ethnic markers associated with the "unstraightened" nose, Ponce, Espichan, and Lira, like hundreds of poor, indigenous and mestiza women in Peru, are turning toward plastic surgery to exchange a nose historically racialized in negative terms for one deemed more "beautiful" by the dominant "white" culture in Peru. As the newspaper article for which the photo was taken reports, "[m]ore than 80% of Peruvians are either Indians or mestizo and suffer discrimination at the hands of a light-skinned wealthy elite. Job offers in newspapers demand a 'good

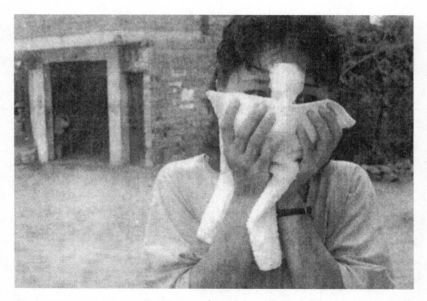

Figure 7.1   Ana Ponce exits a plastic surgeon's office in Lima, Peru after undergoing rhinoplasty.

presence' which sociologists say is code for a non-Indian appearance" (21A). " 'I know my life is going to improve when I look better. . . . A lot of my friends have had plastic surgery and now have boyfriends and jobs,' " says Espichan (21A). However much a solution to Ponce's, Espichan's, and Lira's economic situations, these women, like countless of others, make themselves susceptible to these painful and risky surgical procedures, not necessarily with the end result of looking less indigenous per se but rather as a means of accessing the benefits of socioeconomic power associated with the increasing importation and value of Western beauty ideals.

In this essay, I examine the ways in which institutionalized sexist, racist, and classist ideologies and practices under heteronormative patriarchal capitalist societies make cosmetic surgery, by and large, not a choice but an economic necessity for many Third World women[1] in Peru and elsewhere in the Americas. While recognizing that plastic surgery can function as an enabling science and healing practice—as in the case of reconstructive surgery for female patients who undergo mastectomies—my analysis focuses exclusively on "elective" cosmetic surgical procedures, particularly those under which a patient's racial/ethnic features can be altered or transformed. Arguing that the industry is part and parcel of gender, racial, and class-based systems of domination, I begin with a general discussion on the political implications of cosmetic surgery. Second, I analyze how postmodern, "celebratory" discourses of cosmetic surgery—for example, those appearing in fashion magazine advertisements and medical books— contribute to the effacement of historical asymmetrical power relations that create and normalize dominant Western beauty standards. Third, I look at the ways in which women whose bodies have been historically constructed (in all aspects, e.g., legal, social, and/or biological) as racially "other" and in opposition to "whiteness" use cosmetic surgery as a means toward accessing employment, marriage, social legitimacy, and/or heterosexual desire. I argue that a more "beautiful" face—"beautiful" according to racist, Western standards of feminine beauty—offers women like Ponce the possibility for socioeconomic mobility and power. Lastly, I perform a close reading of the photo-image of Ponce, looking specifically at the ways in which the photograph, like the news article that accompanies it, portrays Peruvian women as passive victims rather than active agents. I argue that the ideological narratives contained within this U.S.-produced photographic and textual narrative perpetuate and participate in the social construction and subordination of "Third World" women.

*   *   *

The relationship between imposed standards of beauty on women and the sexual division of labor is by far anything but new and, in fact, has been widely assessed and discussed by feminist critics. Naomi Wolf, for example, in her bestseller, *The Beauty Myth: How Images of Beauty are Used Against Women,* critically analyzes patriarchal capitalism and the ways in which cultural constructions of feminine beauty function as a way of sustaining and naturalizing the widespread underpayment of women's labor. She discusses how women are doubly affected by dominant standards of beauty in that not only are their wages kept at a low but also women are expected to keep up with the high costs of maintaining a more youthful, wrinkle-free, and/or slender appearance—this, in an effort to remain competitive in the job market. For example, it is not uncommon for professional/working women, particularly in the corporate world or entertainment, media, and sex industries, to undergo liposuction, facelifts, collagen or Botox injections, or other such measures to maintain their jobs and/or secure promotions.

Yet, while the implications of gender and class surrounding feminine beauty norms and the cosmetic surgery industry have been extensively studied and documented, less analyzed are the ways in which feminine constructions of beauty are tied to a racial politics. As feminist scholar Eugenia Kaw notes in her essay, " 'Opening' Faces: The Politics of Cosmetic Surgery and Asian American Women," the male-dominated industry of cosmetic surgery thrives on and depends upon Western notions of beauty that are not only sexist and classist but also inherently racist. Drawing attention to the commodification of double eyelid surgery among Asian American women, Kaw points to the ways in which cosmetic surgery is hardly race-neutral in that, more often than not, becoming more "beautiful" for women of color translates into having their racial/ethnic features "softened" or "reduced." For example, unlike the surgical alterations generally sought out by White women, which tend to revolve around maintaining a youthful face as well as slender and/or voluptuous bodily appearance, Kaw observes that those sought out by women of color are frequently informed by their desires to change or erase facial features predominantly associated with a particular racial/ethnic (nonwhite) phenotype. In an effort to achieve a more Westernized look, African Americans, she notes, often "opt for lip and nasal reductions [while] Asian Americans more often choose to insert an implant on their nasal dorsum for a more prominent nose or undergo double-eyelid surgery . . . [to] make the eye appear wider" (243).

Yet, as Kaw highlights, women of color's efforts at softening their racial/ethnic features are often informed by socioeconomic reasons and, as such, directly tied to a class politics of beauty. Her analysis points to the ways in which, at least for many of the Asian American female subjects interviewed, "looking like a Caucasian is almost essential for socioeconomic success" (254). In fact, one interviewed woman in her study noted that, " '[e]specially if you go into business . . . you kind of have to have a Western facial type and you have to have like their features' " (254). Arguing that "these surgeries are a product of society's racial ideologies, and for many of the women in my study, the surgeries are a calculated means for socioeconomic success" (256), Kaw's ethnographic study and research are important in that they underscore the intersecting gender, race, and class implications of dominant beauty norms and, specifically, cosmetic surgery. Ascribing to these racialized feminine standards of beauty through surgical means, she adds, allows many women of color access to forms of class mobility that they might otherwise be denied. Feminist scholar Kathryn Pauly Morgan echoes these observations in her essay, "Women and the

Knife: Cosmetic Surgery and the Colonization of Women's Bodies," pointing to the ways in which many Jewish, Asian, and Black women's decisions to alter their racial/ethnic features are predominantly informed by their "hopes of better job and marital prospects" (36).

Given that cosmetic surgery is a profitable, multimillion-dollar industry, it should come to no surprise that both the medical establishment and the media downplay the politics behind the reification and marketing of the standardization of Western beauty ideals. As feminist critic Pippa Brush writes, " 'new' and 'different' body images are being presented to women as just so many available commodities through advertising by the industries with a stake in the beauty business" ("Metaphors of Inscription: Discipline, Plasticity and the Rhetoric of Choice" 40). Adding to Brush's observations, Susan Bordo in her essay, " 'Material Girl': The Effacements of Postmodern Culture," discusses the need to be cautious of discourses and slogans that promote cosmetic surgery on, what she calls, "celebratory" postmodern grounds. Bordo signals the ways in which these types of purely positive takes on cosmetic surgery—that is, those that support surgical alterations on the basis that women have a "choice," and that cosmetic surgery allows for transgressive, multiple subjectivities and/or for the (re)creation of the self and body—while not entirely dismissible, efface the historical asymmetrical power relations between, for example, women and men and/or White women and women of color. In other words, they fail to take into consideration how historical constructions of difference—and the ways in which those differences are constructed as inferior and in opposition to dominant (White, Western, male, heterosexual, young, upper class, educated, Christian, etc.) standards—deeply influence women's reasons for undergoing surgical transformations.

Moreover, such "celebratory" takes on cosmetic surgery occur not just at the level of popular magazines and advertisements but also scholarly essays. Feminist critic Kathy Davis, for example, suggests in her essay "Remaking the She-Devil: A Critical Look at Feminist Approaches to Beauty" that women's decisions to undergo cosmetic surgery are not necessarily informed by their desires to be more beautiful per se but rather to be "ordinary." According to Davis, it is up to each woman at the individual level to decide what about her body is "normal" or "deviant" (37). Thus if a woman experiences a "particular part of her body as hateful, disgusting, and beyond what she should have to endure" (37), she may decide to surgically alter it in order to acquire a more "normal" or "ordinary" appearance. Although Davis carefully highlights the ways in which cosmetic surgery is both an oppressive problem as well as a liberating solution to women's lives, her analysis largely focuses on the positive, beneficial aspects of cosmetic surgery, arguing that cosmetic surgery enables women in that there is pleasure involved in the way a woman looks and feels about herself—for instance, getting a breast enhancement might lead to a woman's greater sexual pleasure and/or self-esteem. Furthermore, she writes that cosmetic surgery "might be a way for some women within the limitations of their present situation to end their suffering. When viewed against this backdrop, the decision could conceivably become a moment of triumph—a moment when a woman turns the tables and does something for herself" (22).

While such arguments are not without merit, Davis fails to discuss who determines what constitutes so-called normalcy or, to use her term, ordinariness when she argues that cosmetic surgery is "the right to an ordinary appearance, the right to happiness and well-being" (38). As far as many women might be concerned, sagging breasts and wrinkles could very well be deemed "ordinary," contrary to dominant beauty norms. Additionally, Davis's arguments seem to imply that there is such a thing as an "unordinary" appearance. Although Davis acknowledges the ways in which "unequal power relations between the sexes" (25) and "structures of domination such as racism, classism, ageism, ableism, and homophobia" (26) commonly inform women's demands for surgical transformations, ironically, she often speaks from within the very ideological frameworks that legitimize dominant beauty ideals, as the following passage illustrates:

> I am frequently asked whether the women I interview need cosmetic surgery. In other words, are they "really" ugly enough to merit such drastic measures?. . . In fact, I usually can't even tell what the offending feature is . . . . Once I know what the problem is, I am usually astounded that anyone would consider cosmetic surgery for what seems to me to be a minor imperfection. (36)

By implying that there is such a thing as being "ugly enough" and/or having "offending features" or "minor imperfections," such arguments legitimate and naturalize culturally accepted beauty ideals from which all peoples' physical appearances are measured. Davis furthermore writes: "It is often suggested to me that women do cosmetic surgery for men. This rests on the belief that no woman in her right mind could do such a thing for herself" (34). Again, this statement (however well intended) oversimplifies the reasons that influence women to feel "inferior" or "ugly" in the first place. While it is true that many women undergo surgery for socioeconomic reasons as opposed to doing it "for men," we might inquire why economic success is aligned with beauty standards in the first place. Is it even possible for a woman to get cosmetic surgery "for herself," given the asymmetrical gender, race, and class power relations? And, what about increasingly competitive job markets, especially in economically volatile places like Peru?

While I agree that we should be able to explain cosmetic surgery without "undermining the women who choose to undergo it" (Davis 23) and that cosmetic surgery is a complex issue that should not be solely explained in reductionist, negative terms, critical takes on the subject must nonetheless assess and take into account historical uneven relations of power. This becomes especially important when analyzing women of color's desires for "straighter" noses or "bigger" eyelids. For this matter, I find it useful to revisit the Marxist concepts of *use-value* and *exchange-value*.[2] For example, there is no difference between the *use-value* of the "straight" and the "curved" nose—they both allow us to breath and smell as well as perform other functions that are essential for human life. Similarly, eyesight is not diminished nor restrained by eye/lid size. The difference between a "curved" and a "straight" nose rests on the culturally determined (and therefore arbitrary) *exchange-value* given to one nose over another. Given that it was the Europeans who conquered and colonized Native peoples in the Americas and not the other way around, it seems historically congruent that a nose more aligned with what some would call "Caucasian physiognomy"[3] would be allotted greater cultural currency—that is to say, more value and worth as the title of "The Face Value of Dreams" suggests. This is especially the case in Peru where strong racial divides are not only commonplace but also deeply institutionalized.

With the effects of global capitalism and the growing importation of Western trends—particularly from the United States and European nations to Third World countries—it would be seemingly difficult to argue that the historical legacies of conquest, colonialism, capitalism, and imperialism play no part in women's decisions, particularly Third World women's decisions, to undergo forms of cosmetic surgery. Understanding the political implications of cosmetic surgery entails comprehending the ways in which the industry is both part and parcel of these larger, global systems of domination. Much in the same way as economic, social, and political systems of domination have historically necessitated and depended upon the invention and reification of racist ideologies,[4] the industry of cosmetic surgery relies on the naturalization of not only a sexist logic but also a racist one. Patriarchal capitalism, for example, depends upon the labor exploitation of not just women but, increasingly, Third World women. As such, without the institutionalization of racism and other intersecting systems of oppression, the idea that there is such a thing as a more "beautiful" or "desirable" nose would probably not exist.

In fact, as scholars Sander L. Gilman and Elizabeth Haiken note in their respective studies on cosmetic surgery, deep and disturbing parallels exist between the historical rise and acceptance of cosmetic (or aesthetic) surgery and the racial sciences of the nineteenth and early twentieth centuries.[5] They note that, just as the racial sciences—for example, eugenics (the "science" and movement of racial betterment)— became largely discredited following World War II and the Nazi fiasco, cosmetic surgery became more widely accepted, becoming part of the established, respectable medical profession. Both authors concur that such wide acceptance is intimately tied to the racial sciences in that the latter gave rise to not only the belief in "races" but also the belief in "superior" versus "inferior" races—the White/Caucasian race being the more beautiful and superior and the Black/Negroid race being the most nonaesthetic and primitive. While other races were identified, none bore the physical and mental superior capacities of the Caucasian race. With the rise and fall of eugenics, cosmetic surgery offered an alternative and acceptable medical method of "cleansing" and "purifying" racial/ethnic phenotype (as opposed to previous efforts at targeting the genotype). Thus rather than dealing with racial stigmas like "too small" or "too large" of a nose, individuals were offered the possibility of altering or erasing socially constructed markers of racial difference via cosmetic surgery, enabling them to potentially "pass" as an "invisible" (or "ordinary," to use Davis's term) member into the desired racial/ethnic, cultural, class, and/or national group. As Haiken writes, "the long tradition of the 'sciences of the race' looms large" (208) in the discourse of cosmetic surgery, whereby Black, Native, and other so-called racial/ethnic faces are scientifically measured against more "beautiful," "aesthetic" Caucasian ones.

One has but to look at, for example, W. Earle Matory's medical book *Ethnic Considerations in Facial Aesthetic Surgery*, which contains multiple before and after cosmetic surgery photographs, to notice that first, most of the rhinoplasty (nose) and blepharoplasty (double eyelid) patients photographed in the book are women, specifically women of color; and second, the facial alterations achieved resemble a more or less Caucasian physiognomy. That these women seem to be undergoing a phenotype "whitening" process is evidenced not just by the photographs themselves but also the author's written narrative assumptions. Illustrated with facial sketches that contain geometric formulas and graphs, the book "scientifically" purports to measure "ethnic" peoples' faces in relation to more "balanced," "symmetrical," and "aesthetic" Caucasian ones. Hence in the before and after pictures, "asymmetries" are "corrected" as "big" noses become "smaller," "curved" noses become "straighter," and "excess flaring" of the nostrils is reduced. By the same token, single eyelids are replaced with the more "aesthetic" double eyelids, which, according to Matory, is done "with the goal of achieving eyelid symmetry" (271). Yet, the book is pregnant with contradiction. For example, on the one hand Matory writes that "it is the European–American depiction of beauty that dominates varied cultural perspectives" (11), yet on the other hand he states that "[i]t would be erroneous to assume that the popularity of the double eyelid operation is related solely to Western influence. Asian cultures have long regarded the bright-eyed look associated with the double eyelid as an aesthetically desirable feature" (267–268). Statements like these, which appear sporadically throughout the book, once again situate cosmetic surgery in an historical vacuum, as if desiring "the bright-eyed look" bore no connection to, for example, colonialism, racism, global capitalism, and class struggle, and, related to all of the above, the rising importation of Western beauty ideals.

When we critically look at the sexist, racist, and class-based dimensions underlying the cosmetic surgery industry, we can begin to see, as Bordo, Kaw, Morgan, Brush, and other feminist scholars have done, that the industry both contributes to as well as is a product of the larger systems of domination of which Colette Guillaumin, David Theo Goldberg, and other feminist and/or cultural critics speak.[6] As Rosemary Gillespie, Sandra Bartky, and others note, cosmetic surgery is first and foremost an industry of patriarchal capitalism that directly contributes to the subordination of women—sexual, racial, economic, or otherwise.[7]

In fact, like Gilman's and Haiken's respective research linking cosmetic surgery to the racial sciences, Morgan points to the ways in cosmetic surgery—and the growing demands and pressures on women to succumb to excruciatingly painful medical procedures—is a direct extension of the historical medicalization of women's bodies:

> The history of Western science and Western medical practice is not altogether a positive one for women. As voluminous documentation has

shown, cell biologists, endocrinologists, anatomists, sociobiologists, gynecologists, obstetricians, psychiatrists, surgeons, and other scientists have assumed, hypothesized, or "demonstrated" that women's bodies are generally inferior, deformed, imperfect, and/or infantile. (39)

Adding to Morgan's observations, Gillespie highlights the ways in which, although the widely circulated illusion exists that these oppressive systems and prevailing attitudes toward women have successfully been eradicated (especially in the "first world"), and that women are now free and liberated, women's bodies continue to be pathologized, controlled, and disciplined through "simulation, consumption, and normalising ideals of beauty, physical appearance and shape, by which women's social value has come to be judged" (73). Indeed, as feminist critic Adrian Howe notes in her research on women in prison, *Punish and Critique: Towards a Feminist Analysis of Penality*, there are real, material consequences for women who deviate gendered norms, for instance, they may be locked up, refused job success and/or entry into the marriage market.[8] In fact, Morgan suggests that as cosmetic surgery becomes more of the norm and less of the extraordinary, "women who refuse to submit to the knives and to the needles, to the anesthetics and the bandages, will come to be seen as deviant in one way or another" (40). What we are experiencing, she argues, is "a *normalization* of elective cosmetic surgery" (28; italics in original). Certainly this is evidenced in the recent explosion of television shows in the U.S. that sensationalize cosmetic surgery, for example, *The Swan, Nip and Tuck*, and MTV's *I Want a Famous Face*.

For Brush, cosmetic surgery, is "a disciplinary regime . . . of cultural standards for the body [that] constructs an illusory 'rhetoric of choice' . . . enforcing the inscription of 'willing' female bodies through the construction of desire for the 'perfect body' " (24). Borrowing from Michel Foucault's idea that the body as an "inscribed surface of events," she highlights the ways in which cosmetic surgery figuratively and literally imprints dominant social values onto women's "willing" bodies:

Giving this metaphor of inscription literal significance points to how changing the body can write cultural values directly on to the body of the "willing" female subject . . . The metaphor of inscription becomes alarmingly literal as the surgeon's knife carves socially endorsed yet essentially arbitrary ideals of beauty on to the plastic bodies of women who "choose" to conform more closely to the norms of ideals society constructs, effacing the material reality of women's bodies for the sake of conforming to one of a limited set of culturally specific inscriptions. (24)

As Brush observes, the process of inscribing or "carving" value onto women's bodies is very much a real, material experience. Thus the surgeon's knife to which Brush refers points to the ways in which women's bodies are carved both by socially constructed beauty norms—endorsed by both the selling doctor as well as the buying patient—and the actual process of cosmetic surgery itself which involves the physical, literal cutting up of women's bodies. Notwithstanding the pain, blood, and swelling involved in having one's body physically opened, more often than not, advertisements for or articles on cosmetic surgery—for example, those which circulate in fashion-beauty magazines—focus on the gains and "improved," pleasurable results of surgery while de-emphasizing the medical risks and complications that can occur. As one article reports:

> Slick marketing campaigns make it easy to think of cosmetic surgery as just another off-the-shelf consumer product, its purchase about on a par with buying a new computer system. But surgery is surgery. There is pain. Recovery can be lengthy and uncomfortable. Moreover, "there can be complications of anesthesia, infection, bleeding and unfavorable scars," says Ross Rudolph, head of plastic surgery. (Doug Podolsky, "The Price of Vanity" par. 5)

As Brush highlights, however, precisely because cosmetic surgery is a capitalist industry whose profits rely on commodifying and selling "ideal" bodies and faces, these painful considerations are often overlooked in advertisements, as providing the gruesome details of the process could dissuade many potential buyers. She writes that while "the bruises and the swelling are as much a part of the process as the operation or the finished 'product'[,]. . . . [i]t is in the best interests of surgeons and theorists alike to efface the materiality of the process" (34).[9]

Considering that pain is something that often gets glossed over in most discussions about and advertisements for cosmetic surgery, one has to wonder why pain is significantly emphasized in "The Face Value of Dreams," both in the news article as in the accompanying photo-image of Ponce. We might ask why pain is such a central issue in this textual and photographic narrative but not an issue in, say, for example, the *San Jose Mercury News'* coverage of Paula Jones's[10] new nose ("People in the News")? Appearing six months after "The Face Value of Dreams," coverage of Jones's surgery—reportedly paid for by an "anonymous donor"—is discussed in a matter-of-fact sort of way, and Jones's new nose is described as "shorter, straighter, slightly upturned and more or less cute as a button" (2A). Before and after photos of Jones are provided, with Jones glaring downward and appearing sad-like in the "before" shot while looking straight ahead and appearing confident and content in the "after" shot. There is no mention or indication of the surgical process involved in the alteration of her nose, and we do not see pain in the photos nor do we read about the surgical knives in the article. Bandages do not cover Jones's nose as they do Ponce's in "The Face Value of Dreams," and this representation of Ponce, wherein pain is brought centrally into focus, merits interrogation.

Ponce, who takes up half of the photo, is covering most of her face with a white cloth, and there appear to be bandagings of the nose underneath the cloth. Her expression is one of pain, and we can barely see Ponce's eyes, which avert the camera. In fact, we do not know if the subject is even aware that her photograph is being taken. In their analysis of *National Geographic* visual representations, Catherine Lutz and Jane Collins suggest that averted gazes that "run off into the distance beyond the frame" can "portray either a dreamy, vacant, absent-minded person or a forward looking, future-oriented, and determined one" ("The Photograph as an Intersection of Gazes: The Example of *National Geographic*" 372). In the case of Ponce, the former as opposed to the latter seems to be the case. According to Lutz and Collins, this type of "vacant" gaze often gives subjects "a disconnected and unfocused look" (372). Ponce's photograph, aside from connoting vacancy or absentmindedness, depicts not "a forward looking, future-oriented, and determined" person but one who is suffering and under a significant amount of pain.

Unlike in the photos of Jones, pain is what we see in the photograph of Ponce's face. We do not see before and after shots as we do in the case of Jones as well as most cosmetic surgery ads. Instead, what we see in Ponce's photograph is that which usually remains hidden from view: the "in-between" phase—that is to say, the unrepresentable phase that lies in-between the before and after stages of cosmetic surgery. In fact, aside from the article's negative racialization of indigenous noses, we do not know what Ponce's nose looks like at all, having no notion of what it might have looked like before and/or after (healing from) surgery. Since we know that Ponce has just emerged from the surgeon's office, we can assume that the nose that lies beneath the bandages is nowhere near healing—probably a most unfavorable, bloody sight—which must therefore be kept hidden from view.

While the media in the United States often assuages the pain and medical risks involved in local cosmetic surgical practices, curiously, when it comes to cosmetic surgery performed in the "third world," the U.S. media seems to make it a point hyper-sensationalize the pain and medical risks involved in the process. During the same year "The Face Value of Dreams" was published, for instance, the *San Jose Mercury News* printed another article on cosmetic surgery in the "third world," entitled "Woman Dies After Inexpensive Plastic Surgery: Dominican Republic Clinic Has Reputation as Quick and Cheap." The article, authored by *Associated Press* journalist Michelle Faul, begins in the following sensationalized manner: "All she wanted was shapelier legs. Two weeks later she was dead." No doubt, by isolating these events as specifically "third world" surgical fiascoes, the media creates the illusion that these painful procedures and medical complications are strictly "third world" phenomena, reinforcing an "us" ("first world") and "them" ("third world") binary. The (false) assumption seems to be that these surgical complications do not occur in the scientifically, medically, and technologically advanced "first world."[11] Furthermore, many of these type of sensationalized articles, for example another one entitled "Mexico Puts on a Foreign Face: To Look More 'American,' They Opt for a Poor Man's Nose Job," written by journalist Katherine Ellison and also published by the *San Jose Mercury News*, fail to link "third world" women's efforts to look more "American" to issues of class struggle.

Lutz and Collins moreover suggest that photo-images of Third World peoples in *National Geographic* (or other such magazines and/or newspapers that circulate in the United States) perform a specific ideological purpose and function:

[their] efficacy lies not so much in facilitating social control of those photographed but in representing these others to an audience of "non-deviants" who thereby acquire a language for understanding themselves and the limits they must live within to avoid being classed with those on the outside. . . . The magazine's gaze at the Third World operates to represent it to an American audience in ways which can but do not always shore up a Western cultural identity or sense of self as modern and civilized. (366)

Such photographs, they argue, reinforce the "us" and "them" difference, prompting the "that is not me" response from its First World audiences. By the same token, feminist critic Chandra Talpade Mohanty writes that, "[w]ithout the overdetermined discourse that creates the *third* world, there would be no (singular and privileged) first world. . . . I am suggesting, in effect, that the one enables and sustains the other" ("Under Western Eyes" 74; italics in original). In fact, Mohanty suggests that dominant representations of Third World women ideologically create and naturalize what she calls the "average third-world woman":

> This average third-world woman leads an essentially truncated life based on her feminine gender (read: sexually constrained) and being "third world" (read: ignorant, poor, uneducated, tradition-bound, religious, domesticated, family-oriented, victimized, etc.). This, I suggest, is in contrast to the (implicit) self-representation of Western women as educated, modern, as having control over their own bodies and sexualities, and the "freedom" to make their own decisions. (56)

Considering the *San Jose Mercury News'* positive coverage of Jones's nose job, one can certainly identify a photographic and textual narrative wherein Jones is represented as the educated Western woman of which Mohanty speaks—a woman who is professional and modern and, consequently, has agency and control over her body and sexuality. After all, we might add, we are talking about the woman who filed a sexual harassment federal civil suit against Bill Clinton, former President of the United States. Although the media seldom favorably depicted Jones during her civil suit, the *San Jose Mercury News'* coverage of her surgery and new nose is done in a positive light. By sharp contrast, Ponce's photograph emits a narrative quite the opposite of the one we find in Jones's. For one, Ponce's surgery is not naturalized as it is in the coverage of Jones's. We see nothing wrong or unusual with Jones's new nose and/or her decision to undergo cosmetic surgery. In fact, we see nothing wrong with the fact that her nose was paid for an anonymous (possibly male) donor (a point which seriously calls into question the extent to which Jones has "control" over her own body). The photos themselves (a sad "before" look versus a confident "after" look) and the accompanying article seem to speak approvingly of Jones's new nose, which is said to be comparable to "the 'Pretty Woman' look" (2A). Not only does Ponce's photograph, by contrast, conform to representations of the "average third-world woman" (poor, victimized, unemployed,[12] ignorant, etc.) but it also carries within it narratives of deviancy, abnormality, perversion, and horror.

Because of where Ponce is standing (to the right) and because of the subject's positioning of arms and hands (close to and/or touching the sides of the face), Ponce's photo-image bears striking resemblance to Edvard Munch's infamous painting "The Scream"—a haunting representation that evokes madness, terror, fear, anxiety, and pain. In the background and to the left of Ponce we see a dingy building, which according to the newspaper article, is the "bogus" plastic surgeon's office from which Ponce has just emerged. This windowless, rundown "office"—described as a place in which "risk[s] of infection, disfigurement and even death" occur (21A)—is indicative of the Third World metonymical space in which Ponce lives: a far away location photographically and textually marked by unruliness, dirtiness, infection, disease, peril, underdevelopment, excess poverty, and a lack of professional medical expertise. The news article reports furthermore that "[f]our operations later, [Lira's] nose is too small for her face and one nostril is visibly larger than the other. After the first surgery her nose was flat 'like a boxer's' and after the third her nose collapsed, with loose skin dangling in front. Despite those precedents, Lira wants a fifth operation" (21A). No doubt such descriptions, coupled with the photo of the dingy building from which a painfully bandaged Ponce emerges, also evoke a *Dr. Jekyll and Mr. Hyde* narrative whereby the surgeon's makeshift office becomes a dark, mysterious space in which monstrosities occur—a dangerous place where poor, docile women are "lured" (as the subtitle of the article suggests) by evil pseudo-doctors, becoming disfigured and deformed. While we do not know what lies beneath the white cloth/bandages covering Ponce's face, we can guess that whatever is hidden from view must certainly be a most frightening, unpleasant, and terrifying sight.

One can interpret Ponce's hiding of her face in several ways. The most obvious, literal reading is that she is hiding the unrepresentable, gruesome "in-between" phase of cosmetic surgery—that is to say, she is hiding the recently performed surgical inscriptions on her nose: the blood, the open wound, the swelling, and so forth. Yet, one can also read Ponce's hiding of her face in a metaphorical, figurative sense, suggesting that the white cloth/bandages that cover Ponce's face symbolically point to the whitening process of cosmetic surgery. For example, just as the surgical knives alter and/or erase the racial/ethnic markers associated with the "unstraightened" nose, the white cloth/bandages in the photo might also represent another layer of hiding or erasing the indigenous/mestiza face. Thus we might interpret the photograph as indicative of Ponce's desire to hide/erase her nose by way of the surgical knives as well as by way of the white cloth/bandages that conceal her face. In the end, that which is painfully nonaesthetic and must therefore remain hidden from view is not just Ponce's nose but her entire racial/ethnic face itself. The fact that not just her nose but three quarters of her face is absent is significant. That her mouth is missing might also reinforce the stereotype of the "mute" and passive indigenous woman. Overall, the message that we get is that Ponce's racial/ethnic markers must be physically erased (via cosmetic surgery) and/or hidden from view (via the white cloth/bandages). In the end we are presented with the double erasure of Ponce's racial/ethnic features, left only with a fragmented, incomplete image of Ponce, her face superimposed with multiple layers of "whiteness." And, such a superimposition of whiteness—ideologically, culturally, physically—is poignantly marked by pain.

Yet, pain, as Gillespie and other feminist critics argue, is only one side of the coin when it comes to cosmetic surgery. The other side, they note, is the way in which cosmetic surgery can lead to socioeconomic mobility. Having recently undergone various high-level corruption scandals along with a turbulent presidential transition from Alberto Fujimori's 10-year authoritarian leadership to Alejandro Toledo's populist government, Peru continues to suffer from excess poverty, hunger, soaring inflation rates, and high levels of unemployment. Marked by a long history of Western colonialism and neocolonialism,[13] Peru's present status is that of a dependent capitalist country—that is to say, a country whose economy is dominated by foreign capital interests. In 1999, just a year after "The Face Value of Dreams" was published, official figures estimated that unemployment, in a nation of approximately 24 million people, was at a 50 percent high (Lawrence J. Speer, "War and Poverty: A President Seeks Re-election Amid Controversy" 3rd par.). As reported in WIN News, women in Peru—especially poor, indigenous women—have been most affected by the rising economic disparities and soaring levels of unemployment ("Status of Women in Peru Under Specific CEDAW Articles" 1st par). Unable to get by and/or rely on a single family member's (i.e., a husband's) salary alone, women must also search for ways to make money while at the same time caring for children and/or siblings as well as tending to the household chores.

In her book When Women Rebel: The Rise of Popular Feminism in Peru, Carol Andreas presents us not with the stereotypical image of the "average third-world woman" but rather offers a more realistic portrayal of Peruvian women—women whose lives are characterized by long histories of political activism, agency, resistance, and social struggle. Demanding basic needs from the government such as jobs, running water, housing, sanitation, electricity, food, health care, child care, reproductive rights, and labor protection laws, Andreas discusses how women in Peru have organized labor strikes, massive street political protests and manifestations, taken over buildings and factories, as well as participated in armed struggles of resistance. While several organized and collective resistance efforts by Peruvian women have been successful, many have been met with harsh state reprisals. In fact, as Andreas highlights, more often than not, women's demands for public health care, running water, electricity, and better wages get read by the powerful ruling Peruvian elite as political acts of "subversion." Notwithstanding the retaliation with which resistance efforts in Latin America are often met, the extensive history and longevity of women's resistance movements and organizing efforts in Peru as well as elsewhere in the Americas highlight the ways in which these women, contrary to dominant stereotypes of Third World women (as passive, docile victims) actively assert and exercise their political agency.

Given that jobs, especially decent paying jobs, are extremely limited in Peru, it should come to no surprise that a nonindigenous appearance has become one of the requirements in a competitive job market where good jobs have historically been reserved for light-skinned males. Thus as job competition increases, so do tensions along racial and gendered lines. Further, as more and more multinational corporations move into the Third World in search for cheaper (female) labor, there becomes an even greater need on behalf of these corporations and local national elites to further strengthen and uphold rigid race and gender classificatory systems—this, in an effort to secure a reliable pool of cheap labor for foreign-owned industries (i.e., *maquiladoras*) while simultaneously reserving the better paying national jobs for the light-skinned populations. As Andreas observes, in 1985 "women who retain[ed] indigenous cultural traits in language and dress [were] considered totally ineligible for [certain] jobs" (125). Today, these types of "qualifications" for better-paying jobs have exceeded language and cultural dress in that they now also include a nonindigenous physiognomy, illustrating the ways in which job competition in the region has further exacerbated forms of institutionalized racism, adding to national exclusionary practices.

When we look at the limited resources and alternatives for poor women in Peru and the systems of domination that exclude Third World women from accessing forms of social power, cosmetic surgery, however much a painful procedure embedded in sexist and racist ideologies, offers women like Ponce the possibility for socioeconomic mobility. In a country like Peru where the professional job sector is marked by deep gender, racial, and class divides, cosmetic surgery becomes both a problem and a solution to indigenous and/or mestiza women's searches for better lives. Clearly Ponce's, Espichan's, and Lira's respective decisions to undergo surgery are deeply influenced by their desires to enter the competitive job and/or marriage market. And, while their surgical alterations may ascribe to racist Western beauty ideals, such acts nonetheless carry the potential promise for social betterment. As Gillespie writes, although women who opt for cosmetic surgery do, on various levels, "conform to dominant images of beauty," this "conformity may function subversively and enable them to achieve social power and have their voices heard" (81). In essence, one type of pain (cosmetic surgery) relieves another kind of pain—the pain of being unemployed, racially discriminated against, and/or deemed sexually unattractive by dominant standards, and so on. As such, it would be a mistake to conclude that Ponce, Lira, and Espichan are blindly seduced and "lured" by a sexist and racist politics of appearance inasmuch as it would be erroneous to read these women's surgical transformations as celebratory moments of "triumph" devoid of history and social struggle. Refusing to engage in false "either/or" dichotomies (i.e., Third World/First World, exploited/liberated, passive/active, backward/postmodern) permits us to overcome dominant, overarching tendencies that read women like Ponce, on the one hand, as agency-less and eternally oppressed, and, on the other hand, as devoid of history and social context.

While this is not to suggest that cosmetic surgery is the answer to all of the socioeconomic problems that affect women of color—indeed, as Gillespie observes, while such a "solution" certainly offers women access to social power at the individual level, at the macro-level, however, such actions can be disempowering in that they fail to challenge an inherently oppressive system—it is an acknowledgment of the global/local systems of domination that, by and large, inform Third World women's decisions to undergo cosmetic surgery. It seems that a critical challenge for both First World and Third World feminists alike would be to work toward subverting dominant, reductive binary narratives (i.e., exploitation versus liberation) while simultaneously redirecting the gaze to the historical forces that give rise to the exploitation of Third World women as well as the various ways in which women actively resist and challenge these forces.

Notes

1. I use the terms Third World women and/or "women of color" throughout my essay much in the same way that Chandra Talpade Mohanty uses it in her respective works. See "Cartographies of Struggle: Third World Women and the Politics of Feminism" and "Under Western Eyes: Feminist Scholarship and Colonial Discourses," *Third World Women and the Politics of Feminism*, edited by Mohanty, Ann Russo, Lourdes Torres (Bloomington: Indiana University Press, 1991), 1–47, 51–80. According to Mohanty, "third world women" is an analytical and political category that refers to "an imagined community" of "potential alliances and collaborations across divisive boundaries" (4). Notwithstanding, I use both terms (Third World and Women of color) provisionally, given the lack of currency that these terms elicit in the context of Latin America.
2. Karl Marx, *Capital: A Critique of Political Economy v. 1*, edited by Frederick Engels, trans. Samuel Moore and Edward Aveling, 1992 ed. (New York: International Publishers, 1967). See Part I, "Commodities and Money" 43–144.
3. See Harold E. Pierce, M.D., ed., "Cosmetic Head and Face Surgery: Ethnic Considerations," *Cosmetic Plastic Surgery in Nonwhite Patients* (New York: Grune and Stratton, 1982), 37–49; see in particular pages 43–44.
4. The following are a few texts that provide important critical analyses of the historical construction and political functions of race: Hannah Arendt, *The Origins of Totalitarianism* (New York: Harcourt Brace, 1948); Samir Amin, *Eurocentrism*, trans. Russell Moore (New York: Monthly Review Press, 1989); David Theo Goldberg, *Racist Culture: Philosophy and the Politics of Meaning* (Cambridge: Blackwell Publishers, 1993); Colette Guillaumin, *Racism, Sexism, Power and Ideology* (New York: Routledge, 1995); David R. Roediger, *The Wages of Whiteness: Race and the Making of the American Working Class* (London: Verso, 1991).
5. Sander L. Gilman, *Making the Body Beautiful: A Cultural History of Aesthetic Surgery* (Princeton: Princeton University Press, 1999); Elizabeth Haiken, *Venus Envy: A History of Cosmetic Surgery* (Baltimore: The Johns Hopkins University Press, 1997).
6. Ibid.
7. Rosemary Gillespie, "Women, the Body and Brand Extension in Medicine: Cosmetic Surgery and the Paradox of Choice," *Women & Health* 24.4 (1996): 69–85; Sandra L. Bartky, *Femininity and Domination: Studies in the Phenomenology of Oppression* (London: Routledge, 1990).
8. Adrian Howe, *Punish and Critique: Towards a Feminist Analysis of Penality* (New York: Routledge, 1994); see in particular chapter five.

9. It should be noted that even new popular television shows that capitalize on cosmetic surgery, i.e., *I Want a Famous Face*, tend to deemphasize the pain by focusing on the desired end results. While the process and procedure of cosmetic surgery is certainly a sensationalized part of the shows—we see the knives and the needles digging into the participants' flesh, and later we also witness the patients' post-operative pain—the painful aspects are ultimately assuaged and subsumed by the desired end results: happy, smiling women (and some men) who immediately forget about the pain following their makeovers. Moreover, even when a patient's pain is emphasized on these shows, many such segments only last a few seconds.

10. Paula Jones filed a federal civil suit against U.S. President William Clinton for sexual harassment in 1994. Without an apology or admission of guilt, the case was settled in 1998 when Clinton agreed to pay Jones $850,000.

11. During a "Third World Feminisms" course in which I incorporated a discussion on some of these issues, a student of mine, Berhan Bayleyegn, suggested that such sensationalized news articles might also serve the purpose of dissuading U.S. consumers from investing in cheaper foreign surgical practices, thereby reducing growing competition between expensive U.S.-based surgeries and cheaper Latin American ones.

12. In fact, whereas Third World women seeking surgical alterations tend to be, for the most part, represented as poor and/or unemployed—their very physical appearance and racial/ethnic features being that which excludes them from entering the job market—White women seeking surgical alterations tend to be represented as already "working professionals." See, e.g., Jill Neimark's article, "Changing of Face . . . Change of Fate" in *Psychology Today* (May–June 1994), which talks about the ways in which White women's desires for surgery are informed by their intent to *remain* competitive in the workplace (as opposed to, e.g., Ponce's desires to *enter* it).

13. Colonized by Spain in the sixteenth century, Peru gained its independence in 1821. Soon after, British economic interests took over the region followed by North American economic and political domination in the late nineteenth century and throughout the twentieth century. During the last 35 years or so, Peru has undergone a series of economic crises, unstable leadership, deep political turmoil, and growing social agitation, all of which have led to the rise of popular and organized armed struggles of resistance (i.e., the Tupac Amaru and the Shining Path guerrillas).

Bibliography

Amin, Samir. *Eurocentrism*. trans. Russell Moore. New York: Grune & Stratton, 1982.

Andreas, Carol. *When Women Rebel: The Rise of Popular Feminism in Peru*. Westport: Lawrence Hill and Company, 1985.

Arendt, Hannah. *The Origins of Totalitarianism*. New York: Harcourt Brace, 1948.

Bartky, Sandra L. *Femininity and Domination: Studies in the Phenomenology of Oppression*. London: Routledge, 1990.

Bordo, Susan. " 'Material Girl': The Effacements of Postmodern Culture." *Michigan Quarterly Review* 29(4) (1990), 653–677.

Brush, Pippa. "Metaphors of Inscription: Discipline, Plasticity and the Rhetoric of Choice." *Feminist Review* 58 (1998), 22–43.

Davis, Kathy. "Remaking the She-Devil: A Critical Look at Feminist Approaches to Beauty." *Hypatia* 6(2) (1991), 21–43.

Ellison, Katherine. "Mexico Puts on a Foreign Face: To Look More 'American', They Opt for a Poor Man's Nose Job." *San Jose Mercury News* December 16, 1990: 1A. SAVE™ Available: MediaStream, Inc. August 7 1998 <http://newslibrary.krmediastream.com/cgi- . . . document/sj_auth?DBLIST=sj90& DOCNUM=97611>.

Faul, Michelle, "Woman Dies After Inexpensive Plastic Surgery: Dominican Republic Clinic Has Reputation as Quick and Cheap." *San Jose Mercury News* September 4, 1998.

Gillespie, Rosemary. "Women, the Body and Brand Extension in Medicine: Cosmetic Surgery and the Paradox of Choice." *Women & Health* 24(4) (1996), 69–85.

Gilman, Sander L. *Making the Body Beautiful: A Cultural History of Aesthetic Surgery*. Princeton, NJ: Princeton University Press, 1999.

Goldberg, David Theo. *Racist Culture: Philosophy and the Politics of Meaning*. Cambridge: Blackwell Publishers, 1993.

Guillaumin, Colette. *Racism, Sexism, Power and Ideology*. New York: Routledge, 1995.

Haiken, Elizabeth. *Venus Envy: A History of Cosmetic Surgery*. Baltimore, MD: The Johns Hopkins University Press, 1997.

Howe, Adrian. *Punish and Critique: Towards a Feminist Analysis of Penality*. New York: Routledge, 1994.

Kaw, Eugenia. " 'Opening' Faces: The Politics of Cosmetic Surgery and Asian American Women." In *Many Mirrors: Body Image and Social Relations*. Nicole Sault, ed. New Brunswick: Rutgers University Press, 1994, 241–265.

Koop, David. "The Face Value of Dreams." *San Jose Mercury News* February 1998, 14, 21A.

Lutz, Catherine and Jane Collins. "The Photograph as an Intersection of Gazes: The Example of National Geographic." In *Visualizing Theory*. Lucien Taylor, ed. New York: Routledge, 1994, 363–384.

Marx, Karl. *Capital: A Critique of Political Economy v. 1*. Frederick Engels, ed., trans. Samuel Moore and Edward Aveling. 1992 edn. New York: International Publishers, 1967.

Matory, W. Earle Jr., M.D., F.A.C.S., ed. *Ethnic Considerations in Facial Aesthetic Surgery*. New York: Lippincott-Raven, 1998.

Mohanty, Chandra Talpade. "Cartographies of Struggle: Third World Women and the Politics of Feminism" and "Under Western Eyes: Feminist Scholarship and Colonial Discourses." In *Third World Women and the Politics of Feminism*. Mohanty, Ann Russo, and Lourdes Torres, eds. Bloomington: Indiana University Press, 1991, 1–47; 51–80.

Morgan, Kathryn Pauly. "Women and the Knife: Cosmetic Surgery and the Colonization of Women's Bodies." *Hypatia* 6(3) (1991), 25–53.

Neimark, Jill. "Change of Face . . . Change of Fate." *Psychology Today* May–June 1994: 42 (8 pages). MELVYL ® Available: MAGS. August 5, 1998 <http://192.35.215.185/mw/mwcgi.mb#LB>.

"People in the News." *San Jose Mercury News* August 14, 1998, 2A.

Pierce, Harold E., M.D., ed. *Cosmetic Plastic Surgery in Nonwhite Patients.* New York: Grune & Stratton, 1982.

Podolsky, Doug. "The Price of Vanity." *U.S. News & World Report* October 14, 1996, 22 (6 pages). MELVYL ® Available: MAGS. August 5, 1998 <http://192.35.215.185 /mw/mwcgi.mb#LB>.

Roediger, David R. *The Wages of Whiteness: Race and the Making of the American Working Class.* London: Verso, 1991.

Speer, Lawrence J. "War and Poverty: A President Seeks Re-election Amid Controversy." *Maclean's* April 10, 1995: 22 (2 pages). MELVYL ® Available: MAGS. July 31, 1999 <http://192.35.215.185/mw/mwcgi?sesid=2585 . . . 9.3/CM&CScs=9&Cdisplay(3,1cit.txt,abbrev)>.

"Status of Women in Peru Under Specific CEDAW Articles," *WIN News* Autumn 1998, 72 (2 pages). MELVYL ® Available: MAGS. July 31, 1999 <http://192.35.215.185/mwcgi?sesid=2585 . . . 1/CM&CScs=28&Cdisplay (1,1cit.txt,abbrev)>.

Wolf, Naomi. *The Beauty Myth: How Images of Beauty Are Used Against Women.* New York: Anchor Books, Doubleday, 1991.

8

A Fraction of National Belonging: "Hybrid Hawaiians," Blood Quantum, and the Ongoing Search for Purity

J. Kēhaulani Kauanui

She is just the type of child some folks desperately wish I would bring into this world. Why? Because she is classified genuine "50 percent blooded" Hawaiian. This is how some talk about it. Never mind that the other "half" is Chinese; they could care less about the other racial makeup. She could be Puerto Rican, Filipino, Portuguese, White, or Japanese. What counts here, in some minds, is her Hawaiian "blood." This reproductive description—indeed, this reproductive prescription—is not limited to me as a light skinned "less than 50 percent" Hawaiian per se; a 50 percent blood quantum rule continues to define "native Hawaiian" in state policy (see figure 8.1).

This racial criterion of 50 percent originates in the Hawaiian Homes Commission Act of 1920, which allotted lease lands for residential, agricultural, and pastoral purposes. Eligibility for land leasing is restricted to those "descendants with at least one-half blood quantum of individuals inhabiting the Hawaiian Islands prior to 1778." The stated intention of the Hawaiian Homes Commission Act was to provide lands for Hawaiians in need of "rehabilitation." The legislation targeted urban Hawaiians in Honolulu—those who were dispossessed, diseased, and suffering from rapid depopulation. Racial constructions of Hawaiianness reflect dominant understandings of blood-notions—that is, the assumption that "loss of blood" means loss of culture, where blood quantum is calculated on the basis the generational proximity of one's genetic relationship, as a direct lineal descendent, to those who are supposedly "full blood," as in unmixed. This specific blood racialization of Hawaiians, through various drafts of the bill prior to the passage of the legislation emerged as a way to shift the arguments for the bill that were based on Hawaiian land entitlement over to the privileging of White American property interests.[1] (Kauanui 1999, 2002). Since then, the state of Hawaii reified this federal definition when it institutionalized the Department of Hawaiian Home Lands and the Office of Hawaiian Affairs. Hence, Hawaiian anxieties about "measuring up," in terms of having enough "blood," exceed the metaphorical.

As for measurements, that is nearly all the information now available on this girl-child, besides the fact that the photograph was taken in 1930. The back of the original has no name; it reads "Chinese–Hawaiian girl." Her name alone could tell us more about her cultural affiliation. It might have been Napuahiwahiwa, Carolyn, Ling, or Alma. Who are her parents? It is very likely that her mother was Hawaiian and her father was Chinese (one of the most common couplings in Hawai`i during that time). And who raised her? On which island does she stand? Ni`ihau? Kaua`i? Molokai? Lanai? O`ahu? Maui? Hawai`i? There are no coconut trees here, no sandy beach in the background. Where is she? She could be on a school playground, in the yard of an orphanage, or on Hawaiian Home Lands.

These different scenarios help me *imagine* her racial identity/trajectory, her familial and community context. To "know her" would necessarily begin by locating her—to receive her—to engage her, and yes, possibly even rank her (genealogically) depending on her Hawaiian lineage. Perhaps this photo is an ultimate example of a form of visual extrapolation, of individualization. As Jacqueline Urla and Jennifer Terry argue, "bodies—like all objects that acquire the status of the Real through elaborate processes that represent them as material—are condensations and displacement of social relations." In Hawaiian terms, I do not know who she is because I do not know her name or the family she belonged to and who she became.

I came across this photograph (see figure 8.1) at the National Anthropological Archives in Washington, D.C. while researching the papers and field notes of William A. Lessa from the 1930s. Lessa worked in Hawai`i as a field assistant to Harry L. Shapiro of the American Museum of Natural History who directed an anthropometric study of "Chinese–Hawaiian hybrids." Lessa was a graduate student of Harvard where he had earned his B.A. degree in 1928. He was also affiliated with the Columbia Medical Center, studying there for over a year before being sent to Hawai`i. Once there, compared the

Figure 8.1 "Chinese–Hawaiian Girl," 1930 photograph included in papers of William A. Lessa, National Anthropological Archives.

"mixed" Hawaiian–Chinese with the "integrated" Hawaiians and Chinese by locating, photographing, measuring, and securing blood samples from them. For reasons that will become increasingly clear, out of 5,700 participants, there were 4,214 children in all.[2]

This essay discusses the blood quantum requirement for Hawaiians and the study of Hawaiian blood mixture. I focus on the persistence of the 50 percent rule defining "native Hawaiian" and the documentation of the search for the full-blood Hawaiians in Lessa's study and how it resonates with contemporary nationalist impulses among Hawaiians, as a response to the blood quantum rule and scientific discourses of hybridity that characterize Hawaiian people. Besides offering my meditations of the photo itself, I discuss the discourses of blood that saturate current political projects geared toward assertions of indigenous Hawaiian sovereignty and how they specifically implicate Hawaiian women and their potential offspring. I explore what the photo evokes for me as someone invested in these same sovereignty struggles and aim to open up critical conversations about problematics that emerge at the intersections of the state's demand that Hawaiians prove their ancestry and nationalist anxieties about Hawaiian meeting such criteria and visibility linked to physical presence and phenotypical recognition.

The Production of Racial Knowledge

This study was part of a larger project that the University of Hawaii initiated to examine the physiological, sociological, and psychological effects of race-mixing in Hawaii. Besides the involvement of the American Museum of Natural History, other researchers who participated in this Rockefeller-funded study were based at Harvard's Peabody Museum of Archaeology and Ethnology and the Bishop Museum in Honolulu. The stated impetus of the study was to build on the work of Franz Boas by studying the life of immigrants' children's physicality to map any substantial shifts in growth. Besides investigating bodily size and "vigor," Shapiro and Lessa set out to delineate the "laws of inheritance" in mixed-race subjects to examine "the 'Mendelian laws' which operate in such heredity" drawing from a particular set of traits and measurements under investigation.[3] Even though this study was primarily focused on genetics, not surprisingly, the project of photographing each subject was demanded. David Green, mapping photography and anthropology as mutual technologies of power, argues that

> As the position and status of the "inferior" races became increasingly fixed, so sociocultural difference came to be regarded as dependent

upon hereditary characteristics. Since these were inaccessible to direct observation they had to be inferred from physical and behavioral traits which, in turn, they were intended to explain. Sociocultural differences among human populations became subsumed within the identity of the human body.[4]

Green delineates how anthropology was integral to the maintenance of colonial economic and political power and that photography was "paramount in the formation of a particular discourse of race which was located in the conceptualization of the body as the object of anthropological knowledge."[5] Here "othered" bodies of colonial subjects were subjected to the eye of salvage anthropology's camera.

Hawai'i was a desirable location for the Shapiro/Lessa study as it already had the reputation for being a "great laboratory" for racial research. Besides the oft-uttered notation that Hawai'i was the great melting pot, researchers reported that Hawai'i was ideal

> because for some reason people here can supply accurate record about their own genealogies. This may be a survival from ancient Hawaiian days, when a man knew exactly who he was, and no doubt about it, helped perhaps by the attitude of the Chinese, who also know who their ancestors were. Besides that, rumor has it that the Kamehameha School [for children of Hawaiian ancestry] and the Palama Settlement, have very considerable masses of data.[6]

Here, genealogical knowledge was crucial to this genetic study even while the radicalized terms of the study effaced genealogical identification at every turn. Lessa was dismayed that he was

> "finding fewer pure Hawaiians than anyone had ever supposed, and for this he was criticized by some who thought he was being too strict in his criteria, which included not only visual inspection but also public health records, data supplied by the potential subjects themselves . . . [and] . . . hearsay gossip about illegitimacy . . .".[7]

Lessa found the sources of "hearsay gossip" to be important relationships in his work "because of their value as informants in supplying genealogical information."[8] Specifically he was concerned with the " 'purity' of subjects claiming to be Hawaiians or Chinese [sic]-Hawaiians with no Haole (White) or other admixture . . ."[9] Lessa concluded that because of their help, he had to eliminate large numbers of persons as subjects and that "this was contrary to the prevailing opinion regarding the number of pure Hawaiians in the Islands."[10] He cited the census, for example, which "used a broad ethnic identity and counted twenty times the number" that he did.[11]

Lessa's search proved to be a taxing one as his correspondence with supervisor Shapiro reveals frustration at the many "suspicious Hawaiians," who, he would eventually find out, were not "pure" after all.[12] Genealogical informants would often alert him to the fact that so and so's grandfather, for example, was actually English or Tahitian. Lessa's quest for the "pure" Hawaiians and his subsequent disappointment with finding them to be "hybrid" was conveyed repeatedly in his personal letters to Shapiro who advised him "Don't be discouraged about the Haole [White] fly in the Hawaiian ointment. It will surprise you after a while to realize how many we really are getting who are Chinese, Hawaiian, or a mixture without extraneous elements."[13] Long after the study, which was to his disappointment never published, Lessa reflected: "Undoubtedly, considerable skepticism about my work was felt by persons who used a loose definition of 'pure' Hawaiian. I was motivated by accuracy in a study of unmixed subjects."[14]

Besides standardized anthropometric measurement data and photographs, other materials gathered by Lessa include birth and marriage certificates, as well as other genealogical data. Lessa's field notebooks alone contain provocative information such as the names of the people studied, who were not to be identified in the work intended for publication, and whose names are not listed on the photographs and measurement cards. A number of ethical issues emerge. Besides basic issues of privacy for those who were involved in the study, many of whom might be living today, identification politics in Hawai'i now is bound up with rights to land and revenues access and customary gathering practices under state authority—all of which are based on the ability to meet the blood quantum criterion. Some of this evidence could very well harm contemporary Hawaiians whose relations claimed themselves as "full blood" Hawaiians—and from whose claims blood degree was figured within legal documentation.

One letter in particular underscores the delicate nature of anthropometric studies that reveal the sensitive risks involved in securing an individual's hereditary information, especially in regards to forms of personal consent that were rendered moot for the children involved. A Hawaiian mother writes to her daughter's teacher at the school, where the study extends about her daughter's background: "She was found in the graveyard . . . she was taken to the Children['s] Hospital and I went to adopt her. We don't know who her real folks are . . . She goes as Chinese H [awaiian]. Don't tell her any thing she dose [*sic*] not know that she is adopt [ed] by me. As I always tell her that I am her ma."[15]

The above case also reveals how particular forms of knowledge can escape the camera's lens. While bodies "do indeed enjoy the status of the Real and the material, and thus become a powerful source of medical and scientific knowledge as much as they become grounds form articulating political claims . . . they become surface onto which physicians, scientists, and lay people can inscribe and project powerful cultural meanings and moral prohibitions."[16] Similarly, the technology of photography in anthropological discourse became a form of anthropological knowledge.

Mapping Hybridity

Her picture is like a snapshot, unlike the established procedures for scientists producing physical type photographs. Certainly, Lessa would have been familiar that the formula that was intended to provide standardization for scientific study. Given their own criteria, what would have been the purpose to take and keep this image? Perhaps Lessa was keen to show her individual traits rather than put her in a lineup of "racial types." To show her outside, with the sunlight and shade across her face, seems to catch her in the midst of her daily routine; it seems to document her mixed existence as normative. Thus, this photograph becomes a different form of anthropological knowledge about racial hybridity.

The Shapiro–Lessa study was not the first of its kind: earlier studies of this type had attempted to map Hawaiian hybridity through the charting of physical corporeality through measurements, photographs, and reports that represented the different (pheno)types of Hawaiians. Before the Shapiro–Lessa study, Leslie C. Dunn also undertook genetic research on Hawaiians. His work was undertaken at the Peabody Museum of American Archaeology and Ethnology at Harvard University, based on data collected by Alfred M. Tozzer who was collaborating with Hooten in 1916 (both of whom later participated in Shapiro's study). In 1928, Dunn published the results in *An Anthropomorphic Study of Hawaiians of Pure and Mixed-Blood*.[17] There he noted that at that time there was no other data on living "pure" Hawaiians.[18]

I am particularly interested in this study because of its timing in Hawaiian history. How was Dunn's work part of a larger body of constitutive discourses that were later deployed by U.S. government officials in decisions regarding the larger body politic? We should consider the process by which the statistical "disappearance" of the "pure" Hawaiian was constantly re-evoked in political contexts—such as United States Congressional Debates—where definitions of Hawaiianness, based on blood notions, were codified. Although Dunn's analysis of Tozzer's data was not published until 1928, Tozzer's actual work in the field (1916–1920) was just prior to the passing of the Hawaiian Homes Commission Act. Dunn's work details anthropometric descriptions of "Native Hawaiians" (unmixed) and some descendants "from crosses of Hawaiians with other races'— namely offspring from Hawaiian women with European or Chinese men. Dunn concluded that "The evidence of Chinese blood in the hybrids are throughout more easily and certainly distinguishable than the Hawaiian traits."[19] Dunn found that hybrid mixes might bring about positive results, noting "The impression gained by the observer was that the hybrids arising from the cross of Hawaiians and the Chinese were normal persons, frequently combining the more valuable personal characteristics of both parent types . . . persons of this descent are apparently not handicapped, either physically or mentally, in comparison with either parent type."[20] The notion that some mixes produced more viable subjects than others is a common feature in many of these studies that lean toward a form of "positive" eugenics, theorizing which matings could produce the ideal citizen within such a varied island population forcibly incorporated in the American body politic.

These reports treat the Hawaiian body as an historical artifact, a material object of the past. The science of the hybrid Hawaiian is about the authority and pronouncement that worked to reconstitute different racialized fragments into a "neo-Hawaiian" body, with a new label, containing it within an already operative system of classifications and racial schema. While it may be true "[t]o a greater or lesser extent that reorientation of anthropological theory in the 1920s involved the rejection of racial classification as the structuring principal of anthropological inquiry,"[21] I argue that "hybridity" itself became the 1930s racial classification for Hawaiians. David Green argues that "the practices of anthropometry, and the photographic genre which it had fostered, were virtually abandoned by anthropologists whose interests were [re]directed" toward ethnography.[22] But a cursory glance at the studies of the "hybrid Hawaiians" would support the argument that perhaps racially mixed subjects provided a site where this type of work flourished. Green further argues that "the body has become the focus of a social rather than a biological identity and its significance is no longer of a psychological but cultural order."[23]

The hybrid Hawaiian, as studies reveal, provided a subject where concerns of the biological and social were intricately bound. These discourses on Hawaiians produced particular objects of knowledge. Although these racial productions vary, they are stunning exercises evincing that "[f]acination with mixing and unity is a symptom of preoccupation with purity and decomposition."[24] In the taxonomic, one cannot see what is excluded. But in the taxonomy of the hybrid Hawaiian, nothing at all is excluded. Hence, the term "Hawaiian" almost became meaningless, as island version of "American" without its unmarked dominant whiteness. Hence, now it is not enough to say "Hawaiians" to talk about Hawaiians. Instead, Hawaiians and non-Hawaiians alike employ markers to specify—real, indigenous, Native—to refill that which has been emptied of meaning as a signifier.

An early example of this all-inclusive subjectivity is provided in a 1932 report by William Atherton Du Puy. At the time, Du Puy was the executive assistant to the United States Secretary of the Interior. He compiled his research into a work titled *Hawaii and Its Race Problems*.[25] Drawing on work by yet another researcher—Romanzo Adams, who wrote *Interracial Marriage in Hawaii: A Study of the Mutually Conditioned Process of Acculturation and Amalgamation* in 1937[26]—Du Puy predicted that

[T]here ultimately must be a fusion, and that in the end the Hawaiian-American will be a composition of all the people who have settled here as permanent residents . . . On the basis of the present populations he . . . [*sic*] . . . will be something near one-third Japanese, one-fifth Filipino, one-ninth Portuguese, one-tenth Hawaiian, one-twelfth Chinese, one-fifteenth Anglo-Saxon, with a sprinkling of Korean, Puerto Rican, and what-not.[27]

Interestingly Du Puy's term "Hawaiian–American" never took hold in Hawai'i and that in general, hyphenated identities do not hold much currency in contemporary Hawai'i contexts. Also, the term "Hawaiian" is commonly reserved for someone indigenous to Hawaii who traces their ancestry to the people who occupied the Islands prior to Cook's landing in 1778. While—according to the 1990 U.S. census—over 96 percent of indigenous Hawaiians are mixed-race, Hawaiians still make distinctions between someone with this traceable ancestry and someone else who merely resides in Hawai`i.[28] It is important to note that in the 2000 census, 282,667 people in Hawai`i identified themselves as at least part Hawaiian or Pacific Islander—an increase of 74.2 percent from 1990, while 113,539 described themselves solely as a member of that group.[29] This suggests the endurance of Hawaiian indigenous identities, regardless of blood quantum and dominant insistence that those who do not meet the 50 percent blood rule become honorary Whites (or Asians, for that matter).

These studies were an important part of the "remaking" of Hawaiians, not simply attempts to understand and map the genetic makeup and changing construct of Hawaiians. Indeed, they came sites where Hawaii's multiracial visibility marked a new episteme in a rapidly changing Hawaiian geographical–colonial–political landscape. In this context, Hawaiianness was made sense of through a constitution of racialized notions what makes a Hawaiian. These reformulated notions—their indigenous content effaced—were then reinserted into multiracial Hawaii's wider material-semiotic process and inscribed onto a new pluralist body politic, which always already, then, figures Hawai`i as a site of hyper-mixedness.

Women and Children of the Nation

To me she seems hesitant, like she is holding something else besides her right hand. Perhaps censuring a full smile? Or maybe just barely forcing the one she offered along with her upright posture. Her haircut is short, perhaps cut just in time for the photo? She could have been at hula practice and then changed into her Sunday best. Or maybe she was approached just after getting out of church. She looks ready to bolt— back to class, back to Uncle's Kitchen in the tenement project in Chinatown, to the beach, to hold hands with her girlfriend and tell grand stories, to the book she was reading, to the cane fields. Or maybe she was learning how to weave *lauhala* from Aunty. Maybe she was pulled away from her Chinese language class where she was trying to keep up with her brother who was on his way to China (being sent by their father so he would have a customary upbringing and not associate with the Hawaiian boys then marked for doom). Perhaps she was writing a letter in cursive to her oldest sister who was sent away to live with their grandparents, Hawaiian-style, as is common for the first-born grandchild.

Which Hawaiian counts and for whom? During a long-distance phone call from Hawai`i, an activist friend asked me, in desperation,

"What are we gonna do when the full-bloods die out? How will we define our *lahui* [nation of people]?" I feel a strong sense of despair when I think of his alarm. Yet I am also critical of his assumptions and their implications. What he was suggesting is that *piha kanaka maoli* ("full" Hawaiians) currently defines who Hawaiian people are as *lahui*, and that our future rests with them—an impossible burden indeed. The symbolic demand for the "full-blood" or *piha* Hawaiian creates desire over and above the imaginary need. Within Hawaiian struggles, proving indigeneity is critical to recognition of the indigenous collective subjectivty. The state and population at large demand that Hawaiianness be quantifiable. To quantitively measure Hawaiianness is to try to endow the category with quality.

The blood quantum rule leads Hawaiian people to be classed into two categories, the "50 percenters," and the "less than fifties." *Piha* Hawaiians are rarely explicitly named unless in relation to their predicted demise. My friend's anxiety—and that of many Hawaiians—is a haunting refrain. In Hawaiian nationalist contexts, one often hears the political leaders cite numerical figures of Hawaiian mixedness as an index of Hawaiian extinction. Prominent sovereignty activist, Kekuni Blaisdell, M.D. frequently warns that "today there are less than 8,000 *piha kanaka maoli* (pure Hawaiians) remaining."[30] Blaisdell also reports that the United States census evaluation predicts that by the year 2020 there will be no more *piha kanaka maoli*.[31] Linked to these recitations, many Hawaiians urge Hawaiian people to *ho`oulu lahui*—to reinvigorate the nation of Hawaiian people—to create and bear more Hawaiians, preferably the "more than fifties." My friend who phoned was clearly taking refuge in the imaginary need for the authentic sign, with the body as ultimate referent to cope with the political anxieties that come with confirmation, becoming a legal subject and exiting wardship status—two key goals propelling the ongoing Hawaiian struggle for sovereign self-governance.

These issues all resonate strongly with a 1930 article that suggests, as its title states, that the "Perpetuation of Hawaiian Race Rests with Children."[32] While true that the future of any people rests with the welfare of its children, the perpetuation of Hawaiians rests with out collective ability to raise our children well and with the means to do so. This consideration is easily lost in the push for the *production* of Hawaiian children. Why should Hawaiian children bear the burden of bearing Hawaiian children? What is striking in the case of this article is that just as the *piha maoli* are objectified, so are Hawaii's children; a combination that may in itself reveal and infantilization of *piha maoli.* In both cases, there is the concern with developing a degree of competence in order for the survival of the rest of us. This article was printed in the *Honolulu Advertiser* during the same year that Lessa set out to measure and document Hawaiian children of non-mixed and mixed-Chinese ancestry. More specifically, the article speaks to the decade marked a decade since the passing of the Hawaiian Homes Commission Act of 1920. In the United States federal hearings prior to the Act, notions about who constituted "native Hawaiians" were drawn from both scientific and common knowledge about whether "part-Hawaiians" were endowed with enough difference to warrant their access to land leasing. In the earliest draft bill preceding the Act, Congress first mooted the blood quantum criterion by evoking the living conditions of mixed-race Chinese–Hawaiians who were described as not being "in need" of "special legislation." These "part-Hawaiians," in particular, were configured as a political threat to White plantation interests. Hence, Hawaiianness was constituted in the name of "rehabilitating the Native" while limiting the empowerment of Hawaiians who were also of Asian ancestry.

The continued legal "demand" for Hawaiians who can document their blood quantum at 50 percent or more has in turn fueled an anxiety among many Hawaiians, as evinced in nationalist calls to "replenish the race" by reproduction. These calls have significant bearing on Hawaiian women as well as the transformation of genealogical reckoning. Perhaps more importantly, it is Hawaiian women that are calling on other Hawaiian women. At a feminist family values forum, sovereignty leader Mililani Trask also made note of this push, stating that "There is a saying in the Hawai'ian [*sic*] culture that you can marry whomever you wish, but mate with your own kind. In this way, we regenerate our numbers."[33] The heterosexual configuration of such a dictate is unmarked, but the concern Trask articulates is one of mass depopulation. She explains that "When Cook arrived there were one million Kanaka Maoli [Hawaiians]; a generation and a half later, at the time of the US overthrow, 39,000 of us remain. Today we are 200,000 Kanaka Maoli. You see that our population is increasing, because we love each other."[34] Trask is not alone marking the impetus on reviving a people. In the collection *Autobiography of Protest in Hawai'i*, Hawaiian sovereignty activist Lynette Cruz offers a point that speaks volumes to the issues of pedagogy and reproductive behavior. Cruz also evokes a set of alarming statistics, noting that "It has been projected that by the year 2044, there will be no more Hawaiians with 50 percent or more Hawaiian blood. This means, in effect, there will be no more Hawaiians by our definition, and the federal government no longer has to deal with us as a people."[35] It is not clear why Cruz says "our definition," given that Hawaiian genealogical practices are far more inclusive in defining who counts as Hawaiian. Hawaiians tend to define Hawaiianness through ancestral lines of descent, familial relationality that marks kinship to the land. For one thing, Hawaiianness has historically been reckoned bilineally—through maternal and/or paternal lines—as well as allowing for non-Hawaiian peoples to be adopted into Hawaiian familial structures. These persistent genealogical practices are the key form of contestory modalities through which Hawaiians alternately identify themselves in relation to the land and other Hawaiians—something that cannot be done by merely invoking one's fractional "degree" of Hawaiian "blood." As for lessons for other Hawaiians, Cruz maintains that "When we talk about educating people we're talking about educating them *right now*. Time is short. We're telling people, especially Hawaiian women, that we need to have some Hawaiian babies from Hawaiian men who are full-blooded. We need to have these things documented. This is one strategy that we can use to make sure that Hawaiians do not become extinct by somebody else's definition."[36] Clearly Cruz's plea has a sense of urgency. But who is the "we" that needs the babies and why? Where is the collective and material support that should come with such a demand? What about Hawaiian men? Supposing that Hawaiian women were interested in (ful)filling such a tall order, what would be the method of doing so? How could such a method avoid objectification? Fetishization? Why not instead infuse Hawaiian political projects with a similar sense of urgency toward the goal of wrestling definitions of Hawaiianness away from state-imposed neocolonial definitions as a profound course of self-determination?

Cynthia Enloe has acknowledged that "Women in many communities trying to assert their sense of national identity find that coming into an emergent nationalist movement through the accepted feminine roles of bearer of the community's memory and children is empowering."[37] Indeed reproduction as part of Hawaiian women's self-determined autonomy is potentially empowering as a form of resisting the overdetermined narratives of Hawaiian dilution, the legacy of Hawaiian depopulation that has attributed to Hawaiians' status as a minority in Hawai'i, and the assault on Hawaiian families via state policies and discourses that, in turn, shape concerns about blood quanta criteria and notions of indigeneity making it no surprise that Hawaiians are feeling anxiety about bearing children with more "Hawaiian blood." The issue of population recovery is the impetus for the call to reproduction, not a call for women to bear sons for the nation, which has characterized many other nationalist struggles. These calls to *hoʻoulu lahui* certainly have the potential for uneven gendered impact. Hawaiian women's reproductive rights are reserved without the alternate construction of Hawaiian women's bodily agency, as a site of inevitable betrayal.[38]

Conclusion

I return to the photograph of this mixed-girlchild. She could be on a Hawaiian homestead on the island of Molokai with eight brothers and sisters—their family being boasted and cited as corporeal evidence that the Hawaiian Homes Commission Act did aid in Hawaiian "rehabilitation." I look at her and think of her 1930 girlhood being inscribed with and imposed upon by other people's moral and behavioral imperatives—to marry Hawaiian and "make" more Hawaiians to counter the persistent threat of population demise. Or, maybe she was to "go Chinese" and marry a Chinese man and bear a son that would then carry on his father's line, which might very well entail an erasure of her own mother, who, as the "Hawaiian great-grandmother" would likely be unknown to her "Chinese" descendants. Did she marry? If so, he was probably Hawaiian, Chinese, Hawaiian– Chinese, or Hawaiian-*haole* (White). Who knows—maybe she fell in love with a woman and decided to go to another island, or even San Francisco, Portland, or Vancouver. The hopeful (or disturbing?) part is that she could very well be alive today. If she had children, maybe they would recognize her upon viewing this picture.

Although the blood quantum criterion is state-imposed, some Hawaiians are clearly invested in it as some stand to benefit from that racial form of order. While the criterion seems firmly entrenched, Hawaiians still employ and deploy Hawaiian genealogical links whether or not they meet the criterion. Hawaiian genealogical practices serve as an alternate mode of identification—one that draws from the source of Hawaiian kinship to the land—is the foundational basis of all sovereign claims.

What is to gain in the quest for the "pure" Hawaiian? While some may want to move steadfast on this quest, like Lessa they will certainly become disappointed, not to mention tired of always finding the "suspicious" Hawaiians who—even though perhaps a fraction shy of national belonging—constitute most Hawaiians today. She may not be the type of girlchild I will have.

Notes

1. See Kauanui, J. Kehaulani, "The Politics of Blood and Sovereignty in *Rice v. Cayetano.*" *Political and Legal Anthropology Review* 25(1) 2002: 100–128. and Kauanui 1999. "For Get" Hawaiian Entitlement: Configurations of Land, "Blood," and Americanization in the Hawaiian Homes Commission Act of 1920. *Social Text* 59:123–144.
2. *Deviant Bodies*, edited by Jennifer Terry and Jacqueline Urla (Bloomington and Indianapolis: Indiana University Press), 6.
3. "Scientist to Examine Cops for 'Points,' " *Honolulu Advertiser*, July 17, 1930, n.p., n.a.
4. David Green, "Classified Subjects: Photography and Anthropology: The Technology of Power." *Ten* 8(14) 1984: 30–37.
5. Ibid., 31.
6. *University of Hawaii Quarterly Bulletin*, vol. IX, No. 3, May 1932.
7. William A. Lessa papers, National Anthropological Archives, notation provided by Lessa, under "FRIENDS FROM THE HAWAIIAN COMMUNITY 1930–1932" (n.d.).
8. Ibid.
9. Ibid.
10. Letter to Andrew Lind, William A. Lessa papers, National Anthropological Archives.
11. Ibid.
12. Letter to Harry L. Shapiro, William A. Lessa papers, National Anthropological Archives.
13. Letter to, William A. Lessa, William A. Lessa papers, National Anthropological Archives.
14. Letter to Andrew Lind, William A. Lessa papers, National Anthropological Archives.
15. William A. Lessa papers, National Anthropological Archives.
16. Terry and Urla, ibid.
17. Dunn, Leslie C., *An Anthropomorphic Study of Hawaiians of Pure or Mixed-Blood*, Papers of the Peabody Museum of American Archaeology and Ethnology (Harvard University, Cambridge: Peabody Museum, 1928).
18. Ibid., 100.
19. Ibid., 147.
20. Ibid., 147.
21. Green, ibid., 34–35.
22. Ibid., 35.
23. Ibid., 37.
24. Donna Haraway, *Modest Witness* (New York and London: Routledge, 1997), 214.
25. William Atherton Du Puy, *Hawaii and Its Race Problems* (Washington: United States Government Printing Office, 1932).
26. Romanzo, Adams, *Interracial Marriage in Hawaii: A Study of the Mutually Conditioned Process of Acculturation and Amalgamation* (New York: AMS Press, 1937).

27. William Atherton Du Puy, 115–117.
28. Blaisdell, Kekuni and Noreen Mokuau, "Kanaka Maoli, indigenous Hawaiians," in *Hawai`i Return to Nationhood*, edited by Jonathan Friedman and Ulla Hasager, 49–67, IWGIA Document 75 (Copenhagen: The International Working Group of Indigenous Affairs, 1993), 5.
29. Bricking, Tanya and Robbie Dingeman. 2001. Census lists more "Native Hawaiians" than ever. *Honolulu Advertiser*, March 20:3.
30. Ibid., 50.
31. Ibid.
32. Ibid.
33. "Mililani Trask," *Feminist Family Values Forum: Gloria Steinam, Angela Davis, Maria Jimenez, Mililani Trask*, presented by the Foundation for a Compassionate Society, edited by Susan Bright (Austin, TX: Plain View Press, 1996), 13.
34. Ibid.
35. "Lynette Cruz," *Autobiography of Protest in Hawai'i*, edited by Robert H. Mast and Anne B. Mast, Honolulu: University of Hawai'i Press), 381.
36. Ibid., 381–382.
37. Cythia Enloe, *Bananas. Beaches & Bases: Making Feminist Sense of International Politics* (Berkeley and Los Angeles: University of California Press, 1989), 55.
38. See 1998. Kauanui, Off-Island Hawaiians "Making" Ourselves at "Home": A (Gendered) Contradiction in Terms? *Women's Studies International Forum* 21(6): 681–693.

Part III

Resistance Images

Bearing Bandoleras: Transfigurative Liberation and the Iconography of la Nueva Chicana

Maylei Blackwell

Deploying a popular Chicano movement photo as a point of departure, this essay charts how dominant visual tropes within Chicano movement print culture helped to produce and maintain gendered political scripts about the terms of women political participation. In turn, Chicana activists engaged with political icons and politicized iconography in order to negotiate their own political agency and (re)figure themselves within movement iconography by creating new images of women's revolutionary participation. More than just forms of visual representation, political iconography can be seen as a site of articulation, negotiation, and struggle. This essay explores how the figure of la Soldadera was transformed during the Chicano movement and how cultural icons and movement iconography served as a terrain of struggle over the signification or meaning of women's political agency in the Chicano movement. This photograph (figure 9.1), which first appeared in the *Chicano Student Movement* newspaper in 1968 and was republished in numerous places, including the first issue of *La Raza* magazine (where it was advertised as a political poster), represents larger discursive and ideological struggles around the role women played in the Chicano movement. It marks one point where "the transfigurative liberation of the icon"[1] began to take place as Chicana feminists reclaimed narratives of women's participation in the Mexican Revolution of 1910 as a way to negotiate a different political agency within the masculinist registers of Chicano nationalism.

Figure 9.1 "La Soldadera," *Chicana Student Movement* newspaper, 1968. Photograph by Raul Ruiz.

This essay explores the ways in which gender was constructed through nationalist discourse and how Chicana feminist interventions recast and (re)imagined history in an effort to break open the confines of the Chicano Nationalism and the symbolic economy of nation, or Aztlán (the mythic homeland of Chicanos). Visually mapping the figure of the Soldadera is one way to understand the cultural work that these reclaimed historical narratives performed in creating new spaces for women within male dominated movement discourses and practices.[2] It situates this photo and the production of Chicana feminist iconography within a larger visual cultural history that unfolded from the circulation of visual images in movement print culture, slide shows, and the first filmic images produced by Chicanas. I trace the dominant mode of address and representational strategy of the Chicano movement through the idealization of the people and the construction of "heroes" of the people. Movement archetypes, such as the pachuco, the stoic worker, or romanticized revolutionary, constituted a field of subject positions that were negotiated over within the social spaces of the movement. The historic development of an iconography of the Nueva Chicana can be seen in the ways in which women's agency and political subjectivities were not only constituted by movement imaging practices, but by the ways Chicana feminists refigured themselves through the circulation and production of their own images. The iconography of the Nueva Chicana reworked the gendered nationalist constructions of the Adelita, la Revolucionaria and other figures (such as the martyr and the revolutionary (m)Other). Deploying different frames of reference and modes of address in its visual strategies, these representational practices show us how Chicana activists shifted nationalist representational registers and figured themselves as new historical subjects.

In the photo, the image of a young woman, member of the Brown Berets, captures the contradictions and contestations around the figure of the Soldadera and the position of women both within narratives and movement practices of Chicano nationalism. She is politically and visually present in the movement, but her gaze is turned away; deflected. The photograph frames her at a medium shot; the top of her head reaches out of the frame. Because her head is turned, gaze laterally oblique, the viewer's focus is pulled to the center of her body—her corazon, pecho—bearing bandoleras. The crossed bandoleras represents an intersection—simultaneously symbolizing her revolutionary commitment while invoking the complex ways women and women's bodies are made to stand in for the nation within both historic projects of nation building as well as numerous revolutionary struggles.[3]

The photograph was taken in the late 1960s at the Fiesta de los Barrios at Lincoln High School invoking the historic East Los Angeles blow outs where students walked out of their high schools demanding an end to racist education. It is a grainy black and white image common to the kind of photojournalism that circulated in movement print culture. Its impact as a document of the Chicano struggle relies on the form of realism created by photojournalistic techniques. It is a powerful movement photo document because, while the context of the rally is evident, the focus of the image is on one actor, captured by zoom lens. The quality of realism or its realistic aura key to many political photographs is also reliant on the seemingly unstaged nature of the image. In documentary fashion, it claims to represent and document a moment in political history represented as innocent of staging. The woman seems unaware that her photo is being taken. Yet, she bears the bandoleras (signifier of both present and historic revolutions) across her heart and in that way is represented both as a documentary image of an activist at a political event and a symbol of it. The image of the woman in combat gear is complicated because it signifies her participation in a revolution of national liberation while simultaneously representing the conflation of her body as a symbol of that nation. This dual signifier has been used in other anti-imperialist movements for national liberation before and after the height of the Chicano Movement. Recent scholars have commented on these contradictions by stating:

> Often made to metaphorize the nation, the image of the revolutionary woman carrying a bomb or waving a flag was celebrated precisely because her precarious position within the revolution called attention to its fissures. Thus, the same Third Worldist discourse that valorized the revolutionary female figure has also condemned Third World feminists as "traitors to the nation" in response to their critique of the masculinist narration of the nation.[4]

The figure of the Soldadera and her manifestation in the image of this young brown beret activist also calls attention to the fissures of the nation Aztlán and the manner in which it engenders its subject-citizens. Many movements in the United States articulated their discursive project of decolonization and anti-imperialism through an ideological alignment with Third World Liberation Movements where masculinist nationalism was manifest through a construction of a specific revolutionary masculinity, ala Che Guevara. As argued by male gender critics, then and now, this form of masculinity was seen as an act of decolonization and reclamation of the dignity men of color had lost in this particularly patriarchal view of power.[5]

While this photo first appeared in the early political publication, *Chicano Student Movement* newspaper, more recently, this image has continued to circulate 35 years after its first appearance as a compelling tribute to Chicana Power on T-shirts and stickers, in a book dedicated to the basic historical writings of Chicana Feminism and even on the cover to a Chicano Oldies album.[6] As much as this image represents a site of contestation and negotiation of women's political subjectivity and agency within the Chicano movement, it also represents a continued struggle over popular memory and identity formation. As a mediation on the representations of women's widespread participation in the Chicano movement, the continued circulation of this image also invokes the empowering message of Chicana resistance as well as a mode in which gender is emplotted in the structures of remembrance within the movement. It also calls our attention to the ways in which women and Chicana feminism are the eccentric subjects of Chicano movement narratives because they recycle the narrative of male dominance, instead of representing the complicated ways in which women participated, transformed, and provided leadership in the movement.

I began to track the cultural work of producing and circulating an iconography of la Nueva Chicana while conducting an oral history project with members of las Hijas de Cuauhtémoc. I first noticed the transfiguration of la Soldadera as an icon while closely studying the *Hijas de Cuauhtémoc* newspaper in order to historicize the political work of Chicana activists of this era.[7] What I found was that more than their conventional political work, the work of engendering the political culture of the movement helped women to articulate a different political agency within the imaginary of Chicano nationalism and different political roles for women within the larger political arena of Chicano Civil Rights in the 1960s and 1970s.[8] The iconography of Chicano Nationalism has been discussed by historian Vicki Ruiz who points out the limitations it set for women's agency. She notes the way that the figure of the Soldadera, although a politicized image, often functioned as a conservative model of the role Chicanas were expected to play in movement. While la Soldadera was seen as loyal camp follower or as a woman who "stands by her man" to provide comfort to the revolutionary hero, it also circulated with the figure of la Adelita that conjured up an image of the revolutionary sweetheart. Chicana women leaders and feministas also reclaimed counter-narratives of revolutionary women and reclaimed the images of the Soldadera to help contest the conservative cultural images of women circulating in the Chicano movement and resignify them through the lens of Chicana resistance.[9] The Soldadera signified either foot soldiers of the movement or revolutionary sweethearts who served the men who were seen as the real actors in the struggle. In their first issue of the newspaper, the Hijas de Cuauhtémoc began to resignify the image of the Soldadera through historical narratives to produce a revolutionary historical agency. This was part of a larger discursive struggle to craft new genealogies of revolutionary women who worked for women's liberation within the framework of the national revolution. The 1960s Hijas de Cuauhtémoc took their name from a women's underground newspaper which called for the end to the Porfirio Díaz dictatorship and for women's civil and political rights in the years before the Mexican Revolution.

As much as Chicano Nationalism was a project of racial justice and cultural pride, it was a gendered project. The roles of women that were often viewed as romantic reclamations of traditional mexicano culture[10] were in themselves gendered constructs that established a mode of representation of women in movement culture and a code of conduct of what it meant to be "down" (or a true revolutionary woman). Chicana activists in the student movement contested the way in which their participation was often reduced to their reproductive labor, and how they were seen as the symbolic bearers of the nation, sites of cultural authenticity, or only as revolutionary sweet hearts. The fissures this image calls into question are located at the crossroads of the bandoleras women bear symbolically and politically.

Visuality and Social Movements: Print Cultures, Imaged Communities

Benedict Anderson's influential work articulates a conceptualization of the Nation as imagined community and explores how Nation is constituted through print communities.[11] Anderson's study has produced new insights about social movements, communities of resistance and anticolonial struggles like the Chicano movement.[12] For example, Partha Chatterjee, a historian involved in the Subaltern Studies Group, reconfigures Anderson's formulation for the historical specificity of anticolonial nationalisms by arguing that it is not through engagement in conflict with the state but within the cultural realm that prefigures this struggle where decolonizing nationalist imaginaries are consti-tuted. He argues that anticolonial nationalism creates a domain of sovereignty within colonial society and that this domain is produced through "an entire institutional network of printing presses, publishing houses, newspapers, (and) magazines . . . created . . . outside the purview of the state . . . through which the new language (nationalist liberation) . . . is given shape."[13] The Chicano movement deployed a form of decolonizing nationalism and the circulation of print media in the form of student and community newspapers, political pamphlets, and movement magazines, which played a formative role in articulat-ing new political subjectivites as well as a shared, collective (if not uncontested) notion of Aztlán as the Chicano nation.

Since, the Hijas de Cuauhtémoc deployed strategic feminist recon-figurations of nationalist discourse in the newspaper they published, they played a vital role in the critique of the national subject as male and struggled to refigure the Nation (Aztlán) as a space for difference along axes of gender, sexuality, and class. By reworking notions of tradition, culture, and history that circumscribed racial, sexual, and gendered exceptions of women, the work of the Hijas de Cuauhtémoc multiplied the critical dialogues within their own communities and between constituencies constituted through an imagined alternative print community. The members of the Hijas de Cuauhtémoc engaged in what Kobena Mercer describes as critical dialogism. He writes that, "critical dialogism has the potential to overturn the binaristic relations of hegemonic boundary maintenance by multiplying critical dialogues *within* particular communities and *between* the various constituencies that make up the 'imagined community' of the nation."[14]

I have refashioned Anderson's notion of imagined communities to include "image(d) communities" by examining the way that the circulation of print media within the Chicano movement was crucial to the formation of political community. Photos, images, art, photo journalism and collage produced the larger imagined community that linked activists together through the circulation of print media within the Chicano movement. The visual culture within these media often imaged a mode of self-representation and echoed struggles that were occurring within organizations and movement culture. The reason the notion of "image(d) communities" is useful is because the production of visual images and the project of imaging new political agencies for Chicana through the circulation of these new symbols articulates a political practice and collective conversation of reimagining historical subjectivity across temporal and spatial borders. The distribution, production, and circulation of these print texts in the forms of political pamphlets and newspapers were critical to the formation of a Chicano historical consciousness and the images that traveled embedded within this vibrant print culture was also key to creating image(d) communities which enlisted new political subjects into Chicana subjectivity. Furthermore, the circulation of image was a powerful constitutive practice in forming Chicana counterpublics whereby members of this alternative discursive space produced and were interpellated by an alternative subjective registers of Chicana feminisms.[15]

I examine the production of this Chicana feminist iconography by tracing a larger visual culture that unfolds from the work the Hijas de Cuauhtémoc—from the circulation of visual images in print cultures, to forging new image(d) communities through wider networks of conversation, collaboration, and distribution, to the production of a "Chicana Feminist Slide Show" that Anna NietoGomez developed as part of her Chicana Studies curriculum, to finally, the transformation of photographic images compiled by Anna NietoGomez into moving images for Sylvia Morales's 1976 film, *La Chicana*. Emphasizing the image(d) community of Chicana feminists that were constituted through the circulation of images in print media, I explore the historical specificity of Chicano Nationalism and the kind of historical narratives and narrative images it employed.

Negotiating Icons: Mapping Chicana
Historical Imaginaries in/through
Nationalist Terrains

> *A nation is not only a political entity but something which produces meanings—a system of cultural representation. People are not only legal citizens of a nation; they participate in the idea of the nation as represented in its national culture.*[16]
>
> —Stuart Hall

Chicano cultural nationalism was forged through the recuperation or rediscovery of a historical legacy suppressed by colonization. More than the act of reclamation, it was the production of a Chicano identity. If we understand how the formation of a Chicano identity was crafted through narratives of working-class labor history, migration, and resistance to colonization, then it is vital for us to also understand that identities are not fixed in the past and merely recovered through historical memory. Rather, political identities are constructed through the narratives of the past and *produced* through the positioning of the subject in relationship to those narratives. Stuart Hall's critical intervention reminds us:

> Far from being grounded in a mere "recovery" of the past, which is waiting to be found, and which, when found, will secure our sense of ourselves into eternity, identities are the names we give to the different ways we are positioned by, and position ourselves within, the narratives of the past.[17]

An examination of the historical narratives the Chicano movement marshaled to produce new political identities and create new narratives of resistance helps us to understand how Chicana subjectivities were constructed through and positioned by narratives of the past and how specifically, the figure of the Soldadera was a significant site through which the meaning of women's political participation was articulated, contested, and negotiated. While recuperating histories suppressed by colonial institutions and epistemologies has been a critical impulse in decolonizing movements, what mapping historical imaginaries that facilitate the emergence of new Chicana political subjectivities requires us to consider is that narratives of the past are also gendered and imbued with silences and power differentials.

An understanding of how gendered and sexual power function within these narratives is what Chicana feminist historian Emma Pérez calls "sexing the decolonial imaginary."[18]

If we study how the figure of the Soldadera was recuperated by the Hijas de Cuauhtémoc to forge a space for dialogue around women's issues within the Chicano movement, then we can see how they helped to change the gendered political modes of movement organizing and resignify the narratives of nationalism. By questioning and reimagining historical narratives, they contested the way they were positioned by the nationalist narratives ultimately disrupting the gendered project of Chicano nationalism that articulated the subject-citizen of Aztlán as male. The original Hijas de Cuauhtémoc was a feminist club comprised of largely middle-class women who marched in protest against the Porfirio Diaz dictatorship in Mexico City at the beginning of the Revolution (September 11, 1910). They got 1,000 Mexican women to sign a petition asking for Diaz' resignation which finally caused his wife to advise his withdrawal. They continued organizing and a suffragist sentiment solidified early in the Revolution and in May, 1911 when several 100 women signed a letter to interim President de la Barra which requested votes for women by pointing out that the 1857 Constitution did not bar them from voting since it made no mention of the sex of the voters. Declaring it to be time that Mexican women recognized that their "rights and obligations go much farther than just the home," a manifesto of the Cuauhtémoc feminist league called for political enfranchisement and the full emancipation of Mexican women in the "economic, physical, intellectual and moral struggles."[19] In addition to women's suffrage, another group by the same name advocated for women's right to education and were pivotal actors in the cause of the Flores Magon brothers whom they assisted by publishing propaganda in the form of newspapers, trafficking arms and supplies, and safehousing political dissidents. The Hijas de Cuauhtémoc of the 1910s were part of women's active role in the revolution and as a movement for women's emancipation gained force in Mexico, revolutionary leaders began to support this cause for women's rights.

This information gave the Hijas de Cuauhtémoc of the 1960s and 1970s a sense of legitimacy as women political agents within the Nationalist Movement. It authorized them to organize around the immediate survival of Chicanas on campus and to work on a feminist political project by showing that it was indeed part of a nationalist tradition. By moving from the mythic terrain of Aztlán into a political historical consciousness, the Hijas were able to disrupt the nationalist meaning of "Chicana." George Lipsitz argues that,

> myth and folklore are not enough. It is the oppressions of history—of gender, of race, and of class—that make aggrieved populations suspicious of dominant narratives [of history] . . . Storytelling that leaves history to the oppressor, that imagines a world of desire detached from the world of necessity, cannot challenge the hegemony of dominant discourse. But story-telling that . . . employs the insights and passions of myth and folklore in the service of revising history, can be a powerful tool of contestation.[20]

Lipsitz then suggests another mode of remembrance, that of counter-memory, which names the practice the Hijas de Cuauhtémoc utilized in looking to the past for submerged histories excluded from dominant historical narratives. By crafting an identity through the Mexican Revolution and women's participation, they struggled over the meaning of Chicano Nationalism and gendered politics. Countermemory, unlike myth, does not detach itself from a larger historical context. As Lipsitz defines it, "counter-memory forces revision of existing histories by supplying new perspectives about the past. Countermemory focuses on localized experiences with oppression, using them to reframe and refocus dominant narratives purporting to represent universal experience."[21]

The Hijas de Cuauhtémoc found historical and political agency by reclaiming submerged histories of women's revolutionary participation and this discovery helped them to develop a sense of countermemory. One of the most significant interventions the Hijas de Cuauhtémoc made was that they shifted the historical imaginary and site of political agency away from the mythic terrain of Aztlán to the revolutionary participation of women in the Mexican Revolution. By crafting an identity through this alternative sense of women's role in movement politics, they complicated static meanings of gender within Chicano Nationalism thereby multiplying the forms of gendered subjectivity available to activist women. Their reclamation of earlier feminists and women political leaders was a way to constitute a historical tradition, gain political legitimacy within Chicano Nationalism and most importantly, create a new historical imaginary which authorized an autonomous female political agency. By basing their agency on the historical traditions of Mexican "feminist foremothers," Chicanas contested how cultural icons—la Malinche, la Virgen, la Adelita—circulating in the Chicano movement functioned as conservative proscriptions for women's behavior that enforced dominant patriarchal gender ideology.

Taking on the name of the Hijas de Cuauhtémoc helped this group of Chicanas align themselves historically and politically with a decolonial imaginary. It located them within a genealogy of resistance by invoking Cuauhtémoc, the last Aztec emperor who defied colonization and refused to cede power to the Spanish colonizers. The act of taking on the name of Hijas de Cuauhtémoc had the effect of subverting the silencing mechanism or Malinche complex deployed by Chicano nationalists who felt that a women's agenda in the movement was divisive. By locating themselves within an untold feminist history of the Mexican Revolution, they shifted the mode of gendered representation and the political possibilities for women in the movement. As much a struggle over politics, creating new spaces and gendered possibilities for women in the movement involved a struggle over representation and the meaning of historical narratives. As Stuart Hall reminds us, those narratives themselves do not merely reflect political identities, they also produce them. Stuart Hall argues that

> . . . it is only within the discursive, and subject to its specific conditions, limits and modalities, do they have or can they be constructed within meaning . . ., how things are represented and the "machineries" and regimes of representation in a culture do play a *constitutive*, and not merely a reflexive, after-the-event role. This gives questions of culture and ideology, and the scenarios of representation—subjectivity, identity, politics—a formative, not merely an expressive, place in the constitution of social and political life.[22]

The Hijas de Cuauhtémoc of the 1960s worked to disrupt the confining discursive formations of gender within nationalism because they had to, first, constitute the space within this context of meaning to mount their political challenges to the sexism of the Chicano Student Movement and, second, mobilize an historical imaginary to confront the multiple oppressions and forms of discrimination they faced in the dominant society. They did this by constituting a political subjectivity that lay within the frame of reference of nationalism while at the same time shifting, and sometimes subverting, that meaning.

Transfigurative Liberation of the Icons

Published in 1971, the *Hijas de Cuauhtémoc* newspaper addressed Mexican women in historical perspective and focused on the transfiguration and reclamation of la Soldadera and la Adelita figures of the Mexican Revolution.[23] It included an article on women's history in Mexico as a liberatory move and historical validation for their own political activism. Student activist and member of the Hijas de Cuauhtémoc, Marta López, wrote about "La Mexicana," and women in the Mexican Revolution. Her story elucidates the rich historical consciousness and connections this group used to forge both a national imaginary of raza women and a tradition which authorized a space for themselves vis-à-vis their detractors who claimed that women's autonomous organizing was anti-Raza/Chicano. As a young woman, Marta Lopez writes the following of the Mexican feminists at the turn of the century:

> In the Revolution the strength of the Mexicana was seen by all. With these experiences and an evolving political background she was able to organize herself into lasting women's groups . . . Organizations working directly with the community worked hand in hand with those involved in women's legal rights. One of the outstanding political organizations was Hijas de Cuautémoc. It is after them that we have named our paper.[24]

Previously La Soldadera was portrayed as a loyal camp follower or as a woman who "stands by her man" to provide comfort to the revolutionary hero. She was construed as a foot soldier of the movement who would follow the nationalist line on the ground level. The resignification of the image of the Soldadera through historical narratives was part of the production of a gendered revolutionary historical agency and part of a larger discursive struggle. The newspaper began to craft new genealogies of revolutionary women who were worked for women's liberation within the framework of the larger revolution.[25]

Imaged Communities: Mapping the Gendered Political Scripts of the Chicano Movement through a Political Iconography

What I want to do now is to map a visual cultural history of the production of the Nueva Chicana of the 1960s and 1970s through a politicized iconography and circulation of these images in the Chicano Movement print culture. The production of a politicized historical subjectivity of what was termed in the movement as the Nueva Chicana was created, in part, through the images circulated in newspapers, political pamphlets, photos, and film media. I focus on this visual cultural history and these modes of representation because images are ideological and political and were important coordinates within the struggle for gender equality in the Chicano movement.

The 1967 Chicano historical epic, *Yo Soy Joaquín*, written by Rodolfo "Corky" Gonzales, founder of the Civil Rights organization Crusade for Justice in Denver, Colorado was widely read, circulated, and performed at rallies and by teatro groups as the self-proclaimed, "epic of the Mexican American people."[26] Rather than focus on an analysis of the written text itself which other Chicano scholars have done,[27] I examine the way gender was deployed in the visual images that accompany this popular text as an example of Chicano nationalist iconography. I use this text as a series of establishing shots to illustrate the way the iconography of nationalism operated within this time period. I discuss the print images of *Yo Soy Joaquín* because it circulated widely in movement print culture by mass photocopying and popular distribution and was extremely popular among activists because it articulated in poetic form, the emerging ideology of Chicano cultural nationalism. The introduction to the 1972 edition speaks to this broad circulation:

> Since 1967, the Crusade for Justice has published in mimeographed, photocopied, and printed editions, over 100,000 copies which have been given away or sold . . . *I am Joaquín* has been reproduced by numerous Chicano Press newspapers, which print 10,000 to 20,000 copy editions . . . it has been copied and reproduced by student groups, farm workers organizations, teachers, barrio groups, professionals and workers (all sectors of Aztlán).

Through the print circulation of images in *Yo Soy Joaquín*, I analyze some of the more dominant visual tropes that both produce and maintain the relations of gender in Chicano movement political culture and organizational life. My rendering examines both the formal and ideological aspects of these images as well as considers the way in which they were used as a pedagogy of nationalism. I am interested in the visual processes by which the iconography of nationalism is gendered. Again, this reinforces the idea that these visual tropes are not just "representations" of what already exists within Chicano culture but rather, political and cultural practices which play a constitutive role in the domain of culture.

The images in *Yo Soy Joaquín* depict how revolutionary male prototypes were constituted and circulated in the movement. These visual images were recoded over and over until these visual tropes of the worker, pachuco/cholo/street warrior, Brown Beret, farm worker became archetypes of Chicano nationalism visually encoding the political subjectivity of the movement as male. Other visual tropes of the revolutionary male hero and the familia as allegory for the movement established the dominant mode of address and representational strategy of the Chicano movement. The images, photographic slides, and illustrative drawings depict the creation of movement archetypes through icons of the pachuco, the stoic worker or romanticized revolutionary, which came to constitute a field of subject position where la Raza (the people), the "heroes" of the people, and the national subject were viewed as male. This visual field marginalized women's political subjectivity to that of the suffering witnesses to historic oppression, the bearers of pain and cultural survival, revolutionary mothers or supporters/helpmates to revolutionary male leaders. Rosa Linda Fregoso argues these images posit

> . . . a "collective" cultural identity that is singularly male-centered. Multiple identities are subsumed into a collectivity whose narrative voice is enacted in this historical male subject, Joaquín. The males who inform Chicano cultural identity have names (Cuauhtémoc, Moctezuma, Juan Diego, and so on), but the females are nameless abstractions. Indeed, as opposed to appearing as historical subjects, women are positioned as the metaphors for the emotive side of Chicano Collective cultural identity, as "faithful" wives or "suffering" Mexican mothers.[28]

Nationalist iconography images the subject-citizen of the nation (Aztlán) as male. The cover of Yo Soy Joaquín illustrates the reclamation of subaltern masculinities—pachucos, cholos, homeboys—working-class young men as the privileged site of political subjectivity. The book features images of Brown Berets from what I call the Che Guevara Low Shot because low shots valorize the young militant man as revolutionary subject/hero. It shows the masculinized pride of la Raza (and its resonance, borrowing, and transforming of Black Panther and Young Lord images of resistance). As the coinciding poem states, having nothing more than our "bold with machismo" stance and courage in the face of oppression. Another photo depicts the family as the structuring metaphor for la Raza and for the movement as a whole. Visually, the man is centered and the photograph's formal and gendered composition elucidates the hierarchy of power. Several other images depict the family as la Raza or el movimiento as a prevalent visual trope that helped to produce expectations about leadership and power within the movement. The man in the image (Chávez) leads his people, the women, visually, follow. Another image combines both visual tropes by depicting "revolutionary hero" as the patriarchal head of family.

The text is full of representations of individual men who represent the subjects of la causa creating the visual tropes of the citizen/subjects of Aztlán as the stoic worker, protestor, or revolutionary hero. Visually they are idealized through low shots and lighting to elucidate the humbleness of the people (who are men) and the righteousness of their struggle. The way the retelling of the epic past is staged in the text functions to establish male lineage and revolutionary legacy within the Chicano movement through masculinist notions of historical subjectivity. One photo illustrates the reclamation of Indigenous roots within the framework of the nation and a national project of Mexico that has flattened out racial/ethnic difference. These roots are inscribed on the bodies of the man sitting below a portrait of Benito Juárez. The framing device of Juárez delineates male lineage and ancestral struggle. The images of women in Yo Soy Joaquín are based on visual tropes that echo many of the ideological sentiments forwarded by the movement. Women are represented as Martyrs, Virgins, or Mothers. They are not political subjects; not inscribed as subject-citizens of Aztlán. Women are literally (and visually martyred as) the bearers of the pain of injustice. Visually women are configured as mothers of the people (as the text gives voice to the women, "I shed tears of anguish as I see my children" depicting idealized motherhood instead of what women in the movement really did—i.e., engaged in union organizing or demanded child care).

Beyond the Revolutionary (m)Other

Perhaps the most enduring images within the symbolic economy of nationalism is an image I call the Revolutionary (m)Other. This image represents the way in which women are figured as part of the revolution, but only in reproductive ways. Their role is defined by reproducing the nation and fighting on behalf of their sons. The Revolutionary (m)Other images in Yo Soy Joaquín are accompanied by the text: "I must fight and win this struggle for my sons." The image of the Revolutionary (m)Other is common in national liberation struggles that seek to locate women's revolutionary agency within motherhood. To figure women and their participation into the revolutionary process women were represented not just as mothers of the nation as standard fare but mothers of new nation bearing arms of revolutionary struggle. The image of the revolutionary (m)Other in the Cuban and Nicaraguan cases depict a woman with a machine gun over one shoulder as she cradles and nurses a baby at her breast such as those featured on AMNLAE posters in Nicaragua or on billboards in Cuba; they protect the revolution while they bear the new nation. The image of Revolutionary (m)Others epitomizes the way women's bodies stand in for the nation metaphorically and reveal the contradictions and compliticies between colonialism and nationalism's deployment of women's bodies in the (post)colonial project.[29]

I want to now turn my gaze to the ways Chicanas represented themselves and how Chicana feminists refigured themselves through the circulation and production of their own images. The role of self-representation can not be underestimated. For even when Chicanas did not actually produce or take the photographs, the way they chose to utilize them, figure them in their publications, circulate them within their existing print communities and negotiate the terms on which they would constitute an image(d) community tell a lot about the development of both Chicana cultural practice and subject formation.[30]

One of the most revealing visual patterns in the *Hijas de Cuauhtémoc* newspaper is that more than just the historic photos and drawings contributed by students, the photos taken at conferences and events are displayed in collage format, thereby creating a collective Chicana subject of resistance rather than individual icons. Within Chicana newspapers the photojournalism selected and displayed illustrate that women represented themselves differently. They put themselves into the narrative of revolution but instead of using singular low shot images, they used the effect of photo collage to create a sense of sisterhood and collaboration, creating visually the forms of female and feminist solidarity that they sought to create in their political work. The different use of visuality and images of revolutionary participation created a different mode of address within Chicano movement visual culture which enlisted or hailed women into the project of liberation on their own terms. This new iconography encouraged women's participation, created new forms of political subjectivity based on an historical consciousness of women's participation in the Mexican Revolution and through other visual techniques like collage, posited a female sense of solidarity and collectivity.

Political Icons and Political Subjectivity

What I propose is that we see iconography as a site of struggle over the terms in which women participated in the Chicano movement and were included within its discourses. Instead of just reclaiming women's participation in the movement and illustrating female icons, I want to complicate our understanding of the cultural work of political iconography and read the struggle around these icons as visual negotiations of political subjectivity, forms of political participation, and the way spaces of belonging were articulated. The figure of the Soldadera had many kinds of signifying possibilities and was a site of struggle over the meaning of gender within the movement. Sometimes the image of the Soldadera, especially the Adelita figure, represented the revolutionary sweetheart whose role was to inspire and support their compañeros. This revolutionary sweetheart image circulated in movement culture and more broadly within Chicano popular culture, even airbrushed on customized cars and tattooed on backs and arms.[31] Other images of the Soldadera featured the self-abnegating foot soldiers of the movement who did the reproductive and back room labor of the movement, never questioned their role and upon whose bodies were projected the nationalist project and Chicano pride.

The figure of the Soldadera was also widely reclaimed by women and Chicana feminists to signify women's historic role in revolution and the idea that women's participation, leadership and autonomous agenda was not foreign to the culture, selling out the movement, or being white washed. The Hijas de Cuauhtémoc played a formative role in seeking and producing new forms of knowledge about themselves as Chicanas because they had grown tired of the faded yellow images of Aztec poster princesses that the movement held up to them us mirrors. For example, Anna NietoGomez, along with other Los Angeles-based activists, edited the first journal of Chicana scholarship, *Encuentro Femenil*, which was outgrowth of the Hijas de Cuauhtémoc newspaper. In one of the editors' introduction to the journal, it read:

> In 1969, there was a great eagerness to experience the first Chicano Studies classes. The women were very excited to learn about their heritage both as Chicanos and as mujeres. However, the women were very disappointed to discover that neither Chicano history, Mexican history, nor Chicano literature included any measurable material on the mujer. At best she would be referred to mystically as "la India," the bulwark of the family, or she would be referred to romantically as "la

Adelita," "la Soldadera" of the movement. La mujer either had a baby in her arms or a rifle in her hand or both. But few dealt with the identity of la mujer in the family, or even knew who was "la Adelita." They were merely symbols for her to look towards, and if she was any Chicana at all, the spirit of either model was expected to appear instinctively.[32]

Chicana feminists established discursive and visual spaces in which to negotiate alternative subjectivities by reworking the icons and cultural narratives of the Chicano movement. This tradition "of working simultaneously within and against dominant cultural" within an over-all project of reclamation has been expanded and theorized by cultural critic, Yvonne Yarbro-Bejarano, in her study of the representational strategies deployed by Chicana lesbians.[33] In theorizing of the "cultural specificity of the lesbianization of the heterosexual icons of popular culture," within Latina cultural production, she calls upon what Amalia Mesa Baines calls "the transfigurative liberation of the icon."[34] By refiguring the symbols of nationalist patrimony (cultural legacy), the Hijas de Cuauhtémoc helped to change the hailing mechanism by setting up an alternative feminist apparatus of interpellation of the subject of Aztlán. This politics of disidentification did not reproduce the same national symbols, but engaged in a resignifying practice of reworking a figure such as Cuauhtémoc in order to create or recall a women's "revolutionary legacy." They built a new discourse of Chicana femenismo by busting the sutures of Chicano nationalist discourse and refigured an alternative genealogy of the revolutionary participation by shifting the historical imaginary of the Chicano movement.

   Besides taking on the name of an earlier Mexican feminist organization, the Hijas de Cuauhtémoc newspaper began transforming the figure of the Soldadera reclaiming it through the publication of archival photos and reappropriating nationalist iconography. One way the Hijas de Cuauhtémoc reworked nationalist imagery was on the cover page of one of their newspaper editions which features a drawing of a woman liberating herself from a net that represents oppression. There is the figure of the eagle that overshadows the woman as she uses her machete to cut herself free. The meaning of the image is ambiguous as it is unclear if she is fighting for the nation or liberating herself from the fetters of the nation. Beyond photos of la Soldadera of the Mexican Revolution, other images also positioned women as participants in the revolution. One photo in particular looks over the shoulder of a Chicana Activist while she reads a newspaper with a huge masthead declaring "Mujer Como Revolucionaria."

This image accompanies the manifestos and position papers produced at the Los Angeles Chicana Regional Conference, which was a regional preparatory conference for the first-ever-national Chicana conference in Houston in 1971. These images change the dominant tropes within the pedagogy of the nationalism to suggest that this revolucionaria has her own sense of political agency and is not a naturalized male subject of the movement but is gaining knowledge about herself as a political subject.

Several of the images within women's newspapers also dialogically rework and engender some of the visual tropes that establish male revolutionary patrimony in the Chicano movement. In another report back from the Chicana Regional Conference, there is a second image that references how women (re)imaged themselves into the legacy of struggle. This shot uses a framing device similar to that referencing the historical legacy of Benito Juárez photo mentioned earlier. Yet, this image begins to disrupt the male lineage of nationalist patrimony; it depicts a Chicana Brown Beret as the revolutionary descendent of Che Guevara, as she sits below his larger-than life photo. Other images of women that were dialogically engaged and resignified other popularized images of women's passivity. Specifically the image of the Martyr was invoked by women wearing rebozos on their heads but the women are (re)presented in an active position on the verge of action—often appearing as if they carried arms or some weapon of resistance under their rebozos.

These images map the migration from suffering, submission, or passivity to active subjects of history and politics. These images signal the emergence of the iconography of la Nueva Chicana and were common figures in the visual and discursive struggle Chicana Feminists engaged within the imaged community of the nation. They created new images, reworked older more traditional representations and used innovative designs to create a new subjectivity. The mode of photo layout and collage—almost like a family album—in the movement newspapers, are illustrative of how Chicanas image themselves collectively. The sequence of images shows the historic development of an iconography of the New Chicana and traces the ways in which women's agency and political subjectivities were constituted in a new imaged(d) community of Chicana feminists.

Both the political and the cultural work done by the Hijas de Cuauhtémoc created a crisis within the signifying systems of nationalism to break the sign function of various figures of woman thereby creating disorder in the symbolic order of Nationalism. This double act of disarticulation and resignification occurred around particular signifiers of woman deployed by Chicano nationalist discourse. Instead of performing the typecast roles for Chicanas, they retrofitted them to change the gendered hailing mechanism (or the way women were called into) the project of liberation. In addition to the early resignification of the Adelita figure by the Hijas de Cuauhtémoc, Chicana feminists have had a long-standing cultural project of reworking Malinche.[35] Artists like Yolanda Lopez, Ester Hernandez and more recently, Alma Lopez, all rework the signifying possibilities for la Virgen de Guadalupe around women's agency, resistance and sexuality. Chicana lesbian feminist artists have been especially active in creating new signifying possibilities for female icons, expanding the range of meanings to include even resignifying the figure of the Virgen as a matrix of power and desire or the vulva. This form of cultural work is a form of retrofitted memory because it changes the relationship Chicanas have as historical subjects to the sexed and gendered narratives of the past. In an important essay, Laura Pérez explores these early and continuing acts of resignification that articulated a kind of feminism within nationalism, but they were the roots of a political movement that eventually moved between nationalist imaginaries and then beyond them.[36] This cultural work has revealed and disrupted the virgin/whore dichotomy and engendered the very symbols of national liberation. Articulating new modes of representation within movement iconography, political discourse, and historical memory played a constitutive role in engendering a space for Chicanas in the movement opening the way for new political possibilities.

The Iconography of the Nueva Chicana reworks the gendered nationalist constructions of the Adelita and Revolucionaria movement figures, forges an image(d) community of Chicana feminist counterpublics by representing themselves in collectivity, and deploys different frames of reference and modes of address in its visual strategies. By tracing the development of Nueva Chicana iconographic practices, we can see how the images of the movement Martyr, the mother and revolutionary (m)Other, the Soldadera, and Revolucionaria are alternatively imaged in ways that shift the nationalist representational regime. These images serve to multiply the possible subject positions and options for women in the movement. This essay has begun to map the historic development of the image(d) community of the Nueva Chicana, which served to forge new social and political spaces. Chicano art critic, Tomás Ybarra-Frausto's discusses the transformative role of new cultural productions and their circulation in public cultures which he argues opens up new social spaces and oppositional publics.[37]

Conclusion: Continued Movement, Resurfacing Icons, and the Politics of Re-Membering and Forgetting

The photo of the woman bearing bandoleras discussed in this essay continues to circulate, not just in Chicana/o Studies, but within popular culture, music culture, and political culture. But what happens in the circulation and migration of this image? Because movement histories are sites of contemporary identity construction and maintenance, we must be attentive to how modes of remembrance are structured by gender, sexuality, and relations of power in ways that are bound by the historical conjunctures that produce them. In Chicano movement histories, the organizers and organizations that articulated Chicana political subject positions have been erased or relegated to the margins of the cosmology of masculinity—the mode of gender through which Chicano liberation was initially articulated. Although this was immediately challenged, these challenges and the feminist history of Chicana struggles with the movement have been excluded. Because the "Movement" is constructed as a monolithic and unitary narrative of origins where the often-bitter struggles of gender and sexuality are forgotten, when it is invoked in an act of remembrance these same structures of gender are reenacted.

When these images circulate in popular culture, they often come to stand in for the movement themselves and in this instance, the erasure of women in the movement. They are images that evoke powerful narratives that have traveled through time and they testify to the pull and power of Chicano nationalism. Yet, often they erase the mass participation of women in radical movements of the 1960s and the 1970s as well as the simultaneous struggles around gender and sexuality that women engaged in while in those movements. Activist, scholar, and historian Angela Y. Davis has written a critical reflection of the ways in which her own image is associated with a kind of a kind of Black nationalism that she herself contested. "What I am trying to suggest is that contemporary representations of nationalism in African-American and diasporic popular culture are far too frequently reifications of a very complex and contradictory project that had emancipatory moment leading beyond itself." Suggesting that we

explore the "suppressed moments of the history of sixties nationalisms,"[38] Davis calls upon the still revolutionary potential of the
images, icons, and narratives of the 1960s and the 1970s as they circulate in popular culture when they accurately portray the complexity
of those political traditions and legacies. "Young people with 'nationalist' proclivities ought, at least, have the opportunity to choose which
tradition of nationalism they will embrace. How will they position
themselves en masse in defense of women's rights and in defense of gay
rights if they are not aware of the historical precedents for such posi-
tionings?"[39] In recovering the suppressed feminist history of the
Chicano movement, the visual terrain is a critical aspect of understanding the role, political work, and the legacy of Chicanas in the
movement. The visual terrain is critical because if history is only
knowable through representation, we can also study representation as
a site of historicity and a place in which historical subjectivities were
imaged and imagined.

Notes

1. Amalia Mesa-Baines, "El Mundo Femenino: Chicana Artists of the
Movement—A Commentary on Development and Production," in *Chicano
Art: Resistance and Affirmation* (Los Angeles: Wright Art Gallery, UCLA,
1991), 131–140.
2. See also, the important essay by Laura Elisa Pérez that examines feminist representational practices and Chicano Nationalism: "*El desorden*, Nationalism, and
Chicana/o Aesthetics," in *Between Woman and National: Nationalisms,
Transnational Feminisms and the State*, edited by Caren Kaplan, Norma Alarcón,
and Minoo Moallem (Berkeley, CA: Third Woman Press, 1999), 19–46.
3. In this photo, there is a man in the background of the photo who seems like he is
attempting to talk with the woman. She looks like she is at a political rally; listening to a speaker perhaps. Is the young man propositioning the young woman?
In most circulations of this photo, the background has been cropped out. Just as
in most movement histories, narratives, and even within the circulation of movement icons, the background of the lived working and organizing conditions of
women in the movement, or even their stories, have been cropped out.
4. Ibid., 7.
5. See Armando B. Rendon, *Chicano Manifesto* (New York: Macmillan Company,
1971); *Alfredo Mirandé, Hobres y machos: Masculinity and Latino Culture*
(Boulder, CO: Westview Press, 1997).
6. See *Chicano Power! Latin Rock in the USA, 1968–1976: 2* CD Set & 40 Page
Booklet. Soul Jazz Records CD 39, Released 1999. For contemporary examples
of how this image is being circulated in political art on T-shirts and stickers, see
the politically conscious social justice art of Faviana Rodriquez at
<www.faviana.com/port_other/other1.php> (site visited on May 15, 2004).

7. Under the direction of Chicana activist and theorist Anna NietoGomez, the Hijas de Cuauhtémoc negotiated both the Chicano cultural nationalism of the 1960 and the 1970s and the overlaying simultaneous locations of gender, class race, and sexuality by creating a Chicana feminist counterpublic through gendered print culture, campus and community political organizing, cross-regional Chicana feminist dialogue, and by reworking and engendering the political icons of Chicano nationalism. They began organizing in 1968 and began publishing their newspaper in 1971.

8. I first presented these findings on movement visual culture in 1996 at the NACCS conference in a paper entitled, "Mapping the Iconography of La Nueva Chicana in and through Nationalist Terrains." I explored how Chicanas reclaimed an earlier tradition of Mexican feminism at the turn of the twentieth century, specifically by reclaiming narratives and images of female participants in the Mexican revolution.

9. For Vicki Ruiz's rich discussion, see "La Nueva Chicana: Women and the Movement," in *From Out of the Shadows: Mexican Women in Twentieth-Century America* (New York: Oxford University Press, 1998), 111–112 specifically discuss the figure of la Soldadera.

10. See Kaye Brigal, "Our Culture Hell", unpublished movement manuscript.

11. Benedict Anderson, *Imagined Communities: Reflections on the Origin and Spread of Nationalism*, Revised edition (London: Verso, 1991).

12. For example, see Chandra Mohanty's use of Anderson's "imagined communities" in her Introduction to *Third World Politics and the Politics of Feminism*, ed Chandra Talpade Mohanty, Ann Russo, and Lourdes Torres (Bloomington: Indiana University Press, 1991).

13. Partha Chatterjee, *The Nation and Its Fragments. Colonial and Postcolonial Histories.* (Princeton, NJ: Princeton University Press, 1993), 7.

14. Kobena Mercer, *Welcome to the Jungle: New Positions in Black Cultural Studies.* (London: Routledge, 1994), 64–65 (italics in the original).

15. Chicana film scholar, Rosa Linda Fregoso, discusses the imaginative possibility of film stating that "the Chicano nation [is] captured in these films represents an 'imagined community.' Far from fabricating or inventing a community, Chicana and Chicanos have reinvented (imagined anew) a 'community' of Chicanos and Chicanas." *The Bronze Screen: Chicana and Chicano Film Culture*. Minneapolis: University of Minnesota Press, 1993, xxiii. For a different rendering of the ways in which alternative discursive formations cause a crisis the system of signification and mode of address of a national culture, see Homi K. Bhabha, "DissemiNation: time, narrative, and the margins of the modern nation," in *Nation and Narration* (New York: Routledge, 1990), 297.

16. Stuart Hall, "The Question of Cultural Identity," in *Modernity and Its Futures*, edited by S. Hall, D. Held, and T. McGrew (Cambridge: Polity Press), 274–316.

17. Ibid.

18. See her groundbreaking work by the same title. Emma Pérez, *Sexing the Decolonial Imaginary: Writing Chicanas into History* (Bloomington, Indiana: Indiana University Press), 1999.

19. Quoted in Fredrick Turder, *The Dynamic of Mexican Nationalism* (Chapel Hill: University of North Carolina Press, 1968), 193.

20. George Lipsitz, *Time Passages: Collective Memory and American Popular Culture* (Minneapolis: University of Minnesota Press, 1990), 213.

21. Ibid., 213.

22. Ibid., 27.

23. See, Norma Cantú's, "Women, Then and Now: An Analysis of the Adelita Image versus the Chicana as Political Writer and Philosopher," in *Chicana Voices*, edited by Teresa Córdova et al. (Austin: Center for Mexican American Studies (CMAS), University of Texas), 8–10. Also, several Chicana and Mexicana scholars have done in-depth research on the role of women in the Mexican Revolution. See Elizabeth Salsas (UT Press, 1990) and Ana Lau (Planeta, 1987).

24. Marta Lopez, "La Mexicana," *Hijas de Cuauhtémoc*, n.d. First Issue (early 1971).

25. See Vicki Ruiz, *Out of the Shadows: Mexican Women in Twentieth Century America* (New York: Oxford University Press, 1998), Chapter five for a larger discussion of the soldadera contextualized within the movement.

26. Gonzales, *I am Joaquín/Yo Soy Joaquín: An Epic Poem* (with a chronology of people and events in Mexican and Mexican American history) (New York: Bantam Books, 1972).

27. For a discussion of the ways in which *Yo Soy Joaquín* functioned in the Chicano Movement as a narrative of racial unity, see Angie Chabram Dernersesian's " 'Chicana! Rican? No, Chicana-Riqueña!' Refashioning the Transnational Connection," in *Multiculturalism: A Critical Reader*, edited by David Theo Goldberg (Cambridge: Basil Blackwell Ltd., 1994), 269–295; and for a Chicano literary history of this text see, Rafael Pérez-Torres, *Movements in Chicano Poetry: Against Myths, Against Margins* (Cambridge: The Cambridge University Press, 1995).

28. Fregoso, *The Bronze Screen*, 6.

29. See, Anne McClintock, Aamir Mufti, and Ella Shohat, eds., *Dangerous Liaisons: Gender, Nation, and Postcolonial Perspectives* (Minneapolis: University of Minnesota Press), 1997.

30. Print Culture and its visual images were often the basis of early Chicano film. *Yo Soy Joaquín* was made into a film directed by Luis Valdez in 1969 and Anna NietoGomez's "Chicana Feminist Sideshow" was the basis for the 1976 film *La Chicana*, directed by Sylvia Morales who was assisted by another Hijas de Cuauhtémoc member, Cindy Honesto. Rosa Linda Fregoso has developed an incisive comparative rendering of these two films in her book, *Bronze Screen: Chicana and Chicano Film Culture*.

31. The most common of this genre of image is a drawing of a woman on one knee, holding a rifle, her abundant chest crossed with bandoleras. This image is highly sexualized as the center of the image is the visibility of her erect nipples, her hair is tossed, and her mouth and lips are posed seductively in an half opened position.

32. "Introduction," *Encuentro Femenil*, 1(2), 1974: 4.

33. Yvonne Yarbro-Bejarano, "The Lesbian Body in Latin Cultural Production," in ¿Entiendes? Queer Readings, Hispanic Writings, edited by Emilie L. Bergmann and Paul Jullian Smith (London: Duke University Press, 1995), 182.
34. Amalia Mesa-Baines, "El Mundo Femenino: Chicana Artists of the Movement—A Commentary on Development and Production," in Chicano Art: Resistance and Affirmation (Los Angeles: Wright Art Gallery, UCLA, 1991), 131–140.
35. See Adelaida R. del Castillo, "Malintzin Tenepal: A Preliminary Look into a New Perspective," in Essays on La Mujer, edited by Rosaura Sánchez and Rosa Martiníz Cruz (Los Angeles, CA: Chicano Studies Center Publications, University of California, Los Angeles, 1977); Cordelia Candelaria, "La Malinche, Feminist Prototype," Frontiers, 5(2), 1980: 1–6; Norma Alarcón, "Traddutora, Traditora: A Paradigmatic Figure of Chicana Feminism." Cultural Critique, 13, Fall 1989: 57–87.
36. Laura Elisa Pérez, "El desorden, Nationalism, and Chicana/o Aesthetics," in Between Woman and National: Nationalisms, Transnational Feminisms and the State, edited by Caren Kaplan, Norma Alarcón, and Minoo Moallem (Berkeley, CA: Third Woman Press, 1999), 19–46.
37. Tómas Ybarra-Frausto, "Interview with Tómas Ybarra-Frausto: The Chicano Movement in a Multicultural/Multinational Society," in On Edge: The Crisis of Contemporary Latin American Culture, edited by George Yúdice, Jean Franco, and Juan Flores (Minneapolis: University of Minnesota Press, 1992), 207–216.
38. According to Angela Y. Davis in her essay, "Black Nationalism: The Sixties and the Nineties," in Black Popular Culture, edited by Gina Dent (Seattle, WA: Bay Press, 1992), 317–324, key among these is Huey Newton's urging an end of verbal gay bashing and an examination of Black male sexuality after Jean Genet's sojourn with the BPP.
39. Ibid.

10

Aztec Princess Still at Large

Catrióna Rueda Esquibel

Representations of Native women in the United States and Mexico are largely limited to the mythologies of the Indian Princess.[1] In history and popular culture of the United States and Mexico, she is Pocahontas or La Malinche.[2] In everyday encounters she's more like the figure in the poem by Diane Burns (Anishinabe/Chemehuevi), "Sure You Can Ask Me a Personal Question":

> Your great grandmother, huh?
> An Indian Princess, huh?
> Hair down to there?
> Let me guess. Cherokee?

As Peter Hulme argues, "The major feature of this myth is the ideal of cultural harmony through romance" (141). In his discussion of the photographs of Robert Mapplethorpe, Kobena Mercer defines stereotype as "a fixed way of seeing that freezes the flux of experience" (174). In my discussion of Robert Buitrón's photograph *Ixta Ponders Leverage Buyout* (figure 10.1), I discuss this freezing of experience in relation to a mythic Indian princess, whose image circulates primarily in Mexican and Chicano popular cultures.

Buitrón's photograph immediately engages the viewer with fantasies about Native American women. A dark-haired woman sits at a table in the corporate boardroom, surrounded by mature White males. She wears a dark business suit with a high collar. She is the only one of the nine people in the photograph facing the viewer and her gaze is serious. She wears an enormous feathered headdress, which marks her as Indian.

Figure 10.1   "Ixta Ponders Leverage Buyout," Robert Buitrón, 1989.

As the title of the photograph suggests, Buitrón is not only concerned with Anglo American stereotypes about Indian women, but also with Mexican and Chicano/a fantasies about them. "Ixta Ponders Leverage Buyout" identifies the woman as the legendary Aztec princess Ixtacihuátl. According Mexican legend, Ixta—Ixtacihuátl—was an Aztec princess who fell in love with Popo—Popocatépetl—a low-born warrior from a rival tribe. To win Ixta's hand in marriage, Popo goes off to battle to prove his valor. Ixta receives erroneous reports of his death in battle and kills herself. Popo returns victorious, finds only Ixta's body, and takes her to the mountains where he crouches beside her, burning incense and mourning her eternally. This is a story of the origin of the volcanoes Ixtacihuátl and Popocatépetl, which loom above Mexico City. Like the stories of Pocahontas and La Malinche, this legend owes much of its current form to the nineteenth-century constructions of national identity through a national mythology.

In contemporary Chicano and Mexican cultures, this legend circulates primarily through the calendar paintings of Mexican artist Jesus Helguera, dating from the 1940s and the 1950s. These paintings dramatize scenes from Mexican myth and history: romantic tales of the tragic love of the Aztec Princess Ixtacihuátl and her lover Popocatépetl, of "Amor Indio."³ They form a visual link between modern Mexicanos (and by extension Chicanas/os) and the Aztec heroes of a bygone era.

Helguera often combined Maxfield Parrish sunsets with Indian princesses resembling Mexican actresses Lucha Reyes and Dolores Del Rio, and settings that owe more to Tinseltown than to Tenochtitlan. The paintings feature a muscular and active Aztec warrior carrying or mourning the scantily clad and voluptuous body of an Aztec princess. This image inscribes particular fantasies about essential Mexican identities: the male is cast in the subject position, a virile and potent warrior, while the female is an object of visual pleasure, a voluptuous receptive body.

It is important to note that representations of Ixtacihuátl render her as passive and sexualized. Helguera's series of calendar paintings—including *Amor Indio, Gesto Azteca, Grandeza Azteca, Ixtacihuátl*, and *La Leyenda de los Volcanes*—depict the Indian princess with her eyes closed and her body in various stages of undress. Even when fully clothed, her garments are distinct in their transparency and the emphasis they place on her erect nipples.

Tomás Ybarra-Frausto discusses the Aztec imagery of these calendars in the catalog to the 1986 exhibit *Chicano Expressions: A New View in American Art*. He sees them as a significant source of inspiration for Chicano artists, who "emphasized forms of visual expression functioning as integral elements of the decorative scheme in the home environment" (21). Specifically, Ybarra-Frausto discusses "two pervasive graphic traditions . . . exemplified by the almanaque (calendar) and the estampa religiosa (religious imagery)."

> Traditionally, the annual almanaque is given to favorite customers by local merchants. . . . Although created as advertisements, the almanaques exclude any specific product from the visual representation itself. Rather, the illustrations often feature Mexican genre scenes, interpretations of indigenous myths [such as] the Aztec warrior holding a dead maiden in his arm . . . a pictorial representation of the myth of Ixtacihuátl and Popocatépetl made famous by the Mexican calendar artist Jesús Helguera. These . . . illustrations are often saved and displayed as household icons. (21)

These calendars are available in the United States from restaurants, hair salons, gift shops, "mexicatessens," botanicas, and auto mechanics as well as from Chicana/o art galleries. Not only are the Helguera calendars themselves pervasive, but their themes are also recreated by other artists.[4]

Helguera's calendar paintings continue to circulate widely, so much so that Ixta and Popo have found their way into popular culture, through murals, custom car murals and detailing, T-shirts, ceramics, and black velvet paintings. Chicana and Chicano artists regularly invoke Helguera's imagery in their representations of Chicano/a culture. Why are these images so prevalent? What pleasures are derived from viewing the sleeping or dead body of the Aztec Princess? On the one hand, it may mark a nostalgia for the lost ideal of pre-Columbian culture. Popo mourns his lost love, dead by her own hand before their wedding, and contemporary Chicanos mourn the lost "empire" of the Aztecs. At the same time, the sensual detailing of Ixta's body seems to represent a disavowal of colonial violence. The first part of that disavowal would state, I know very well that Indians died horrible deaths in the colonial institution of New-Spain-which-became-Mexico. Yet, the disavowal continues, I prefer to imagine Indian death as the romantic tale of tragic love, through the visually pleasing image of Ixta's body. The disassociation of Ixta's death from colonial violence is crucial to the success of both the image and the legend. Finally, the death of Ixta is a visual signifier of the constant reinvention of Native Mexicans as extinct: Native Mexicans are represented as always-already dead. As Norma Alarcón has argued, "the historical founding moment of the construction of [national Mexican] mestizo subjectivity entails the rejection and denial of the dark Indian Mother as Indian . . . and to actually deny the Indian position even as that position is visually stylized and represented in the making of the fatherland" ("Chicana Feminism" 374). Thus the construction of the nationalist subject as mestizo—and as the legitimate inheritor of Mexico—rests on this depiction of Aztecs as extinct, and as wholly separate from contemporary indigenous populations and social movements.

Ybarra-Frausto's reference to the calendars as "integral elements of the decorative scheme in the home environment" provides entry into a new theorization of the calendars. According to Victor Burgin,

> Photographs are not seen by deliberate choice, they have no special space or time allotted to them, they are *apparently* (an important qualification) provided free of charge—photographs offer themselves *gratuitously*; whereas paintings and films readily present themselves

to critical attention as objects, photographs are received rather as *environment*. ("Looking at Photographs" 143)

I argue that Helguera's paintings of Ixta and Popo—like photographs— are received as environment, and that this distinction is important to understanding the significance of Buitrón's photograph *Ixta Ponders Leverage Buyout*.

Buitrón is clearly engaging this popular representation of Ixta, the Aztec princess, even as he problematizes it. In the background of the photograph, on the dark walls of the boardroom, hang four formal oil portraits. All of the portraits are of mature White men in business suits. These four paintings, then, make up a series that seems to represent the legacy of Anglo men in the boardroom. There is a fifth picture in the series, one which has no ornate frame: a paper calendar is tacked up, the central image of which is Helguera's, *Gesto Azteca*, which features Popo holding Ixta's body in his arms. Below the painting, the calendar features an advertisement for "La Fortuna" restaurant.

Ixta Ponders Leverage Buyout is part of Buitrón's 1989 photo- graphic series *The Legend of Ixtaccihuatl y Popocatepetal*: twelve photographs compiled in a printed wall calendar. Buitrón deliberately engages Helguera's calendar paintings through narrative photography that combines social commentary with a rasquache aesthetic. Although often interpreted simply as "Mexican kitsch," to be rasquache means, in a sense, to revel in those aspects of working-class Mexican- American culture that are most devalued by the bourgeois aesthetics of American hegemonic culture. Rasquachísmo delights in its own exces- sive hybridity. It is the sombrero embroidered in sequins, it is the low- rider car with air-brushed detailing, it is the purple house, the Chihuahua, and the black velvet painting. Yet Buitrón's photograph does not merely represent the rasquache aesthetic: by incorporating the physical presence of one of Helguera's calendars, it also partici- pates in rasquachísmo by presenting itself as just such a calendar.

The photograph and its title highlights simultaneous stereotypes of Native American women, stereotypes held by both Mexicans/ Chicanos and Anglo Americans. The Mexican/Chicano stereotype is of Ixtacihuátl, the dead maiden in the arms of her warrior lover. The Anglo American stereotype images Native Americans as "caught between two worlds": the old traditional world, symbolized by the feathered headdress and the modern-day world, symbolized by the woman's power suit.

Legacy of the Aztec Princess

We are Ixtacihuatls,

sleeping, snowcapped volcanoes

buried alive in myths

princesses with the name of a warrior

on our lips

                                          —Ana Castillo

An early feminist reading of the legend of Ixta and Popo might contend that it buries Chicanas "beneath the weight of a subject-position meant to be self-sacrificing and reverent" (Rafael Pérez-Torres, 192). Chicana and Chicano artists and writers who take up Ixtacihuátl have often done so primarily in terms of what Kobena Mercer describes as "binary alternatives between positive and negative images" (172): either protesting the objectification of Ixta, or participating in it.

Luis Jiménez is a Chicano artist who repeatedly works with the theme of Ixta and Popo in his Southwest Pieta[5] sculptures. In framing Ixta and Popo as a Pietà, the religious icon of the Virgin Mary mourning with her son's dead body in her arms, Jiménez makes central the image of the warrior Popo holding the dead body of his lover. These sculptures, then, focus on the pathos of the mourning Popo. In his drawing *Mexican Allegory on Wheels* and watercolor *Cholo with Low-Rider Van*, Jiménez depicts the legend of Ixta and Popo on a customized low-rider van driven by a contemporary Chicano/cholo. In both of these works there is a connection between the Chicano driver and the Aztec Popo, brought out by the colors in their clothing and headgear. Ixta is bared to the waist, and her face is obscured by her hair. With their almost exclusive emphasis on the male protagonist, Jiménez's works continue the objectification of Ixta.

On first reading, the excerpt above from Castillo's poem "Ixtacihuátl Died in Vain" appears to discuss Ixtacihuátl strictly as a negative role. Both the title and the speaking subject of the poem create a critical distance from Ixta: the "We" refers to Chicanas, who feel the heavy burden of this myth covering them and freezing them like snow on the mountains. The poem contrasts the speaker with Ixtacihuátl, and the speaker wants more from her life than to become an icon, either sexualized or self-sacrificing. Yet, the poem also describes a more complex ambivalence, similar to the one Mercer claims in his own readings of Mapplethorpe's photographs of Black men: "An ambivalent structure of feeling, in which anger and envy divided the identifications that placed me somewhere always already inside the text" (193).[6]

Like the Chicana narrator of "Ixtacihuátl Died in Vain," the woman in the photograph finds herself "always already inside the text" of the Helguera calendar. Yet, *Ixta Ponders Leverage Buyout* seems to me to constitute a rendering of Ixta and her myth that is radically different from either Castillo or Jiménez, because it changes Ixta's position both within and outside of the frame of the photograph. Popo—with whom the Mexican/Chicano male viewer is usually expected to identify—does not even appear in the main space of the photograph at all. He is not "replaced" by the White men in the boardroom so much as he is displaced by the context of the photograph. The subject of the photograph is Ixta. The photograph renders Ixta, not in relation to Popo, but as a player in a contemporary capitalist enclave. The calendar in the background creates a critical distance for us, the viewers of the photograph, and this distance highlights "the imaginary projection of certain racial and sexual fantasies" (Mercer 173). The men in the boardroom are not looking at Ixta: we are. At the same time, she is meeting our gaze. The gaze of the Aztec princess meets our fantasies head on, but does not submit to them.

What does Buitrón's photograph have to say about the roles available to contemporary Chicanas? The placement of the "La Fortuna" calendar featuring *Gesto Azteca* next to the oil portraits seems to highlight the Chicana's newly arrived status in the boardroom: the formal portraits represent the legacy of the White men; the calendar, unframed and hastily tacked up, suggests that up till now, Ixta's role has been that of the object, not the subject, of the gaze. The other portraits are evenly spaced from one another. The Mexican calendar, however, is placed in the smallest space between the last portrait and a corner of the room: it has been mounted in a space that was never designed to hold it. The incongruity of the calendar raises questions about Ixta herself: does she belong in this boardroom? Was she ever intended to have a place there? What is her role? Will she make her fortune? Will she tell her fortune?

The other participants in the board meeting are looking toward the head of the table; like Ixta, we presume, they ponder leverage buyout. It is unclear, however, just who or what is being bought out. Has Ixta at last become La Malinche, the vendida, the sellout, through her participation in the corporate world? Is she the one with the power, buying out this otherwise White male corporation? Perhaps she is the negotiating representative for a pan-Indian, intergalactic battle force. Is she a positive role model? A negative one?

Another possibility is that the woman in the boardroom is a contemporary Chicana businesswoman, conventionally dressed, but that someone is viewing her as the Aztec princess. This may be the fantasy of the men in the room, or the fantasy of the woman herself. She may be viewed by the White men as an exotic, and thus may embody to them the Aztec princess. She may, like the driver of the low-rider van in Jiménez's work, imagine herself as an ancient Aztec. However, unlike the cholo driver, if she is to imagine herself as a character in an Helguera painting, she must change the terms of the painting. She cannot be both the subject and Ixtacihuátl. Thus she is not the sleeping woman, looked at, but not looking, but rather the woman staring boldly into the camera. By claiming the name or the fantasy of Ixta, the woman changes what it means to be Ixta.

These questions remain unanswered and unanswerable by the photograph, which plays upon the ambivalence of fantasies of Indian women, but refuses narrative resolution. Through Buitrón's deployment of the Mexican calendar of the Aztec Princess, *Ixta Ponders Leverage Buyout* makes these fantasies visible, even as it deploys them to undermine the Anglo male hegemony of the corporate boardroom. While the boardroom may never be the same, neither will Ixta herself. I titled this discussion "Aztec Princess Still At Large" because Buitrón's photograph seems to me to constitute an escape for Ixta. She has stepped down from the "La Fortuna" calendar, changed from a diaphanous robe into a suit, opened her eyes and faced her future head-on. Perhaps she is realizing her own American dream. Perhaps her freedom is just another fantasy. Perhaps she has moved only from one calendar to another, and will move into an infinite series of calendars/fantasies. At any rate, it seems clear that her current role is one she has chosen, and not the snow-capped destiny predetermined by myth.

Ixta Ponders Leverage Buyout is so provocative precisely because it raises questions that it refuses to answer. At the same time, the woman in the photograph challenges the viewer, forcing us to recognize that she is not merely a frozen mythic figure, but her own agent. Again, like the narrator of Burns's poem, the direct look seems to clearly articulate

> This ain't no stoic look.
> This is my face.

Notes

1. Joanne Barker further explores representations of Native American women in her essay on "Beyond Pocahontas," also in this volume.
2. Hulme discusses the myth of Pocahontas as having "its own interest. . . . Strictly speaking it is a product of the early nineteenth-century search for a . . . national heritage" (141). "It is difficult to disentangle the confluence of the literary topos of the 'enamoured princess' from the historical examples, of whom Pocahontas and Malinche are only the best known. Much can be put down to male fantasy . . ." (300 n. 15). While Mexican nationalism in the nineteenth century displaced the "cultural harmony through romance" myth for La Malinche (replacing it with a narrative of feminine betrayal of the Aztec people), in the case of Pocahontas the myth is still very much a part of U.S. cultural identity.
3. Literally, "Indian Love," *Amor Indio* is the title of one of Helguera's paintings of Ixta and Popo.
4. Because the Aztec themes of the calendars is well established, the imitation of Helgueran themes by other Mexican calendar artists may be largely pragmatic: Mexican calendar publisher Calendarios Landin holds the copyright to Helguera's work, and thus, to be competitive, other publishers must supply Native themes by different artists.
5. These include *Southwest Pieta, Popo and Isle*, and *Pieta del Suroeste*.
6. While these examples suggest that Ixta is rendered in exclusively heterosexual contexts, this is by no means the case. In *Movements in Chicano Poetry*, Rafael Pérez-Torres argues that "Ixtacihuatl Died in Vain" "asserts a lesbian agency in the face of patriarchy" (192). Joey Terrill's painting *La historia de amor* is based on Helguera's *Amor Indio* in which Popo, seated, holds Ixta in his lap: her eyes are closed, and it is unclear whether she is dead or merely sleeping. Terrill's *La historia de amor* replaces Ixta with an Aztec male youth, thus laying claim to a history of gay Chicanos dating back to pre-Conquest times. Elsewhere, I have argued that Terri de la Peña's short story "La Maya"—about a Chicana lesbian vacationing in the Yucatán, who has an affair with her Mayan tour guide—can best be understood as participating in the same racial/sexual economy as the Death of the Aztec Princess.

Bibliography

Alarcón, Norma. "Chicana Feminism: In the Tracks of 'the' Native Woman." *Critical Studies* 4(3) (1990): 248–256. Rpt. in *Living Chicana Theory*. Carla Trujillo, ed. Berkeley, CA: Third Woman Press, 1998, 371–382.

Burns, Diane. "Sure, You Can Ask Me a Personal Question." *Songs from this Earth on Turtle's Back*. Ed. Joseph Bruchac. New York: Greensfield Review Press, 1983, 40.

Castillo, Ana. "Ixtacihuatl Died in Vain." In *My Father Was a Toltec*. New York: Norton, 1995, 39–41.

206   Catrióna Rueda Esquibel

Esquibel, Catrióna Rueda. "Velvet Malinche." *Velvet Barrios*. Alicia Gaspar de Alba, ed. New York: Palgrave, 2003.

Jiménez, Luis. *Cholo with Lowrider Van*. 1993. Watercolor on paper 43″ × 52″. *Man on Fire: Luis Jiménez*. The Albuquerque Museum, Albuquerque: 1994, Plate 46, 89.

———. *Mexican Allegory on Wheels*. 1976. Colored pencil on paper, Diptych, 28″ × 20″ each. *Man on Fire: Luis Jiménez*. The Albuquerque Museum, Albuquerque: 1994, Plate 43, 87.

Mercer, Kobena. "Reading Racial Fetishism: The Photographs of Robert Mapplethorpe." (1986, 1989) Rpt. in *Welcome to the Jungle: New Positions in Black Cultural Studies*. New York & London: Routledge, 1994, 171–219.

Pérez-Torres, Rafael. *Movements in Chicano Poetry: Against Myths, Against Margins*. Cambridge Studies in American Literature and Culture 88. Cambridge and New York: Cambridge University Press, 1995.

Terrill, Joey. *La Historia De Amor*. Calendar (almanaque). VIVA Lesbian and Gay Latino Artists. Los Angeles, Plate, 1994.

Ybarra-Frausto, Tomás. "Grafica/Urban Iconography." *Chicano Expressions: A New View in American Art*. Inverna Lockpez, Tomás Ybarra-Frausto, Judith Baca, and Kay Turner, eds. New York: INTAR Latin American Gallery, 1986, 21–27.

11

Embodied at the Shrine of Cultural Disjuncture

Luz Calvo

And so it was not I who make a meaning for myself, but it is the meaning that was already there, pre-existing, waiting for me.

—*Fanon 134*

She has this fear/that she's an image/that comes and goes/clearing and darkening/the fear that she's the dreamwork inside someone else's skull/ she has this fear.

—*Anzaldúa 43*

Exceeding is not escaping, and the subject exceeds precisely that to which it is bound.

—*Butler 17*

Laura Aguilar's *Three Eagles Flying* (1990, silver gelatin print, triptych, 24 × 60 inches) (figure 11.1) depicts the bound body as (dis)juncture: between Mexico and the United States, between subordination and desire, between fantasy and geopolitical reality, between artistic production and its reception. Reprinted in Coco Fusco's *English is Broken Here*, Deborah Bright's *The Passionate Camera*, and Carla Trujillo's *Living Chicana Theory*, Aguilar's image has achieved notoriety, elegantly speaking to the intersection of nation, race, and sexuality.[1] My aim in this essay is to begin to unravel the significance of *Three Eagles Flying*, an image I believe to be both brilliant and

Figure 11.1   Laura Aguilar's *Three Eagles Flying* (1990, silver gelatin print, triptych, 24 × 60 inches). Courtesy of the artist and Vielmetter Los Angeles Projects.

disturbing. It is an image that speaks the language of the unconscious—presenting itself at once as dream, as fantasy scenario, and as a series of desires and identifications that follow no politically prescribed direction. It is also an image whose power constantly evades my interpretive ability. Bound by the same flags as the subject of the photo, I find myself constrained by my own resistences: after years of studying this image, I continue to feel unable to "see" its meaning or translate the strong emotional reaction I have to the image into an analysis of its impact. This is an image that thwarts my desire for mastery—an image that eludes, slips, exceeds interpretation. The best I can do is to write a series of fragments that only just begin to approach the image and my relation to it.

*   *   *

The Surface

In *Three Eagles Flying*, Aguilar photographs herself bound by a thick cargo rope that wraps around her neck and across her chest, tying her clenched fists in front of her body. Her head is wrapped tightly by the Mexican flag whose central image—an eagle devouring a serpent sitting on a nopal—covers her face. Her hips are wrapped in the U.S. flag, with stripes to the left and stars to the right. Aguilar's breasts and arms are bare; a tan line—perhaps from a tank top— reveals skin that is lighter on the chest and darker on the arms, while a substantial scar is visible on the right forearm. *Three Eagles Flying* is a triptych: the center photograph of Aguilar is flanked by photographs of an American flag, on the left, and the Mexican flag, on the right. The visual structure of the triptych is compact and symmetrical: the flags, the body, and the rope are all carefully arranged.

I have just revealed that this image is of Aguilar herself, a fact that would be evident to those familiar with her larger body of work, in which self-portraiture is pivotal. In addition, Aguilar's lesbian identity, not immediately obvious in this image-context, is staged explicitly in the "Latina Lesbian Series," a photo-essay of the Los Angeles Latina lesbian community in the 1980s, which includes a photo of Aguilar herself. Of what use, if any, is this biographical information about the artist? My aim is to read this photograph as a text: to find in it—rather than in the artist—multiple, layered, and potentially contradictory significations. Yet, as I approach this image-text, I find it imbued with meanings from other texts—including Aguilar's oeuvre and the critical analysis of her work—from which I can no longer isolate *Three Eagles Flying*.[2] I must, then, read Aguilar's image intertextually: that is, in or against other texts that speak to the image. In turn, this essay may become part of the intertexual landscape through which Aguilar's image is read and understood. Thus, Aguilar's *Three Eagles Flying* cannot be kept "pure" as it is always already "contaminated" by other texts—texts that imbue it with, among other things, "lesbianicity."[3]

*   *   *

Beginnings

I don't know where to begin my analysis: word or image? inside the frame or outside? left or right? center? top or bottom? political or psychic? dream? nightmare? or fantasy? If I were an eagle, I could circle the image from far above in ever-tightening concentric circles. In my fantasy, I would find a center, a core, an answer. In the analysis that follows, I propose no center, no core, no answers.

*   *   *

No Translation

The Spanish word for eagle: águila. The artist plays on her last name in the title, *Three Eagles Flying*. While other critics (Yarbro-Bejarano,

Hulick) have noted the confluence of "águila" and "Aguilar," I wonder about the disjuncture: the additional "r" on the surname, the accent mark over the "a" in águila. For me, the surname is almost, but not quite, eagle—a difference overlooked by the title introducing three eagles: the Mexican eagle, the American eagle, and the Chicana lesbian artist.[4] The águila in Aguilar is further enforced by the image of the eagle that literally replaces the artist's face. (This is the Mexican eagle, sitting on a nopal, devouring a serpent.) "Eagle" is defined by the American Heritage Dictionary as "any of various large . . . birds of prey . . ., characterized by a powerful hooked bill, keen vision, long broad wings, and strong, soaring flight." The artist presents herself without the ability to "look back" at the spectator of this image, yet because her entire head is covered by the Mexican flag, the image suggests paradox: the subject cannot look back but she nevertheless is endowed with "keen vision."

*   *   *

"Don't Stare"

In *Male Subjectivity at the Margins*, Kaja Silverman distinguishes between the look and the gaze. Drawing on Lacan's *Four Fundamental Concepts*, Silverman notes that the gaze is exterior to the subject. Indeed, Lacan likens the constitution of the subject to "the photo session" and the "clicking of an imaginary camera" (Silverman, 128). For Lacan "what determines [the subject] at the most profound level in the visible is the gaze that is outside" (Silverman, 128). Silverman explains that although the gaze might be said to be "the presence of others as such, it is by no means coterminous with any individual viewer or group of viewers. It issues 'from all sides,' whereas the eye [sees] from only one point" (130). Thus, the look issues from the subject, while the gaze is focused on the subject. "The relationship between [the look] and the gaze" proclaims Silverman, "is thus analogous in certain ways to that which links penis to phallus; the former can stand in for the latter, but can never approximate it" (130).

As a spectator, I look at Aguilar's image, much like a voyeur might look through a keyhole. For hours, I sit alone at my desk, staring at Aguilar's image as I try to write. My eyes wander from the two flags to the two breasts to the rope that binds them all together; my eyes circle the parameters of the image but always return to the breasts. Then, I avert my eyes. Look away. Stop myself from staring. It is "at precisely that moment when the eye is placed to the keyhole," Silverman explains, "that it is most likely to find itself subordinated to the gaze" (130). So, as I look at the photograph, I become the subject of the gaze. Perhaps someone will walk into the room and catch me staring at the image. Lacan elucidates this (awkward) moment: as I look through the peephole "a gaze surprises [me] in the function of voyeur, disturbs [me], overwhelms [me], reduces [me]to shame" (Lacan, 84, qtd in Silverman 130).

I am not sure what impels this shame. Certainly, one is "supposed" to look at a photograph. Even if it is a nude. Even if it is an "artful" S/M image. What is it in this image that provokes me so?

*   *   *

Fantasy

If as Jean Laplanche and J.P. Pontalis suggest, fantasy is "not the object of desire, but its setting," we might look at Aguilar's photograph as staging a mise-en-scene in which the Chicana subject of the photograph locates herself (fantasmatically) in a "sequence of images." Mise-en-scene is a cinematic term used to denote the setting—including props, costumes, set design—of a film scene. The mise-en-scene is critical; it sets the scene in time and space, and it marks class and culture specificities. Mise-en-scene can be extended to the setting of a fantasy; indeed, LaPlanche and Pontalis argue that fantasy is mise-en-scene. The setting of *Three Eagles Flying*'s fantasy is, first of all, between two flags. The flags are hanging (not flying). The mood produced is sullen; the flags seem drained of color. Inserted between the two hanging flags is Aguilar's body bound by two more flags (or, one imagines, the same flags, now binding her). A thick cargo rope ties the flags to Aguilar's body and puts her in bondage.

Three Eagles Flying is a "scene" in more that one sense: overtly, it is a photographic scene staged for the camera, but it also suggests an S/M "scene." According to Thomas Murphy and Thomas Murrel, "In a sadomasochistic encounter, [a scene is a] script of events or activities previously negotiated or agreed upon and then followed by all participants" (119). The authors then quotes a personal interview with "Lucinda" who provides ostensibly "inside" information: "[Scenes] are usually worked out to right to the finest detail. I mean, they have to be. There are a lot of crazies out there" (119). The detail of Aguilar's image—the position of the flags, the careful placement of the rope, the pose of the body—suggest a bondage scenario in which the aim is to take one's place in a highly charged visual image. There is an overriding sense of exactness to this image: think of the time it took to collect and arrange the props "just so." If *Three Eagles Flying* stages a fantasy, which I think it does, that fantasy is not in the subject of the photograph offering herself as object of desire, but, rather in the fastidiously constructed setting: the rope, the flags, and the body all meticulously placed in their position. Thus, I offer this definition of "scene" from S/M culture simply because it underscores the fetishizing processes that go into the production of a "scene." I do not mean to imply that S/M culture can be easily placed alongside Freud's discussion of sadism and masochism; nor that S/M culture provides some privileged ground from which to read *Three Eagles Flying*.

I do think that Aguilar's image produces a fantasy scenario that recalls Freud's 1919 essay "A Child Is Being Beaten" with its critical insight that each fantasy contains the multiple and concealed possibilities. Freud finds that the subject of fantasy may oscillate between various positions: feminine/masculine, active/passive, sadistic/masochistic and scopophilic/exhibitionist. He demonstrates that fantasies undergo a historical development in which they vacillate in relation to "the author of the fantasy, and as regards their object, their content, and their significance" (*SE*: 17: 184). In other words, the simple presentation of a fantasy such as "A child is being beaten" speaks to only one configuration in a scenario that yields multiple permutations. How, then, might Aguilar's image—which presents us with a visualization of the fantasy "A Chicana is in bondage"—be variously construed?

In the first instance, the image presents itself as a scene of subordination. In the words of one critic, *Three Eagles Flying* "confronts competing poles of her own cultural identity—the American and Mexican ones. Never totally accepted by either she is inextricably bound to both . . ." (Marcellino 19). In this view, *Three Eagles Flying* illustrates the "conditions of subordination" of a Chicana subject, who lives under two symbolic orders—that of the United States on one hand and Mexico on the other—that act upon her, weigh her down, anchor her to a reality not of her choosing. Aguilar's scene speaks to a geopolitical drama that leaves its mark on the bodies that inhabit the greater Mexico–U.S. borderlands. However, if the analysis is left here, then the Chicana is imagined to have no desire except to escape, an impossible desire. I believe, however, that this image provides the possibility for alternate scenarios. The image exceeds, which is not to say that it escapes, its geopolitical grounding.

Contained within the fantasy scenario staged by the image is a second spectatorial fantasy: "I am in bondage." While the first "fantasy" was political in nature, the second is clearly sexual. Here, a sadomasochistic economy of desire emerges from the previously "political" scene as the spectator identifies with the bound subject: the spectator imagines herself to be the woman bound. Thus, the original "she is in bondage" is replaced by "I am in bondage." Thus, "I" imagine myself bound and blindfolded; entirely helpless—at the will of my captors. In order to flesh out this fantasy I create—consciously or not—an imaginary captor. I realize as I am writing that I have always imagined the subject in this photograph (and me in my identification with her) to be at the will of a group of women. In my fantasy she/I are captured by a group of Chicana lesbians! Lest the reader think I am out of my mind, I might refer to the authority of Freud and especially his analysis of the girlhood fantasy "A child is being beaten."[5] Freud finds that concealed in the fantasy "A child is being beaten" is the fantasy "I am being beaten"; and in yet another turn, he finds that the producer of the fantasy often constructs an "artistic super-structure"[6] that involves elaborate rituals and a series of "whipping boys" who are beaten. In this context, then, my fantasy, does not seem at all unusual; in fact, it seems rather in line with those discussed by Freud.

I believe that my fantasy—being put in bondage by a wild gang of Chicana lesbians—is further provoked by the implicit photographic relation: I am put in the position of spectator of this scene by the Chicana lesbian artist. I am already under her spell, if you will. (However, I am not sure when or how the singular artist acquired a gang.)

At any rate, it should be clear to the reader that I am offering my spectatorial fantasy, in the hope that others might be spurred to locate themselves in the scenario. I do understand, however, as Teresa de Lauretis has astutely noted in regard to film: "it does not always follow that every film or every film's fantasy is capable of engaging every spectator . . . spectatorial admission into the film's scenario of desire is complex, overdetermined, and not always possible" (98). The same would be true of entry into the "scenario of desire" staged by *Three Eagles Flying*; indeed, all I can do is to attempt to unravel my own identifications and desires in relation to the image.

Thus, I would like to return for a moment to elaborate on the initial, political, fantasy "A Chicana is in bondage" that now can be seen to conceal a similar, but sexual, fantasy: "A Chicana is put in bondage

by a gang of Chicana lesbians and I am watching." Here, the specta-
tor revels in her position as voyeur; this is the position of Mercedes
McCambridge in *Touch of Evil*, when she declares, "Lemme stay,
I want to watch."

*   *   *

Ambivalence

Far from staging a straightforward critique of racial and sexual
oppression in the Mexico–U.S. borderlands, *Three Eagles Flying* produces a thoroughly ambivalent position for both the spectator of the
image and for the Chicana lesbian subject of photograph. In his essay
"Busy in the Ruins of Wretched Phantasia," Kobena Mercer identifies
the "fear/fantasy formulation" as the expression of social and psychic
ambivalence. Excessive, irrational fear might signal a sexual fantasy
that cannot be acknowledged by the subject, who projects instead fear
and repulsion. (This is the terrain of Frantz Fanon's *Black Skin, White
Masks*: the psychosexual underpinnings of racism.) The psychoanalytic
conception of ambivalence is crucial to the fear/fantasy formulation
deployed by Mercer. Defined by J. Laplanche and J.-B. Pontalis as "the
simultaneous existence of contradictory tendencies, attitudes or feelings
in the relationship to a single object," ambivalence, I argue, structures
U.S. discourses about Mexico as well as Mexican and Chicano/a
responses to U.S. hegemony.

Playing in the field of this ambivalence, Aguilar's image presents
three possible identificatory positions to the spectator: the position of
watching the scene, the position of being bound, and the position of
restraining and tying up the Chicana subject. (I have commented on
the first two of these, I leave it to the reader to find my [their] sadistic
desires embedded in this image/analysis.) To think literally for a
moment, we might consider how in staging her own bondage in this
photo(graphic) scene, Aguilar occupies both active and passive
positions—she ties up a woman in the staging of this fantasy *and* she
is tied up—she looks at the photograph as the photographer *and*
she is looked at as the photographed subject. The scene of *Three
Eagles Flying* is completely structured by what Kobena Mercer
identifies (in another context) as an oscillation between the position
of subject, object, and spectator. Discussing the relation between
ambivalence and this oscillation, Mercer writes, "the ambivalence of

identification can be seen to arise from the effect of unconscious phantasy in which the self oscillates between positions of subject, object or spectator of the scene" (40). What I have tried to bring to surface are the unconscious fantasies provoked in me by *Three Eagles Flying*. My resistances, repressions, and internal censors—not to mention the bounds of common decency—preclude any further disclosure.

*   *   *

The Subject

I begin reading Judith Butler's *The Psychic Life of Power* and I find her introductory chapter seems to speak to the scenario portrayed in *Three Eagles Flying*. Butler asserts a paradox at the heart of subjecti-ficaton: that it is necessary "to desire the conditions of one's own subordination" (9). Like Aguilar's image, Butler's assertion disturbs: it gets under my skin. Productively, Butler challenges a liberal–humanist formulation of the individual "whose agency is always and only opposed to power." We might back up for a moment to consider the distinction between "subject," used by Butler and others working within psychoanalytic or post-structuralist paradigms, and "person" or "individual" used in liberal and humanist discourses. "Subject" is distinguished from "person" and "individual" because the latter two imply a kind of free agency—someone who can act autonomously or is self-ruling. Butler's opening epigraph is the *Oxford English Dictionary*'s definition of subjection: "The act or fact of being subjected, as under a monarch or other sovereign or superior power; the state of being subject to, or under the dominion of another; hence *gen.* subordination . . . The condition of being subject . . ." Thus, unlike the individual who is imagined to exist apart from or opposing power, the "subject" is understood to be always already subjugated.

Aguilar's *Three Eagles Flying*, then, is seen to stage a subject (not an individual) who exists—or more accurately, comes into being—inside of complex matrices of power: apparatus of state power, as well as the fields of sexual, racial, and national difference. This image might be the nativity scene of "the" Chicana subject. It is not a scene that can be undone, however, without the very dissolution of the Chicana sub-ject. In other words, there is no (Chicana) subject, without the moment of becoming subjugated to the (state, national, patriarchal, Oedipal, familial, etc.) powers that constitutes one as subject.

*   *   *

Aesthetics of Pessimism

Speaking to psychic processes as well as political ones, Aguilar's photography marks a decisive shift away from the emphasis on "positive" images that were prominent in earlier eras of self-representation.[7] The numerous photographs, murals, and silkscreens of Chicanas with fists raised in defiance—the popular iconography of the brown power movement—are undone by Aguilar's image: her fists are not only not raised they are tied in front of her. Aguilar belongs to a generation of postcolonial artists who explore what Mercer describes as "the fluid, mobile and highly unpredictable arena of fear and fantasy."

*   *   *

This collection of fragments continues to swerve around what only seem to be disjunctive categories: from politics to fantasy, desire to subordination, artistic production to its reception, Mexico to the United States. How is it possible to write while keeping present the mutual imbrication of these categories over and against discourses that need to keep them separate and divided? How also to recognize the moments of disjuncture—when the categories disintegrate and only bodies remain? My reading opens but deliberately leaves unclosed the nature of the relationship of the psychic to the political: I suggest that neither is primary and that both exist in tension with the other.

Notes

1. In addition to its circulation in these books, Aguilar's image has also been reprinted in the following journals: *Latin American Art* 5(3), *High Performance*, *Artweek* (October 18, 1990), *Commoción*.
2. Several critics have written about Aguilar's work; the most definitive article to date is Yvonne Yarbro-Bejarano's "Laying it Bare: The Queer/Colored Body" in Photography by Laura Aguilar. See also Hulick, Alfaro, Salzman.
3. I am drawing from Barthes reading of "Italianicity" in Rhetoric of the Image 33–34.

4. These three designations are "figures," i.e., signifiers imbued with a complex set of cultural connotations. Not a question of "essential" differences, the adjectives "Mexican," "American," and "Chicana lesbian" modify nouns, "eagle" and "artist" in ways that change the cultural connotations. See Gloria Anzaldúa's discussion of the connotations of "Chicana lesbian writer" as opposed to "writer" in her artile "To(o) Queer the Writer."
5. Of course, for some readers it is my appeal to the patriarchal authority of Freud that might signify that I have "lost my mind."
6. In the edition edited by Rieff, Phillip ed. (118) the term is rendered "Artistic superstructure"; in the Standard Edition "elaborate superstructure" (190).
7. Silverman notes that the call for "positive images of women, blacks, gays, and other(s) . . . all too often work to resubstantialize identity, even at times to essentialize it" (154).

References

Alfaro, Luis. "Queer Culture: 'Exposing Ourselves': Photography Expression Workshops by Laura Aguilar." *Vanguard* (August 7, 1992): 17.
Anzaldúa, Gloria. *Borderlands/La Frontera: The New Mestiza.* San Francisco, CA: Aunt Lute Books, 1987.
———. "To(o) Queer the Writer—Loca, escritora y chicana." *Living Chicana Theory.* Carla Trujillo, ed. Berkeley, CA: Third Woman Press, 1998, 263–276. *Series in Chicana/Latina Studies.*
Barthes, Roland. "The Rhetoric of the Image" in *Image, Music, Text,* Stephen Heath, trans. New York: Noonday Press, 1977.
Bhabha, Homi K. "The Other Question: The Stereotype and Colonial Discourse." *The Sexual Subject: A Screen Reader in Sexuality.* London: Routledge, 1992, 312–331.
Bulter, Judith. *The Psychic Life of Power: Theories of subjection.* Palo Alto: Stanford University press, 1997.
Burgin, Victor, James Donald, and Cora Kaplan, eds. *Formations of Fantasy.* London: Methuen, 1986.
de Lauretis, Teresa. *The Practice of Love: Lesbian Sexuality and Perverse Desire.* Bloomington: Indiana University Press, 1994.
Fanon, Frantz. *Black Skin, White Masks,* Charles Lam Markmann, trans. New York: Grove Weidenfeld, 1967.
Farr, Ragnar, ed. *Mirage: Enigmas of Race, Difference and Desire.* London: Institute of Contemporary Arts, Institute of International Visual Arts, 1995.
Freud, Sigmund. "A Child Is Being Beaten." in *Sexuality and the Psychology of Love,* Philip Reiff, ed. Alix and James Strachey, trans. New York: Collier, 1963, 107–133.
———. *The Standard Edition of the Complete Psychological Works of Sigmund Freud,* James Strachey, trans. and ed. London: Hogarth Press, 1953–1974. 24 vols.
Hulick, Diana Emery. "Laura Aguilar." *Latin American Art.* 5(3), 1993: 52–54.

Laplanche, Jean and Jean-Bertrand Pontalis. "Fantasy and the Origins of Sexuality." *Formations of Fantasy*. Victor Burgin, James Donald, and Cora Kaplan, eds. London: Methuen, 1986, 5–28.

———. *The Language of Psycho-Analysis*. New York: Norton, 1973.

Marcellino, Michael C. "First Word." *Latin American Art*. 5(3), 1993: 19.

Mercer, Kobena. "Busy in the Ruins of Wretched Phantasia." *Mirage: Enigmas of Race, Difference and Desire*. Ragnar Farr, ed. London: Institute of Contemporary Arts, Institute of International Visual Arts, 1995, 15–55.

Murphy, Thomas and Thomas Murrell. *The Language of Sadomasochism*. New York: Greenwood, 1989.

Salzman, Linda Sher. "The Honest Eye: *Image and Identity* at Loyola Marymount University." *Artweek*, October 18, 1990: 15.

Silverman, Kaja. *Male Subjectivity at the Margins*. New York: Routledge, 1992.

12

"¿Soy Punkera, Y Que?": Sexuality, Translocality, and Punk in Los Angeles and Beyond

Michelle Habell-Pallán

My theory had precedence. Stay with me on this. The Clash, for instance jazzed up their music with this reggae influence—a direct reflection of their exposure to the Caribbean diaspora and its musical expression there in London. Nothing new—the usual white man appropriation of an exotic other story—anyway, the Sex Pistols, my theory went, were going to do the same with Norteno, el Tex Mex. I was going on the assumption that the Pistols probably heard the conjunto on KCOR or Radio Jalapeno on the bus ride down from Austin. But the point is, it worked. Talk about your revisionist histories! Griel Marcus is gonna flip!

—Molly Vasquez from Jim Mendiola's 1996 film, Pretty Vacant.

When Alice, lead singer for the Bags rock group, takes the stage in torn fishnet hose and micro-mini leopard-skin tunic, she explodes into convulsive, unintelligible vocals. The effect is a raw sexuality not for the fainthearted.

—Los Angeles Times, 1978.

The xeroxed flyer advertising *Pretty Vacant*, Jim Mendiola's 1996 independent short film (figure 12.1), depicts the much loved figure of the Mexican *La Virgen de Guadalupe* strutting, of all things, an upside down electric guitar a la Jimi Hendrix.[1] As a U.S. born Chicana who, in the 1980s, was rescued from the suburbs of Los Angeles by the Ramones, X, and Dead Kennedys, I must admit that I was captivated by this image and intrigued by the film's title, an obvious reference to the

Figure 12.1   Flyer insert for *Pretty Vacant* (dir. Jim Mendiola, 1996).

British Sex Pistols. A guitar jets out from *La Guadalupe* at a right angle, transforming the familiar oval shape of *La Virgen*'s image into the shape of cross, or an intersection of sorts.[2] What was this flyer suggesting by juxtaposing these deeply symbolic, yet seemingly unrelated, cultural icons? How did the title relate? And why did this deliciously irreverent image prompt me to think of the critically acclaimed *photonovela*/comic series *Love and Rockets* by Los Bros. Hernandez? And the title? *Pretty Vacant* is one of the "hit" songs of the infamous 1970s British punk band, the Sex Pistols. Again, what is this flyer suggesting? With all due respect, what and who lies at the intersection of *Guadalupe* and punk?

It turns out that main protagonist of *Pretty Vacant*, Molly Vasquez, like the fierce Latina characters of the Hernandez Brothers'*Love and Rockets* photo-novela series, and most importantly, real life Angelino Chicana punk musicians,[3] live at that particular intersection. The film depicts a week in the culturally hybrid "do-it-yourself" world of "La Molly" Vasquez, the off-beat 20-something, English-speaking Chicana feminist, *artista*, bisexual, *punkera* subject who lives in a working-class area of San Antonio, Tejas. Her love of the Sex Pistols leads her to the discovery of a well-kept secret that will allow her, as a producer of 'zines and a beginning filmmaker, to *rewrite* rock 'n' roll history by inserting herself and Tejano culture into its narrative. All this, while she prepares for a gig in her all girl band, "Aztlan-a go-go."

My mention of *Pretty Vacant* serves as point of departure for my discussion of the emergence, during the late 1970s and early 1980s, of a punk "do-it-yourself" Chicana grassroots feminist cultural production that circulated coterminus with other burgeoning Chicana activist and scholarly endeavors, as well as the East Los Angeles/Hollywood punk scenes, but have yet to be examined in-depth. The film succeeds at what scholars of U.S. popular music have attempted—it shifts the paradigm that frames the reigning narrative of popular music produced in the United States.[4] Disrupting the status quo narrative of popular music production (in this specific case U.S. punk) by granting a young Latina (more specifically a Tejana) the authority to chronicle the history of punk, the film compels scholars to acknowledge the complexity of popular music and popular music studies in the United States. Ultimately, the film viscerally unsettles long-held assumptions that unconsciously erase the influence of U.S. Latinos from popular music's sonic equation (and asks what is at stake in reproducing that erasure). It opens a discursive space for my own analysis of the production of punk music by Chicanas in East Los Angeles and Hollywood during the 1970s and 1980s, and the music's relation to punk communities beyond the United States.

Beyond the Frame

The lens, her hands, her eye/body, the door, the house, the yard. She moves toward us, the viewers. The arrangement of elements within

Figure 12.2   Still photo for *Pretty Vacant* (dir. Jim Mendiola, 1996).

this frame evoke a sensation of both depth and movement. The lens of her Super 8 camera is at the front and center of the image. Behind the camera is a close-up of her face, her furrowed brow focusing. From there, her hands, eye/body, door, and house recede from her camera lens until the frame is filled by the house, except for an open space to the right where the yard begins. The composition implies a double-movement: we are pulled toward her center as she simultaneously moves away from the door. She is both the object and the subject of the gaze. She stands unconfined, outside of the black weathered door of the paint-chipped house behind her, outside of the private domestic sphere. She has moved out into the day light, into the public sphere.

The black and white image described below (figure 12.2), circulates as a press photo for *Pretty Vacant.*[5] The photo functions as a visual allegory for the way Chicana feminists and artists—as women of color—at the turn of the century, have turned a critical eye on the public sphere, and in doing so, have envisioned new subjects and subjectivities, as well as mapped out affiliations with racialized-as-non-white women within and across national borders. Who is this young woman at the center of the frame?[6] In part, she is a fictionalized construct inspired by the impact made by young feminist punks from East L.A.

Las Punkeras

What is fascinating about the film *Pretty Vacant* is the overlapping of the fictional character's art-practices with the under-analyzed artistic production of Chicana musicians and visual artists shaping the Los Angeles punk sensibility. In the late 1970s and early 1980s, Chicanas in local bands like the Brat (led by Teresa Covarrubias), and The Alice Bags band (led by Alicia Armedariz Velasquez) reconstructed the sound and subjects of British punk. After providing a brief context for the emergence of Chicana/o punk, I examine excerpts of oral histories that allow these Chicana punkeras to narrate their artistic conditions of production, gender relations, as well as the punk aesthetic that emerged in the late 1970s and 1980s.[7]

Chicana/o punk, like punk everywhere, embodied a sonic response to the "excesses of seventies rock."[8] Rock chroniclers Reyes and Waldman note that, "Indulgent guitar solos, pretentious lyrics, and pompous lead singers went against everything that Chicano rock'n'roll represented from Ritchie Valens forward."[9] The appeal of punk to rebellious Chicana and Chicano youth makes sense for several reasons: (1) the D.I.Y. (Do It Yourself) sensibility at the core of punk musical sub-cultures found resonance with the practice of rasquache, a Chicana/o cultural practice of "making-do" with limited resources.[10] In fact, Chicana/o youth had historically been at the forefront of formulating stylized social statements via fashion and youth subculture—beginning with the Pachuchos, and on to Chicana Mods; and (2) punk's critique of the status quo, of poverty, of sexuality, of class inequality, of war, spoke directly to working-class East Los Angeles youth.[11]

Yet for all its familiar feel, punk's international sensibility also appealed to Chicanas/os despite, or perhaps because of the city's history of physically and economically segregating Chicanos apart from the wealthy West Side, thought to be by Los Angeles's dominant culture the place of important "worldly" cultural invention.[12] It goes without saying that Chicana/o punk did not exist in isolation. Reyes and Waldman observe that

> Chicano punk groups where much more deep embedded in the Hollywood rock scene than were the 1960s bands from East Los Angeles. On any given weekend in the late 1970s and early 1980s, Los Illegals,

I

the Brat, and the Plugs would be playing somewhere in Hollywood. Before they crossed the LA River, however, they played at the Vex; an East LA club devoted to presenting punk rock bands.[13]

Vex emerged as an attempt by Chicano youth in East Los Angeles, "to eliminate the barriers that inhibited Chicanos from playing in other parts of L.A., and that kept outsiders from coming from the neighborhood." Willie Herron of Los Illegal remembers," We wanted to bring people from the West Side to see groups from the East Side.' "[14] At an historical moment when the confluence of cultures began to accelerate in the wake of global demographic shifts these Chicana/o youth transformed punk into a social site where popular music, national identity, sexuality, and gender dynamics were transformed. Band's like East L.A.'s Thee Undertakers used a "global" form of youth subculture to bring together local, if segregated, youth.

She Says

Punk allowed people to just get up there, and even if you were not feeling confident— which was not a problem I ever had—but I think for women who felt like they weren't sure of themselves, it was very easy to get up and do it anyway, because you weren't being judged on how well you played.

—Alicia Armendariz Velasquez, singer-songwriter, 1998, Los Angeles.[15]

Working-class Chicanas such as Alicia Armedariz Velasquez, Theresa Covarrubias, Angela Vogel, and others shaped independent, noncommercial music communities and subcultures in Los Angeles and responded to the shrinking of the public sphere and the increased privatization of daily life in contemporary U.S. culture through their musical practices. Although these women impacted local independent music communities sounds and concerns, almost no formal documentation of their participation exist. The fact the women disrupt categories of identity (such as singer-song writer, Chicana, woman musician, punk, etc.) mitigates against recognition of their influence in discussions of subcultural musical practices and in discussions focused on countering the shrinking of the public sphere.

I am interested in the ways these women appropriated, reshaped, and critiqued imagery from unexpected sources such as British youth musical subculture to invent local cultural practices that allowed them to express their realities in a public context. I argue that Chicanas as producers transformed punk and new wave aesthetics into sites of possibility for transnational conversations concerning violence against women and the effects of the shrinking public sphere. Given that most youth musical practices and communities are understood as male-dominated arenas, and rarely as Latino social spaces, these subcultures may seem an unlikely space for the development of a transnational conversation. Yet, it was a site of possibility for these young Chicanas who engaged these subcultures.

Las Gritonas/The Screamers

The Los Angeles bands I'm interested in produced their music on independent labels, which circulated in grassroots and alternative distribution circuits. However these bands had little access to major distribution networks for at least two reasons: most major record labels at the time could not imagine the market appeal of Chicano alternative music, and (much less Latino rock inflected by a grass roots feminist ideology and punk aesthetic); and the women's stated primary desire was *not* to "make it within the mainstream" music industry, but to create a place for public self-expression.

This context, in addition to larger social prejudices against "women in rock," helps to explain why the innovative use by young Chicanas of alternative music to circulate critiques of social inequality and to express their rage against the domestic machine has often gone unrecognized: their recordings and visual images are extremely difficult to locate. This lack of distribution and exposure also occurred with other artists of the period, such as spoken word artist Marisela Norte, who also articulated a grassroots critique of social inequality that circulated in and outside of the university setting.[16] The cultural production of these young Chicanas paralleled the efforts of Chicana feminist theories of representation at the same time, even though their efforts rarely, if ever, intersected. As scholars of Chicana feminism wrote about multiply inflected subjectivity, the intersection of race, class, and gender, and the production of new Chicana subjects, these young women expressed these experiences in their music.[17]

These working-class Chicanas who helped create the local sound of the Los Angeles underground punk subculture were attracted to it for various reasons, but all of them experienced or witnessed violence against Chicanas at an early age and most had been violently sexualized. In a series of interviews I conducted with Alicia Armedariz Vasquez and Teresa Covarrubias, they asserted that the visual and

I

sonic language of punk subculture allowed them to express their private rage about restrictions place on and the violence done to their bodies and their mother's bodies. In addition, their narratives document the effects of the shrinking of public sphere by forces of economic privatization that plagued the 1980s and continue to this day. In other words, theirs is a story of transnationalism told from the bottom up in the years leading up to accords like NAFTA from the point of view of working-class women. Though each woman's experience was different, each was attracted to punk subculture because it was a place where they reimagined the world they lived in, it was a place where they saw themselves as empowered subjects.

Despite the negative press the punk scene received (as extremely violent and racist) all of the women experienced the punk scene as a liberating space where the lines between gender and race were easily if temporarily blurred. It was a place where class differences and racial divisions where held temporarily in suspension. In fact, all the interviewees attested to the fact that in Los Angeles, the scene was multicultural—it reflected the mix of Los Angeles population. In an era when representation of Latinas was even more rare than today on English-language television and radio, the do-it-yourself attitude and aesthetic appealed to them.

In the Bag

Alicia Armedariz Velasquez, stage name Alice Bag, of the Bags Band, is the daughter of Mexican immigrants. Growing up in East Los Angeles, she came of age in the early 1980s. She, like Teresa Covarrubias, described her engagement with punk as a way out of an environment she found too judgmental in terms of ethnicity and sexuality. She found no recourse in the mythic traditional Mexican family to discuss the domestic violence she witnessed as a child. Her embrace of punk culture occurred in "a period when Chicanas were questioning their traditional roles, increasing their participation within the political arena, and inscribing a budding Chicana feminist discourse and practice."[18] Although Amendariz Velasquez's path diverged from most Chicanas of the day, so profound was her influence on the L.A. punk scene, she was a featured artist in the recent photo exhibition and catalog called *Forming: The Early Days of L.A. Punk*. In fact, punk music chronicler David Jones calls Amendariz Velasquez the inventor of the west coast hard-core punk sound.[19]

In 1978, Amendariz Velasquez was featured in a Los Angles Times article, "Female Rockers—A New Breed."[20] Amendariz Velasquez, then known as "Alice Bag," along with Diane Chai of the Alleycats and Xene of X, were considered the most groundbreaking women of the punk scene because their performances demolished narrow models of "women in rock": "the wronged blue belter a la Janis Joplin or the coy sex kitten typified by Linda Ronstadt. In tune with new wave's spirit of change, women punkers are rejecting the confining steoreotype and demanding more."[21] Although no explicit mention of Alice's ethnicity was made, McKenna describes her with code words reserved for ethnic others: "Alice, an exotic beauty whose frenzied vocal seizures generate such chaos that the Bags has earned a reputation for closing clubs."[22] In retrospect we note that McKenna, perhaps unknowingly, cites two Chicanas, Ronstadt and Armendariz Velasquez, as wildly divergent models of "women in rock."

Often accused of being too aggressive on stage, Amendariz Velasquez would perform in pink mini-dresses and severe makeup. In a clip from Penelope Spheeris's 1981 documentary film, *The Decline of Western Civilization*, we witness Amendariz Velasquez exploding onstage and wrestling the boys who jump on stage during the show. The pink of Armendariz Velasquez's dress clashed with her performance and produced a complex statement about women's realities. Amendariz Velasquez did not reject femininity per se, but rejected the equation of femininity with victimization and passivity. In fact, McKenna states, "women punkers like Alice Bag and Xene project an oddly incongruous sexuality. While not exactly neuter, their shock-level redefinition of the female role will take a while to be assimilated culturally."[23] Yet, Amendariz Velasquez's assertion that "Female performers have always tended to be more reserved but all that is changing . . ." foresaw and provided models for performers like Courtney Love, often noted, if not entirely correctly, for what has been called her unprecedented feminine rock aesthetic.[24]

Amendariz Velasquez also described the appeal of punk to young women in practical terms. She explains, "Punk allowed people to just get up there, and even if you were not feeling confident—which was not a problem I ever had—but I think for women who felt like they weren't sure of themselves, it was very easy to get up and do it anyway, because you weren't being judged on how well you played."[25] One of the best preserved and accessible document of Amendariz Velasquez's fearless performance as Alice Bag is the Bags band recording, "We Don't Need the English."[26] With characteristic sardonic humor, Alice and the band loudly refuses the notion that the only authentic punk scene was found in Great Britian.

> We don't need the English
> Tell us what we should be
> We don't need the English
> With their boring songs of anarchy
> Telling us what to wear
> Telling us to dye our hair
> All they do is dye their hair
> Fuck them, send them
> into East Berlin
>
> (Chorus)
> Telling us how to play
> Telling us what to say
> Saying our scenes are fake
> Their brains are all half-baked. . . .

The song opens by rejecting "the English, with their boring songs of anarchy," a direct reference to "Anarchy in the U.K." by uber-punk band, the Sex-Pistols. The song concludes by metaphorically banning the English from the "Canterbury", an infamous, rundown apartment complex in Hollywood that served as a breeding ground for Hollywood punks.[27] Though Amendariz Velasquez did not write the song, the lyrics hold a different valiance when we consider that Amendariz Velasquez was bilingual in a city that often denigrated Spanish-speaking ethnic minorities and that she has taught Bilingual Education for many years in the Los Angeles Unified Public School District.

Although Amendariz Velasquez emerged as a performer in the 1970s Hollywood punk scene (unlike Covarrubias, who grew out of the East Los Angeles punk scene), Amendariz Velasquez came to Chicana consciousness in the early 1990s. After performing as a Lovely Elvette for El Vez and the Memphis Mariachis, Cholita and other L.A. based bands, she formed a folk group, Las Tres, with Teresa Covarrubias and Angela Vogel, former member of the East Los band, the Odd Sqad.[28] When Vogel left the band, the two remaining members formed the duo Goddess 13.

East Los Angeles's The Brat

What attracted Teresa Covarrubias, who was born to a working-class Mexican American family, to punk musical subculture was its do-it-yourself attitude, what she calls the "non-pretentiousness of it." Covarrubias discovered punk in the mid-1970s when her older sister, went on a backpack trip through Europe and began sending her punk fanzines from Germany and England. She recalls that

> What really attracted me to punk, was the notion that "Gee, I could do that. 'Zines had all these paste-up things and all these crazy little articles, and these girl bands and guy bands, and it just seemed like so open. It didn't seem like . . . you had to play really well. It seemed like a from your gut" type thing, and I just fell right into it. You know, it was really raw, and it was in your face, and I really liked that, it kind of got me goin."[29]

Inspired by this low-tech sensibility, one that she says "emerged" from the gut and seemed open to young men and women, she decided to form a new wave band with Rudy Medina, called The Brat. The Brat is synonymous with East L.A. Punk. In contrast to Amendariz Velasquez's family who was fully supportive of her musical lifestyle, Covarrubias's family discouraged her. Although she found a place in the band to critique gender norms with song titles like "Misogyny," she found that sexism did exist in the scene, especially with her own band mates. At times they dismissed her creative opinions because she did not play an instrument. During those times, she explains that

> Because I couldn't get what I wanted, I started acting out in really self-destructive ways . . . because I just felt like I had no say . . . even now, women don't have a lot of faith in themselves, especially if you are going outside of the norm, when you're treading new ground. Everybody's always telling you what you can't do. . . . people look at you and you're brown and you're a woman, and they think, "she can't do that." It's like they immediately assume less.[30]

Fortunately, visual documentation exists of Covarrubias's performances of her song, "Misogyny." In 1992, the television program *Vista L.A.* dedicated an entire segment, "Chicanas In Tune" to Covarrubias and Armendariz Velasquez. "Misogyny" was originally written while Covarrubias was in the Brat. The *Vista L.A.* clip captures Covarrubias's 1980 punk/new wave mode and documents her performance as she swings to the beat in a shimmering early 1960s style dress. Her voice is forced to compete with the guitar, but she holds the attention of her enthusiastic audience. The lyrics critique the position of women within patriarchal culture.

A woman is a precious thing
Far beyond a wedding ring
You have kept her under your thumb

You don't love her
You abuse her,
You confuse her
You just use her

A woman's mind is a priceless Gift
Talk to her like it is
Women's beauty is in her mind
All you see is the sexual side

You don't love her
You abuse her,
You confuse her
You just use her

Blatant is misogyny
It's captured in our history
You will find it hard to steal
The strength from within a woman's will

The narrator breaks down the elements of misogyny by exposing how they are practiced in everyday life in the following way, "you don't love her, you abuse her, you confuse her, you just use her." The narrator critiques the strictures of matrimony that reduce women to property, to be possessed much like a wedding ring. Again, the narrator exhorts the listener to understand that a woman's strength lies in her mind and will and that it is waste to value women *only* for their sexuality. Moreover, the power of the narrator's critique lies in her acknowledgment of the blatancy and frequency of women's abuse. Violence against women is so prevalent and in the open that its practices can be tracked throughout history and across geography, though its effects often go unacknowledged.

Though the Brat released a successful E.P called *The Brat*, they eventually broke up and morphed into Act of Faith, released a compact disk and then broke up again, Covarrubias has continued to write and perform on top of her duties as elementary teacher in the Los Angeles Unified School District.

Mex Goddesses

Alicia Armendariz Velasquez was part of a group of young songstresses that in the 1970s "blanch[ed] at being described as women's libbers—a tame, middle-aged scene by their standards

[but]. . . . could accurately be described as nihilistic feminists."[31] Meanwhile, at Hollywood punk shows in the 1980s, Covarrubias encountered a "a punk elite," that was "really particular about what you looked like. If you didn't look right, they could be rude. There were a couple of times that they would tell me, 'you don't belong here.' "[32] In the early 1990s, however, first as Las Tres with Angela Vogel, and later Goddess 13, the two forged a sound that disrupted the exclusivity of White feminism and anti-Mexican punk. This sound, Armendariz Velasquez declares, "speaks to women of color about their experiences as women."[33] "Happy Accident" by Armendariz Velasquez typifies the ways the group highlighted violence against women in their performance. The song's narrative centers around a battered woman's response to her partner's violent abuse.

> Please believe me / I didn't mean it /
> All I saw / was the look in his eye /
> and I feared for my life / once again.
>
> I didn't know / it was coming /
> all I know / is the done if before /
> sent me crashing to the floor / but no more. . . .
>
> Oh and / I can't say that /
> Oh no, no / I regret it /
> 'cause after all it be him or me /
> you'd be talking to.
> And if I had the chance / to do it all again /
> I don't think it / would have a different end
> / I'm quite happy with this accident.
>
> I didn't know / it was loaded /
> Yes, I knew where he kept all his guns /
> and I just grabbed the one / that was closest.
>
> So, if you ask / why I'm smiling /
> You may think / that a prison cell's tough /
> but I'm much better off / than before.

Though the narrative is bleak, the mid-tempo beat creates a "Chicana trova sound."[34] The contrast between the sound of the music and the lyrics creates a punk-like disruption. The limited options the woman possesses in response to the domestic violence that has "sent [her] crashing to the floor" end up freeing her from one situation, but contain her in another. She finds that a "prison cell's tough / but I'm much better off than before." This tragic all too real scenario speaks to the alarming rate of women of color's incarceration.[35]

Las Tres recorded a live performance at the Los Angeles Theater Center in 1993 and had recorded enough material to shop a compact disk to labels. However, according to Armendariz Velasquez, the tapes never saw the light of day because she and Covarrubias could not afford to buy the master tapes from the recording engineer. The band had been in hiatus since the mid-1990s, but reunited for El Vez's 2002 Quinciañera Show and for the Eastside Revue, a reunion of East Los Angeles boogie and rock n roll bands from the 1940s on, at the Los Angeles Japanese American Cultural Center in October 2002.

Vexed

Because "the Vex became a center for artistic activity of all kinds" punk musicians began to interact with visual and performance artists.[36] Theresa Covarrubias remembers that the Brat "did a show there with local artists . . . It was through the Vex that I realized there were a lot of artists and poets in East L.A."[37] Equally important, for young Chicanas gathering at Vex, whatever their artistic medium, themes of sexuality, antiwar protests, and antiracism ran throughout the narratives. In fact, Reyes and Waldman claim that bands like the Brat

> . . . produced enough original, exciting material to generate interest in the band throughout the LA punk underground. It was not long before punk fans from the West Side [of Los Angeles], maybe some of those who sneered at Teresa when she traveled to their part of town, came to see the Brat perform at the Vex[38]

It can be argued that Chicana/o youth, marginalized by the West Side rock scene, enticed West Side youth, who refused to see Chicano culture as cosmopolitan, or as worthy of their interest, succeeded in creating integrated places in the most unexpected ways. As Sean Carrillo claims: "the punk scene had done the impossible. It accomplished what few cultural movements before had been able to do: it attracted all people from all over town to see Latino bands, and it brought musicians from all over the city to . . . deep in the heart of East L.A."[39]

Covarrubias and Amendariz Velasquez found punk to be an alternative oppositional movement to the Chicano movement, which they felt excluded from because of their position on gender issues. For these Chicanas from East L.A. punk subculture was not the end of their identity formation, but it was a path to a new way of being in the world and to expose the world to their reality.

Pistols Go Chicano, Hendrix Goes Tex Mex: Plotting New Connections

Understanding U.S. punk within a U.S. Latino/Latin American context produces exciting news questions, problematics, and contradictions around analysis of popular musics. Equally important, it challenges the dominant paradigm framing Chicano Studies. To conclude, I'd like to return to *Pretty Vacant* to explore how it problematizes both Pop Music Studies and Chicano Studies. *Pretty Vacant* turns on three narrative strands that finally intersect at the climax of the film. The first strand involves Molly's avoidance of her father and his attachment to a nostalgia for Mexico that does not incorporate her (so refreshingly different from Monteczuma Esparza and Gregory Nava's representation of Selena as devoted daughter)—Molly's dad has bought her an airplane ticket for the annual family reunion in Mexico that she does not want to attend: the second strand invokes Molly's discovery of a well-kept secret that will allow her, as a producer of 'zines and a beginning filmmaker, to *rewrite* rock'n'roll history by inserting herself, and Tejano culture; while the third strand involves Molly's preparation for a performance of her all girl band called "Aztlan-a go-go" of which she is the drummer. Molly's father eventually catches up to her, and she ends up going to Mexico. But what she finds is not her father's version of *Mexico viejo*, but a dynamic exciting youth culture composed of rockeros/as (young people who listen to and make rock en español) who are also concerned with social change.

Broadcast in Los Angeles on Public Television in May 1998, the film successfully uses humor to deal with usually painful issues, including: daughters fighting patriarchal constraints; the frustration of having one's history erased; and the refusal to recognize the artistic and intellectual talents of racialized young women in the struggle to create the conditions for the emergence of a world free from gendered, racialized, and economic oppression. The film also provokes questions it does not necessarily address: as the daughter of a Mexican maid and a working-class Tejano informed by the Chicano movement in its Texas manifestation, what can Molly, who lives at the geographic meeting place of Mexico and the United States, and who lives at the cultural intersection of Steve Jordon (who is known as San Antonio's "Chicano Jimi Hendrix of the accordion") and the Sex Pistols (Jordon stand for the symbolic intersection of San Antonio's and London's working-class culture)—what can she tell us about this particular cultural moment, about new formations of politics of representation, and how does she speak to unequal economic conditions? What can Molly's character, who sees herself in both a local and international milieu, and recognizes herself as a gendered, racialized, and classed subject, tell us about transnational popular music and its potential for a feminist cultural politics, one that Gloria Anzaldúa, Norma Alarcón, and Sonia Saldívar-Hull specify as a border feminist politics insofar as it "is a feminism that exists in a borderland not limited to geographical space . . . that resides in a space not acknowledged by hegemonic culture" and that illuminates the "intersections of the multiple systems of exploitation: capitalism, patriarchy, and white supremacy"[40]

The Molly character offers us a few important insights: that disempowered youth still make their presence felt in the realm of alternative, though not always oppositional, culture; that rock returns to the United States from Mexico as rock en español in the hands of Chicana/o and Mexican youth who themselves are transformed by the music; that Chicana feminism can not be contained by nationalism and national boundaries; that all forms of resistance to the values of the dominant culture have yet to be incorporated, that resistance exists, albeit not in mass movements, but in local sites; and that 'zines, popular music, and independent film enables conversations to occur across distant geographical locations between young people whose interests are not represented by corporate media. Finally, the character of Molly reminds us that Chicana feminists thinking has enabled the production of this film, and helps us to locate sites of resistance to gendered norms and to the desires of the dominant culture in the most unexpected places.

Remapping Punk

Pretty Vacant takes place on the West Side of San Antonio during the early 1990s. It is a setting far removed from both the time and place of the Sex Pistol's first fame in the 1970s. Yet, it is Molly's investment in rewriting 1980s pop culture that drives her to revise and complicate circuits of musical diaspora as mapped out by British scholars Paul Gilroy's *The Black Atlantic* and Dick *Hebdige's Subculture: The Meaning of Style* by documenting the "Tejanoizaiton" of the Sex Pistols music. Always subverting stereotypical expectations of what constitutes Chicanas's interest, the most recent issue of her zine is dedicated to punk music. She sets out to prove a secret that will forever transform rock and roll history: that her favorite British punk band, the Sex Pistols, had been Chicano-fied by their visit to San Antonio.

Molly believes that the Sex Pistol heard Steve Jordon's funky conjunto called "El Kranke" and that they were going to do a cover of the song for their performance. Her current edition of ex-voto Molly's is dedicated to her two musical obsessions Esteven Jordon (Jimmy Hendrix of the Accordion) and the Sex Pistols. She is determined to prove that Chicano music influenced the Sex Pistols during their performance in San Antonio. As a band that gives her inspiration for thinking about the world in new ways and for plotting new connections, Molly does research on the legendary final performance of the Sex Pistols at a cowboy club in San Antonio called Randy's. According to Molly, it was their last and best performance. Snooping around the back stage of Randy's she finds a piece of paper:

> . . . one hidden behind the stage. Get this—The Sex Pistol s play list! And even more amazing? Scribbled at the bottom?—Listen to this—"el Kranke," someone wrote "El Kranke!" one of Steve Jordon's songs! Shit man the Pistol s were gonna end the show that night with some conjunto!
>
> My theory had precedence. Stay with me on this. The Clash, for instance Jazzed up their music with this reggae influence. A direct reflection of their exposure to the Caribbean diaspora and its musical expression there in London. Nothing new—the usual white man appropriation of an exotic other story—anyway, the Pistols, my theory went, were going to do the same with Norteno, el Tex Mex. I was going on the assumptions that the Pistols probably heard the conjunto on KCOR or Radio Jalapeno on the bus ride down from Austin. But the point is, it worked. Talk about your revisionist histories! Griel Marcus is gonna flip![41]

Inventing her alternatives around British Punk is a response to her limited options circumscribed by Chicano patriarchy and U.S. racism. Her attraction to British Punk is not about Great Britain, but instead her desire for an Other—she exoticizes Britain from a Tejana point-of-view. It's her imaging of Britain as a place where oppositional discourses and styles are produced, styles that she can later mine for their symbolic potential. But her imaging of Great Britain as a place where oppositional discourses emerge is not that far off. This reimaging is the inverse of European youth having their image of the U.S. framed by oppositional discourses articulated by some hip-hop production. Molly mentions that the

> Clash (acclaimed anti-capitalist punk British band popular in the 80s), for instance, jazzed up their music with this reggae influence. A direct

reflection of their exposure to the Caribbean diaspora and its musical expression there in London.[42]

Oppositional discourses emerging in the "Third World" found their way to Great Britain through the musical milieu of progressive Black British immigrant and White British youth. Via the imported British records, Tejana Molly tunes in to the embedded oppositional discourses layered within the music—but the process of layering oppositional discourses within the soundings and lyrics of the music does not end there. Molly narrates the furthering layering of the British sound with conjunto—with its own oppositional history in Tejas. She explains: "I was going on the assumptions that the Pistols probably heard the conjunto on KCOR or Radio Jalapeno on the bus ride down from Austin. But the point is, it worked."

For Molly, her zine Ex-Voto, her band, and short films are the places where she engages what Norma Alarcón describes as the "struggle for histories actual and imaginary that give substance and provide an account of her/their position within culture and the political economy."[43] Molly's art-practices are emblematic of both Chicana feminist art practices and theoretical writings of the 1980s. She self-publishes the zine Ex-voto, "cause no one was addressing my needs," just as Chicana feminist formed organizations like MALCS (Mujeres en Letras y Cambio Social) and writers and artists created venues for their own work. Molly's zine catalogues the influences on her proto-feminist subjectivity. She is still in-formation. She combines the cut and paste aesthetic of punk with Chicana rasquache to create a form that expresses her social location where she prints essays titled, "Never Mind Che, Here's La Molly," ironically riffing off the song "Never Mind the Bullocks, Here's the Sex Pistols," while at the same time implicating "Che Guevara," or at least the memory of him, in gendered power relations and disrupting the iconic Che as the signifier of social revolution. That she publishes the letters responding to zine articles written about "Emma Temayuca, the history of retablos, Love and Rockets, Maria Felix movies, Dolores Huerta, Ester Hernandez, the Ramones, and Sor Juana Inez de la Cruz," speaks to the ways the circulation of popular art-forms are used to create community outside of the bounds of ethnicity.

The Emergence of Chicana D.I.Y. Feminist Politics

Molly *is* linked to an earlier generation of Chicana politics, but the filmic representation of that connection is done in a complex,

antiessentialist manner though the composition of a scene that carefully locates Molly spatially and temporally. On her way to work an
independent record store called Hogwild where she clerks, Molly leads
us through local shots of San Antonio's Mexicano neighborhoods, the
Alamo, and the cities freeways. At the record store, Molly informs us:

> I was born 21 years ago on January 23rd, 1973, a Saturday, the same
> day Raza Unida met for their first—and only—national convention, and
> across the Atlantic, David Bowie released "Ziggy Stardust:" both
> movements didn't last, a radical Chicano political party and Bowie's
> particular strain of androgynous rock, but both had their influences, on
> me, to this day.[44]

Molly's birthday, January 23, 1973, is significant in the development
of Chicana politics. In "Mujeres Por La Raza Unida," Evey Chapa
details the development of the Chicana Caucus in relation to the
January 23 National Raza Unida meeting, a caucus that was formed
by women who felt that more needed to be done to ensure women's
participation in the party's electoral politics and positions of power.
Chapa explains,

> We used already the evident commitment of many mujeres to the Raza
> Unida Party, . . . to implement the strategies for the development of
> Mujeres por La Raza Unida . . . a mini-meeting was held in Cristal
> (Crystal City Texas) attended by those who felt that words are not
> enough, that action is the only possible recourse. We formulated a strat-
> egy to discuss and survey the mujer issue with mujeres themselves. We
> canvassed opinions throughout the state . . . for five months they
> planned . . . On August 4, 1973, in San Antonio, Texas, the first
> Conferencia de Mujeres por La Raza Unida was held. It was attended by
> almost 200 women from 20 different counties.[45]

The formation of the Chicana caucus within a larger political
organization was an important move, but by the time Molly comes of
age, the historical conditions that supported mass movements for
social transformation and Civil Rights had changed. Yet Molly is a
subject born out of the difficult struggles that did win important social
advances. And that recognition allows her to narrate herself as being
born of two movements, one concerned with social justice organized
around more traditional electoral politics of the male domain, and the
other concerned with the critique of traditional masculinity located in
the cultural sphere of popular music. Molly recognizes the value of

both types of organizing. The lasting effects that the two movements had on her was to direct her to the realm of cultural politics, a place where she engages her own cultural work. She finds ammunition for imagining cultural transformation beyond the frame of cultural nationalism in the sphere of oppositional punk popular culture. In the domain of oppositional popular culture, she imagines affiliation with other marginalized youth who also desire a different world. Yet while working in the realm women have traditionally been relegated to—that of the domain of culture reproduction—Molly does not reproduce traditional Chicano, patriarchal cultural, nor the status quo values of the dominant culture. She creates something new, just as her flesh and blood analogues, an alternative public sphere that includes her. Though corporate media chose not to give coverage to most oppositional movements during the Reagan–Bush era—the historical moment when the globalization of capital accelerates and conservative political ideology dominated the public sphere—Molly's obsession with 1980s alternative popular culture speaks to the ways young people fashioned oppositional consciousness then and now out of available resources found in the most unexpected places.

The film *Pretty Vacant* was released around the same time as *Selena*—the first Hollywood "hit" film to feature a Mexican American female pop star protagonist. Unlike *Selena*, with its melodramatic narrative—based on Selena's real life tragic death, *Pretty Vacant* at least engages questions of representation brought up by Chicana feminist theorists. Like Latina punks Hopey and Maggie, whose lesbian relationship Jaime Hernandez depicts with great sensitivity in the *Love and Rockets* series, Mendiola's Molly represents a grassroots feminist punk—still in-formation—who draws inspiration from the signs of British punk, the *Love and Rockets* series itself, Tejano culture in general, and rock en español, to construct an "alternative" location away from patriarchal Aztlán, yet still oppositional to the racism of the dominant culture, a place from which to imagine new ways of being in the world, ways that speaks to similar, but structurally different conditions of working-class feminists, both straight and queer.

Again I ask why is this film and its flyer so provocative? My response is not what one might expect it to be. It is not that the young Tejana filmmaker is unique in her artistic endeavors, but instead that the numerous forms of cultural politics invented by Chicanas who have engaged in subversive art and identity formation have been under-examined despite the fact that we have much to learn from their aesthetic and feminist practices. We have yet to understand fully how they set the stage for a future generation of artists and musicians.

What is equally fascinating is the potential for dialogue between Chicana feminist singer songwriters in the United States and rockeras from Mexico, who of course, are positioned differently by their respective nation-states in terms of racial hierarchies and class location, and whose concerns are certainly not identical. In examining the flow of youth culture back and forth between Mexico and the United States, thorny and complex questions of race and class privilege emerge. Yet, as the musical culture demonstrates, the point of connection, of affiliation between the Chicanas and Mexicanas interested in transforming gender relations stems from the shared recognition of their subordinated position within patriarchal culture. Their discursive interventions concerning gender and class relations points toward the possibility for transnational affiliation around critiques of violence against women, specifically against mestizas and women of color. The remarkable work of Julia Palacios and Tere Estrada, on the history of women in Mexican rock, sets us in that direction.[46]

Notes

An earlier version of this essay appears in *Rockin' Las Americas: The Global Politics of Rock in Latin America*, edited by Deborah Pacini Hernández and Eric Zolv (Pittsburg, PA: University of Pittsburgh Press) 2004. I am forever grateful to Deb Pacini Hernandez, Eric Zolov, and Hector L'Oeste for inviting me to participate in the Rockefeller Foundation Bellagio Research Residency team, *Rockin' Las Americas: The Global Politics of Rock in Latin America*.

1. Thanks to the following institutions that have funded portions of this project: Smithsonian Institutions Latino Initiative Fund; the Woodrow Wilson National Fellowship Foundation Career Enhancement Junior Faculty Postdoctoral Grant; and the Center for Chicano/Latino Research, UC Santa Cruz. Portions of this draft have been presented at the following meetings: NACCS 1998; ASA 1999; MLA, 2000; and LASA2000. I thank Lisa Lowe for her wonderful comments, Rosa Linda Fregoso for Tejana insight, and George Mariscal for clarifying the nuances of Chicana/o cultural nationalism, and Jocelyn Guilbault for her excellent suggestions.
2. Mendiola's flyer is inspired by Yolanda López's "Portrait of the Artist as the Virgin of Guadalupe," 1978.
3. José D. Saldívar, "Postmodern Realism," in *The Columbia History of the American Novel*, edited by Emory Elliott (New York: Columbia University Press, 1991), 521. See also William A. Nericcio "A Decidedly 'Mexican and American' Semi[ero]tic Transference." in *Latino/a Popular Culture*, edited by Michelle Habell-Pallán and Mary Romero (New York; London: New York University Press, 2002).
4. See writings by David Reyes and Tom Waldman, *Land of a Thousand Dances: Chicano Rock 'n' roll from Southern California* (Albuquerque: University

of New Mexico Press, 1998); George Lipsitz, *Dangerous Crossroads: Popular Music, Postmodernism, and the Poetics of Place* (London; New York: Verso, 1994); Steven Loza, *Barrio Rhythm: Mexican American Music in Los Angeles* (Urbana: University of Illinois Press, 1993); Jose D. Saldívar, *Border Matters: Remapping American Cultural Studies* (Berkeley: University of California Press, 1997); *Musical Migrations: Transnationalism and Cultural Hybridity in Latin/o America*, edited by Frances Aparicio and Candida F. Jaques (New York: Palgrave Press, 2003); and Curtis Marez, "Becoming Brown: The Politics of Chicana/o Popular Style," Social Text 48 (1996).

5. The limited black and white color spectrum of the photo image itself, because it cannot represent a visible browness, lends itself to reproducing the problematic binary terms in which dominant debates about race and power relations are couched, terms which render invisible the bodies and concerns of women who are racialzed as neither Black or White (such as mestizas, Native Americans, Asian Americans) but who are nevertheless positioned in economic and/or political margins.

6. Literally, she is Tejana actress and performance artist Mariana Vasquez.

7. The interviews I conducted are part of a longer in-progress book manuscript tentively titled, *Punk Saints and Other Urban Goddesses* which includes an analysis of interviews with Theresa Covarrubias, and Alicia Armedariz and other Latinas involved with punk music in Los Angeles during the 1980s. In the interviews the women discuss their artistic conditions of production, gender relations and their relation to Chicana feminism, as well as the Chicana punk aesthetic that emerged in the 1980s.

8. David Reyes and Tom Waldman, *Land of a Thousand Dances: Chicano Rock 'n' Roll from Southern California* (Albuquerque: University of New Mexico Press, 1998), 135.

9. Ibid.

10. For an excellent discussion of how Chicana artists "made do" with limited resources, see Laura Perez, "Spirit Glyphs: Reimagining Art and Artist in the Work of Chicana Tlamatinime." *Modern Fiction Studies* 44(1) (1998): 36–76.

11. For an insightful essay on Chicana youth culture of the 1940s, see Catherine Ramirez, "Crimes of Fashion: The Pachuca and Chicana Style Politics," *Meridians: A Journal of Transnational Feminisms*, 2(2) (2002): 1–35 and Chicana 1960s youth culture, see Keta Miranda's, " 'The East Side Revue, 40 Hits by East Los Angeles' Most Popular Groups!: The Boys in the Band and the Girls Who Were Their Fans," in this volume.

12. See George Sanchez's *Becoming Mexican American*, Ethnicity and Acculturation in Chicano Los Angeles 1900–1945 for a history of Chicanos in Los Angeles. New York: Oxford University Press, 1993.

13. Reyes and Waldman, *Land of a Thousand Dances*, 136.

14. Ibid., 136.

15. Alicia Armendariz Velasquez, interview with author, Los Angeles, 1998.

16. For more on Marisela Norte, see Michelle Habell-Pallán, "No Cultural Icon: Marisela Norte," in *Women Transforming Politics*, edited by Kathy Jones, Cathy Cohen, and Joan Tronto (New York: New York University Press, 1997), 256–268.

17. For a detailed analysis of Chicana cultural production and Chicana feminist discourses, Sonia Saldivar-Hull's *Feminism on the Border: Chicana Gender Politics and Literature* (Berkeley: University of California Press, 2000).
18. AngieChabram-Dernersesian, "I Throw Punches for My Race, but I Don't Want to Be a Man: Writing Us—Chica-nos (Girl, Us)/Chicanas— into the Movement Script," in *Cultural Studies*, edited by Lawrence Grossberg, Cary Nelson, and Paula Treichler (New York: Routledge, 1992), 81–95.
19. See David Jones, *Destroy All Music: Punk Rock Pioneers of Southern California*. Berkeley: University of California Press.
20. Kristine McKenna, "Female Rockers—A New Breed," *Los Angeles Times*, June, Calendar Section, 78–82.
21. Ibid, 78.
22. Ibid.
23. Ibid, 82.
24. Ibid, 78.
25. Alicia Armendariz Velasquez, interview with author, Los Angeles, 1998.
26. Sincere thanks to Jim Fricke, program curator at the Experience Music Project, for allowing me to access the recording *Yes L.A.* compilation.
27. See Marc Spitz and Brendan Mullen, *We Got the Neutron Bomb: The Untold Story of L.A. Punk* (New York: Three Rivers Press, 2001) for varied testimonies of Canterbury's history.
28. For a discussion of another Chicano artist who finds resources in the most unexpected places see Michelle Habell-Pallán, "El Vez is 'Taking Care of Business': The Inter/National Appeal of Chicana/o Popular Music," *Cultural Studies* 13,(2) (1999): 195–210.
29. Teresa Covarrubias, interview by author, Los Angeles, 1998.
30. Ibid.
31. McKenna, "Female Rockers," 82.
32. Reyes and Waldman, *Land of a Thousand Dances*, 139.
33. "Chicanas in Tune." Produced by Ester Reyes for *Life and Times Television*. *Copyright* Community Television of Southern California. Broadcast on KCET public television. Los Angeles, 1994.
34. Las Tres, *Live at the LATC*. Panocha Dulce-Black Rose-Bhima Music, 1993. Audiocassette. "Happy Accident" written by Alicia Armendariz Velasquez. Thanks to Antonia Garcia-Orozco for inventing the notion of Chicana Trova in relation to Nueva Trova, that is Chicana Trova is sung in English and lyrically calls for a consciousness raising through a form of folk music that can be played on accessible instruments.
35. See Tiffany Lopez's, *The Alchemy of Blood: Violence as Critical Discourse in U.S. Latina/o Literature* (Durham: Duke University Press, in press) and Angela Davis on incarceration and women of color in her recording, *The Prison Industrial Complex*. AK Press, 2000. Compact disk.
36. Reyes and Waldman, *Land of a Thousand Dances*, 136.
37. Ibid.
38. Reyes and Waldman, *Land of a Thousand Dances*,140.

39. Sean Carrillo, "East to Eden" in *Forming: The Early Days of L.A. Punk*, coauthored by Sean Carrillo, Christine McKenna, Claude Bessy, and Exene Cervenka (Santa Monica, CA: Smart Art Press, 1999), 42.
40. Sonia Saldívar-Hull, "Feminism on the Border: From Gender Politics to Geopolitics," in *Criticism in the Borderlands: Studies in Chicano Literature, Culture, and Ideology*, edited by Hector Calderon and José D. Saldívar (Durham, NC: Duke University Press, 1991): 204, 211.
41. *Pretty Vacant*, dir Jim Mendiola, 1996. Molly recuperates the great Tejano "punk" accordion player Steve Jordan into her conceptual map of Chicano culture. According to Rosa Linda Fregoso, Jordan has generally been left out in accounts of Tejano oppositional culture—unlike "Little Joe," a Tejano musician associated with the movement—because of his heroin addiction and unconventional lifestyle.
42. *Pretty Vacant*.
43. Norma Alarcón, "Cognitive Desires: An Allegory of/for Chicana Critics," in *Chicana (W)rites on Word and Film*, edited by Maria Herrera-Sobek and Helena Maria Viramontes (Oakland: Third Woman Press, 1996), 187.
44. *Pretty Vacant*.
45. Evey Chapa, "Mujeres Por La Raza Unida," in *Chicana Feminist Thought*, edited by Alma Garcia (New York: Routledge, 1997), 179.
46. See *Rockin' Las Americas: The Global Politics of Rock in Latin America*, edited by Deborah Pacini Hernández and Eric Zolov. (Pittsburgh, PA: University of Pittsburgh Press, 2004).

Index

absence/presence   9, 111–12
aesthetic(s)
  and cosmetic surgery   138–9
  double-function   54
  patriarchal capitalism   137–9
  postmodern   35–36
  punk   223, 227, 236, 240 n. 6
  rasquache   201, 236
  reworked   21
affirmative action   23, 40, 64, 71
ambivalence   7, 8, 10, 11, 36, 45,
    85, 203, 204, 214–15
appropriation
  of exotic   235
  of political contexts   31–2, 36, 41
  subversive   6, 45
assimilation   22, 41, 74
  class   23, 82, 88
  and colonialism   117
attitude   34–5, 157, 226, 229

blood quantum   153–8, 162

civil rights
  California initiative   40
  claim   78–9
  movement   6–7, 21, 36, 80, 81,
    86–8, 175
consumer choice   85
consumption   26–7, 32, 53, 79–80,
    83, 85–6, 93, 95–7

disidentification   188
division of labor, sexual
    133, 138

feminism(s)
  border   234
  hegemonic   42, 47 n. 10
  homogenizing   38, 68
  and nationalism   190, 192 n. 2,
    193 n. 8, 234
  popular   146
  white   68–9, 231
  women of color   2, 5

gaze   49, 142, 186, 203, 210,
    211, 222
genocide   66
ghostly   10, 111, 122–3

hermeneutics   69
heterosexuality   65, 205 n. 6
  compulsive   164
  desire   133
  lesbianization of   188, 205 n. 6
history   5–6
  and Chicano music   15
  of Indian women   65–6
  feminist (re)imagining of, in the
    Chicano movement   172–3,
    176, 178, 181–2,
    191–2
  rock 'n' roll   221, 233–4
hybridity
  of chicano musical style   15
  and commoditization   31–43, 46
  hawaiian   159–60

identity
  and advertising   93

identity—*continued*
  American Indian 65, 73
  Chicano/a struggles over 21–6,
      178, 180–1
  crafting 180
  crisis 80–1
  essential 199
  formation 1, 36, 178, 232
  Hawaiian 157–8
  lesbian 209
  liminal 24
  national 165, 198
  politics 2
  racial 80, 154
  sexual 50
imaginary
  decolonial 178–9, 181
  postcolonial 45
  racial and sexual 203, 211–13
imagination, sociological 110
imagined community(ies) 149,
    176–7, 193 n. 15
immigration 43, 55–9
indigeneity 73, 163
inscribed bodies 38, 45, 58, 140–1,
    145, 159, 162, 185
interpellation 6, 8, 72, 89,
    177, 188
intersectionality 5, 7, 173, 225

knowledge
  hegemonic 74
  objects of 157–61

local 52, 180, 224
  fame 20–1, 42
  global 147, 148

marketing
  body images in 135
  "lesbian chic" 53
  multiculturalism in 32, 41–4
  niche and target 15, 78–80,
      84–93, 135, 225

memory
  community 166
  counter 180
  -scape 108, 110, 115
  retrofitted 190
mixed race 73–4, 156, 161

nation 39
nationalism
  chauvinistic 123–4
  Chicano/a 171–4, 190–2
  as colonial project 65, 69, 74
  pedagogy of 183, 185, 189
  US 65–6, 68–9, 73–4

postmodern
  celebratory discourses 133–5
  multiculturalism 31, 39, 43
  sensibilities 36
public sphere 10, 44, 222–5, 238
  counter public(s) 177, 190,
      193 n. 7

rasquachísmo 203
reification 3, 135, 138, 154, 192

sadomasochism 211–13
sexuality(ies) 35, 50, 52,
    144, 227
  desire 51, 52
  pleasure 136
  and political 213–14
  and racial 203, 214
  spectatorial fantasy 213
  violence 225–26
sovereignty 9, 176
  and autonomy 6, 69–70, 73
  and identity 65
  and kinship 166
  and self-governance 163
state 96
  and capitalism 27
  and civil apparatuses 5
  and colonialism 165

and identity   21–3, 28 n. 1,
    166
non-state entity   73
and power   96, 98 n. 4, 215
and racism   8, 96
and violence   123–5
subject
    agency   215
    and body   21
    colonial/imperial   117,
        127 n. 13, 157
    constitution of   210
    formation   2, 8, 186
    nationalist   200
    remembering   123
    sovereign   96
subjectivity
    collective   163
    political   8, 27

social   7
transgressive   135
subjection   215
subjectification   7, 111, 120, 215

transnationalism
    affiliations   239
    and capital   32, 53
    consumer goods   150 n. 11
    and labor   32, 37, 42–3,
        137–9
    and nafta   226
    and popular music   234

warrior   66–7
woman of color   3–5, 7, 149 n. 1
    criticism   8

xenophobia   56–7

Printed in the United States
103457LV00001B/70/P

9 781403 965332